Measurement in
Information Science

Library and Information Science

Consulting Editor: *Harold Borko*
Graduate School of Library and Information Science
University of California, Los Angeles

Harold Borko and Charles L. Bernier
Abstracting Concepts and Methods

F. W. Lancaster
Toward Paperless Information Systems

H. S. Heaps
Information Retrieval: Computational and Theoretical Aspects

Harold Borko and Charles Bernier
Indexing Concepts and Methods

Gerald Jahoda and Judith Schiek Braunagel
The Librarian and Reference Queries: A Systematic Approach

Charles H. Busha and Stephen P. Harter
Research Methods in Librarianship: Techniques and Interpretation

Diana M. Thomas, Ann T. Hinckley, and Elizabeth R. Eisenbach
The Effective Reference Librarian

G. Edward Evans
Management Techniques for Librarians, Second Edition

Jessica L. Milstead
Subject Access Systems: Alternatives in Design

Dagobert Soergel
Information Storage and Retrieval: A Systems Approach

Stephen P. Harter
Online Information Retrieval: Concepts, Principles, and Techniques

Timothy C. Craven
String Indexing

Lois Swan Jones and Sarah Scott Gibson
Art Libraries and Information Services

The list of books continues at the end of the volume.

Measurement in Information Science

Bert R. Boyce
School of Library and Information Science
Louisiana State University
Baton Rouge, Louisiana

Charles T. Meadow
Faculty of Information Studies
University of Toronto
Toronto, Ontario
Canada

Donald H. Kraft
Department of Computer Science
Louisiana State University
Baton Rouge, Louisiana

Academic Press
San Diego   New York   Boston   London   Sydney   Tokyo   Toronto

This book is printed on acid-free paper. ∞

Copyright © 1994 by ACADEMIC PRESS, INC.
All Rights Reserved.
No part of this publication may be reproduced or transmitted in any form or by any means, electronic or mechanical, including photocopy, recording, or any information storage and retrieval system, without permission in writing from the publisher.

Academic Press, Inc.
A Division of Harcourt Brace & Company
525 B Street, Suite 1900, San Diego, California 92101-4495

United Kingdom Edition published by
Academic Press Limited
24-28 Oval Road, London NW1 7DX

Library of Congress Cataloging-in-Publication Data

Boyce, Bert R.
    Measurement in information science / by Bert R. Boyce, Charles T. Meadow, Donald H. Kraft.
       p.   cm. -- (Library and information science series)
    Includes bibliographical references and index.
    ISBN 0-12-121450-8 (case)
    1. Information science--Statistical methods.   I. Meadow, Charles T. II. Kraft, Donald H. III. Series: Library and information science series (New York, N.Y.)
    Z669.8.B69   1995
    020'.21--dc20   94-17976
                                                    CIP

PRINTED IN THE UNITED STATES OF AMERICA
94 95 96 97 98 99 BB 9 8 7 6 5 4 3 2 1

Dedicated by the authors to their families

Contents

Preface — xv

One
Introduction to Measurement

1
Quantitative and Qualitative Aspects of Measurement

1.1	The Nature of Measurement	3
1.2	Information Systems	5
1.3	Reasons for Measurement	8
1.4	Composite Measures	9
1.5	Measurement and Human Behavior	10
	1.5.1 Relative Measures	11
	1.5.2 Measuring Quality	12
	1.5.3 The Measurement of Human Behavior and Skills	15
	1.5.4 The Measurement of Values	16
1.6	Summary	19
	References	20

2
Methods of Measurement

2.1	Direct Observation	21
2.2	Indirect Observation	22
2.3	Opinion Measurement	23
	2.3.1 Surveys and Questionnaires	24

3
Accuracy and Reliability of Measures

    3.1 Measurement of Measurement Devices   29
           3.1.1 Resolution   30
           3.1.2 Precision   31
           3.1.3 Accuracy   31
           3.1.4 Calibration   31
    3.2 Tolerance   32
    3.3 Summary: What, Me Measure?   33
        References   33

4
Sets and Scales

    4.1 Sets   35
           4.1.1 Set Definitions   35
           4.1.2 Basic Set Operations   36
           4.1.3 Characteristics of Set Operations   36
    4.2 The Concept of Scale   37
    4.3 Nominal Scales   38
    4.4 Ordinal Scales   39
           4.4.1 The Concept of Ordering   39
           4.4.2 Equivalence Relations   40
           4.4.3 A Basis for Ordering   41
    4.5 Interval Scales   42
    4.6 Ratio Scales   42
    4.7 Summary   44
        References   44

Before section 3, at top of page:

        2.3.2 Comparison to Standards and Norms   27
    2.4 Summary   28
        References   28

Two
Mathematical and Statistical Concepts

5
Statistical Measures—Description by Reduction

5.1	Introduction	47
5.2	Sample Spaces	48
	5.2.1 Probabilities of Events	49
	5.2.2 Statistical Samples	51
5.3	Frequency Measures	52
	5.3.1 Frequency Distributions	53
	5.3.2 Graphical Portrayals	55
	5.3.3 Measures of Central Tendency	58
	5.3.4 Dispersion Measures	61
	5.3.5 Using the Standard Deviation as a Measure	63
	5.3.6 The Law of Large Numbers	63
	5.3.7 The Poisson Distribution	64
	5.3.8 The z Score	65
5.4	Summary	66
	References	66

6
Statistical Tests and Correlation

6.1	Errors and Confidence	67
6.2	Testing of Hypotheses	69
6.3	Measures of Association	72
	6.3.1 Measures of Correlation	73
	6.3.2 Regression	76
	6.3.3 Correlation and Regression in Information Science	77
6.4	Summary	78
	References	79

7
Clustering, Similarity, and Set Membership Measures

7.1	Classification	80
7.2	Data Aggregation	81
	7.2.1 Discriminant Analysis	82
	7.2.2 Factor Analysis	83
	7.2.3 Clustering	85
7.3	Multidimensional Scaling	90
7.4	Matching Functions	92

7.5		Fuzzy Set Theory	93
7.6		Summary	95
		References	96

Three
Measures of Information Phenomena

8
Measures of Language and Text

8.1		Informetrics	99
8.2		The Measurement of Language	100
	8.2.1	The Measurement of Meaning	101
	8.2.2	Indexing	102
	8.2.3	Word Association and Vocabulary Control	105
	8.2.4	Characteristics of Text	108
8.3		Summary	110
		References	110

9
Measures of Bibliographic Phenomena

9.1		Bibliometrics	112
9.2		Citations	112
9.3		Growth	114
9.4		Obsolescence	116
9.5		Scattering	117
9.6		Laws of Source Yield	118
	9.6.1	Bradford's Law	119
	9.6.2	Lotka's Law	120
9.7		Information Theory	121
9.8		Application to Information Systems	123
	9.8.1	Journal Selection	124
	9.8.2	Personnel Evaluation	125
	9.8.3	Collection Maintenance	125
9.9		Data Collection Issues	125
9.10		Summary	126
		References	127

Four

Measures of Databases and Information Retrieval

10
Introduction to Measurement in Information Retrieval

10.1	Models of Information Retrieval Systems	131
	10.1.1 Structural Definitions	132
	10.1.2 Logical Definitions	135
10.2	Types and Goals of Measures	138
	10.2.1 Database Measures	139
	10.2.2 User Measures	140
	10.2.3 Query Language Measures	141
	10.2.4 The IRSYS Software	141
	10.2.5 Operation of the Service	141
10.3	Issues in Information Retrieval Measurement	142
10.4	Summary	144
	References	144

11
Measurement of Databases

11.1	Introduction	146
11.2	Database Characteristics	147
11.3	Survey of Database Measures	149
11.4	Definitions and Terminology	151
	11.4.1 Measures of Occurrence of Values	152
	11.4.2 Additional Measures of Value Co-occurrence	153
11.5	Database Measures	154
	11.5.1 Scope	154
	11.5.2 Attributes Represented	155
	11.5.3 Selection of Entities	156
	11.5.4 Magnitude	158
	11.5.5 Timeliness	158
	11.5.6 Selectivity	159
	11.5.7 Reliability	161
	11.5.8 Cost	163
	11.5.9 Comparability with Other Databases	164
11.6	Summary	166
	References	167

12

Measures of the Retrieval Process

12.1	Introduction	168
12.2	Cost and Resources Used	170
12.3	Time and Command Rate	172
12.4	Errors	173
12.5	Summary	174
	References	174

13

Measurement of Retrieval Outcome

13.1	Introduction	176
	13.1.1 Concepts of Relevance and Utility	177
	13.1.2 Uncertainties in Relevance Measurement	179
13.2	Measures Derived from Relevance	180
13.3	Measuring Relevance	183
	13.3.1 Goals, Objectives, and Standards	183
	13.3.2 Measurement Scale	184
	13.3.3 The Meaning of Relevance Being Used	185
	13.3.4 Relevance as a Relative and a Variable Measure	186
13.4	System-Computed Relevance, Ranking, and Feedback	187
	13.4.1 Ranking	188
	13.4.2 Computing the Quantity of Relevance Retrieved	189
	13.4.3 Relevance Feedback	190
13.5	Measuring the Question	191
13.6	General Measures of Outcome	192
	13.6.1 Definition of the System to Be Measured	192
	13.6.2 The Relationship between Precision and Recall	193
	13.6.3 Overall Measures	196
	13.6.4 The Case of No Retrieved Relevance	198
13.7	Summary	199
	References	200

14
Measurement of Users

14.1	Introduction	202
14.2	User Characteristics	202
	14.2.1 Biological and Psychological Measures	203
	14.2.2 Education and Aptitude	204
	14.2.3 Experience and Knowledge	204
	14.2.4 Organizational Factors	207
	14.2.5 Users' Mental Models	208
14.3	User Performance Measures	209
	14.3.1 User Process Measures	209
	14.3.2 Error Measures	211
	14.3.3 Language Use Measures	213
14.4	Search Termination Measures	216
14.5	Outcome Measures	217
	14.5.1 Set Size	217
	14.5.2 Precision and Recall	218
14.6	Summary	218
	References	219

Five
Information Systems Measures

15
Software Metrics

15.1	Relation to Information Systems Measurement	223
15.2	Software Physics and Measures	223
15.3	Logical Complexity	226
15.4	Algorithmic Complexity	229
	15.4.1 Worst and Average Case Analysis	232
15.5	Applications	233
	15.5.1 Query Complexity	233
	15.5.2 File Structures and Search Algorithms	234
	15.5.3 Algorithm Comparisons	236
15.6	Summary	239
	References	240

16
Measures of Information Services

16.1	Output Services versus Inputs versus Intermediate Outputs	241
16.2	Values and Utilities	243
16.3	Costs	244
16.4	Service Statistics	246
16.5	Data Collection, Analysis, and Standards	246
16.6	Decision Making	248
16.7	Conclusion	249
	References	250

Appendix: Measurement Index	253
Recommended Reading	271
Index	273

Preface

Information science is a growing field. It is characterized by a clearly demonstrated need for persons who are trained in the design and use of information systems and who have an appreciation for the role that humans play in operating or managing systems and training or advising users of systems. While attempts at defining information and other system evaluation mechanisms have received much attention in recent years, information science has not been distinguished by careful measurement. Results of our experiments and studies are lacking in both repeatable experimentation and accepted experimental data upon which other experimenters can build.

The purpose of this book is to aid researchers, practitioners, teachers, and students in defining and using precise, repeatable measurements applied to information retrieval and database management systems and in being productive critics of the literature involving measurement. We do not limit our sense of *information system* solely to computer hardware and software. Information systems, in our view, also encompass the information upon which computers operate and the people who use the systems.

Measurement as a process is, to some extent, independent of what is being measured. Measurement involves precise definition. In information retrieval, for example, we cannot discuss the measure called *precision* without a clear understanding of the measure called *relevance,* upon which precision is based. And since precision is a measure of the outcome of a retrieval operation, it is important to know exactly what constitutes the system whose outcome is being measured. If either the meaning of relevance or the exact definition of the system is unclear, then a measure such as *precision* can have very little meaning.

There must be a general consensus on measures, a standard of comparison. A length of one meter must have the same meaning for everyone. A relevance value of 5 on a scale of 7 should also have the same meaning for everyone. Measures must be repeatable. If a ball bearing is 20 mm in diameter today, then it should be the same size tomorrow. If it is not, then either the measuring process was flawed or some other important factor has been omitted, such as the temperature at the time of measurement or the measuring instrument used.

Our aim in writing this book is to encourage the same regard for measurement in information science that exists in the physical sciences, while recognizing that there is much ambiguity in information systems measurement. That we cannot always resolve the ambiguity does not mean that we should not be aware of it.

Our approach has been to start with the fundamentals of measurement, which are quite independent of application. For those not familiar with statistics, we have included, in Chapters 5 and 6, a brief survey of descriptive statistics and statistical decision-making. These short chapters cover a book-length subject and are necessarily terse. Chapter 7 begins the specialized coverage of some statistical procedures that are commonly used in information science and which are not necessarily found in the average introductory statistical text.

Chapters 8 and 9 cover the measurement aspects of language and of the patterns of use of information, which come under the headings of bibliometrics and informetrics.

Chapters 10 through 14 concentrate on databases, information retrieval systems, and the users of retrieval systems. These three aspects of information systems are not always separable from each other in terms of our ability to measure and evaluate performance of one aspect or another.

Finally, in the last two chapters, we consider the measurement of software and of information services, as a whole.

We include a large number of measures of many different aspects of information science. We cannot claim to have covered all of them. Nor do we claim that all those measures we have described should be used in all cases. What we hope we have done is provide a compendium, for working toward a uniform terminology and symbology (while accepting that both are still imperfect), and a starting place for those unfamiliar with the subject. Following Chapter 16 is a measurement index that lists all measures defined in the text in alphabetical order by name of the measure. Unfortunately, authors in this field have not yet come to a standard usage. A reader may find a bewildering array of symbols in use for the same concepts, seemingly different in every paper or book. We regret that in many cases we have added to this number in an attempt to use a consistent terminology within this book.

In addition to the bibliography following each chapter, we have included a recommended reading list, following Chapter 16, which contains only books, some of which have already been referred to, but all of which touch on some of the topics of this book.

This book is intended as a text at the advanced undergraduate or graduate level in schools or departments of information science, computer science, or library science. Specific courses to which it would be applicable might have such titles as Research Methods, Information Retrieval, Database Management, and Information System Analysis, Design, or Evaluation. It will also be of value as a professional reference book for faculty members, advanced students, and practitioners in the fields of information service provision and management, systems anaylsis, and systems design.

Readers should have a basic understanding of computers, which might have come from a course in programming in a high-level language or extensive use of an online database search or database management system. They should have had about a year of university-level mathematics. The specific course is not as important as the maturity and interest needed to grasp the importance of the careful definition of concepts and relationships.

We thank the following colleagues who have assisted us by reading and evaluating the manuscript: Ethel Auster of the University of Toronto, Terence Brooks of the University of Washington, Doris L. Carver of Louisiana State University, Raya Fidel of the University of Washington, Patrick Gignac of the University of Toronto, William Hersh of the Oregon Health Sciences University, William Losee of the University of North Carolina, and Stephen Robertson of City University, London.

Bert R. Boyce
Charles T. Meadow
Donald H. Kraft

One

Introduction to Measurement

1
Quantitative and Qualitative Aspects of Measurement

1.1
The Nature of Measurement

Measurement is the process of acquiring quantitative data about the physical world through the comparison of a known standard unit with a comparable property of an entity that we desire to characterize in a quantitative manner. Thus, all measurement is relative to a chosen unit. In common usage measurement is often said to be either absolute or relative. In this case *absolute* refers to the existence and use of an official standard which has a high degree of acceptance. The meter and gram are examples. *Relative* measurement would then suggest the use of a standard meaningful only in a particular context. "John is half as tall as his father" makes use of John's father's height as a standard, but such relative measurement is not meaningful outside the community of discussion in which at least an approximate grasp of John's father's height is a matter of common knowledge.

A standard system of physical measures has been evolved and adopted almost worldwide. The basic attributes measured and the units of measure are:

length	meter
mass	kilogram
time	second
electric current	ampere
temperature	°K (degree Kelvin)
luminosity	candela

To create an official standard for any of these, we may keep an actual prototype in a vault under controlled conditions and allow it to be employed to generate approximate copies for use in field comparisons. The standard meter once was a metal bar, stored this way in Paris. The meter was originally defined as 1/10,000,000 of a quadrant of a great circle through

3

the poles of the earth and the city of Paris. It is now defined more precisely as 1,650,763.63 wavelengths of the orange-red line in the spectrum of krypton-86, and a meter bar is no longer the official standard. It can be reproduced in a local laboratory and the trip to Paris to check the meter bar is not necessary. The official unit for time is defined by counting the oscillations of atoms or the revolutions of the earth around the sun, or using any other regularly recurring phenomena to provide a unit.

As with length, different standards for the common units of time have existed over the years and actually coexist now for different purposes. Currently the system of Coordinated Universal Time (UTC), maintained by the Bureau International de l'Heure in Paris, is the most generally accepted standard. The UTC second is the duration of 9,192,631,770 periods of radiation corresponding to the transition between the two hyperfine levels of the ground state of the cesium-133 atom. (*New Encyclopaedia Britannica*, 1989)

The International System of Units, or *Système Internationale,* known as the SI system, provides definitions widely accepted in the international scientific and technical community for units of amount of substance, electric current, length, luminous intensity, mass, temperature, and time. Communication is greatly facilitated if units of measurement are agreed upon and consistently used by all those who wish to discuss observable phenomena. If the universe of discourse is small and highly specialized, there is often considerable discussion over the appropriate unit and the definition of the measure which will be in use. This has certainly been the case in the area of information systems.

> Measurement, in most general terms, can be regarded as the assignment of numbers to objects (or events or situations) in accord with some rule. The property of the objects which determines the assignment according to that rule is called *magnitude,* the measurable attribute; the number assigned to a particular object is called its *measure,* the amount or degree of its magnitude. It is to be noted that the rule defines both the magnitude and the measure. (Kaplan, 1964, p. 177)

An attribute is a characteristic of an object that has a value or a magnitude. A measure is a description of, or an approximation of, this magnitude. A book, one example of an object, or entity, has many different characteristics, or attributes. If we are interested in whether or not the book will fit into a given space on a shelf, we are concerned with its length, width, and height. Each of these dimensions has a certain *magnitude,* a physically measurable characteristic which is inherent in the item. When we say a book's spine length is twenty centimeters we are comparing the *magnitude* of that dimension to the *magnitude* of some standard in order to assign a number, a *measure,* which will describe the *magnitude* to those familiar with the standard. If we can use the same scale to *measure* or represent the *magnitude* of the vertical space available between two shelves that we have used to represent the *magnitude* of the spine of the book, we can determine if the book will fit in the space without an actual trial.

In scientific inquiry we assume that we can conceptualize the objects of our interest in such a way as to be able to measure them. Given the objects of interest and the situation in which we consider them to have importance, we assume that we can find some relationship between objects and numerals (character digits used to name things) so that for each object we can establish a correspondence with one numeral. Several objects may, of course, have the same numeral under our assignment rule and thus be considered equal under the rule. The key problem is the discovery of a rule which will prove useful. In this book, our interest is in the measurement of information systems, and we shall attempt to present those rules which have been and are currently in use in the context of information systems. Before continuing with our general discussion of measurement it may be useful to describe this context, briefly.

1.2
Information Systems

An *information system* is a set of components whose combined purpose is to *acquire, process,* and *transmit* information. A typical modern information system is a set of computer hardware and software, operating rules, and operating personnel that, collectively, acquire, maintain, and distribute records. These systems may acquire, store, and process information related to a company's financial status or bibliographic information about a library's contents. However, there are other examples of information systems as defined in the broadest sense.

A home thermostat is one such example. A thermostat senses temperature in its immediate surroundings, compares this with a preset threshold temperature value, and either sends a message to a heating or cooling system to turn on or off, or in its own mechanical way decides to send no message. The preset threshold value may be called a *database,* in this case consisting of but one number. Another example is an international telephone system consisting of tens of millions of terminal sets (telephones), thousands of switching centers, miles of wire and glass fiber lines, terrestrial and satellite microwave links, and standards and procedures for interconnecting one system with another. Yet another example is a commercial database management system such as dBase IV, a software system. dBase IV must be combined with an appropriate computer and a database, acquired separately, plus a human operator. *Managing* the database means to collect input, possibly perform some selection or verification logic, store it, retrieve it as necessary, and operate upon it, whether mathematically or simply to arrange its order to enhance human perception.

An information system must have a means of acquiring data. In the case of the thermostat, this is a fully automatic operation in which readings are continuous and nonselective. The system accepts any temperatures presented to it. In the case of an accounting system or a bibliographic retrieval system, there must be considerable effort to select only appropriate input and to assure that all appropriate input is made available to the system. The selectivity of the system and the content of the input data are important aspects subject to measurement.

Processing data in an information system may consist of very elaborate mathematical computations, such as are needed in weather forecasting, using data sets descriptive of location, temperature, air pressure, humidity, rainfall, wind velocity, and the like. Or, it may be the trivial act of comparing the ambient temperature with the threshold temperature value. In information retrieval, it can mean storing information in an organized way to enhance subsequent retrieval operations, then carrying out those operations as directed by a user. Speed and cost are important variables here and they are frequently in conflict with each other. Both can be difficult to measure. Accuracy and reliability are important as well.

Data transmission can range from the simple thermostat's sending of an on or off signal up to a coordinated color graphic display combined with audio output. Speed and cost are again important attributes to measure, as is intelligibility of the output message to the intended recipient, often a most difficult attribute to measure.

In the field of information science, information retrieval systems are the central issue, although these are not the only ones of importance. We will, however, tend to concentrate on information retrieval issues and measurements.

One critical issue in the analysis of an information system is specifying the bounds of the system. When we use the phrase *information system* we mean any set of components that provides information, ranging from real-time air traffic control systems to boxes of archival records. We impose no restrictions as to the sort of information entities of concern, be they radar images, accounting records, e-mail messages, or books. An information retrieval service is a large information system that includes databases, information retrieval software and hardware, and intermediaries and interfaces with system users.

For an information retrieval service, it must be clear whether an analyst plans to focus on the hardware and software internals or include individuals interacting with the computer (such as intermediaries or users). If we are concerned with only the computer system, then such facets as performance, accuracy, and reliability of the computer and the software are things to be measured. However, if we include users, such things as user satisfaction must also be considered as something to be measured. We will use the phrase *information retrieval system* to refer to the hardware and software aspects of an information system and the phrase *information retrieval service* to include not only these components but also users, intermediaries, and materials for inclusion.

An information retrieval service selects materials for possible later use. It may create and store surrogate records for this material or may store the original material. It is often impractical to store the entity itself. For example, in an air traffic control system storing the in-flight aircraft is impractical, but storing supplemented radar images as surrogates makes the information system possible. An information retrieval system determines how records and queries are to be represented and matched for retrieval purposes.

An information retrieval system establishes the record formats and data structures required for updating and searching. It accepts queries, attempts to assure that these queries represent the needed information, and carries out a matching process. It also distributes the results and determines the best methods of evaluating the success of the total process and its components. The study of the analysis and design of such systems is known as the discipline of information retrieval. Systems so designed, whether they handle documents produced for other purposes or records designed specifically to meet anticipated information needs, are information systems.

Often these processes are carried out by manual systems using paper as a medium, but they can be, and often are, carried out by computer programs. In many cases an intermediary in the person of an information professional is to be found between the retrieval system and the individual with the need for information. This intermediary carries out those retrieval processes that the person may not feel confident in performing, and particularly provides an effective interface between the user and the system. (Kraft, 1985; Salton and McGill, 1983)

Information professionals use various means to bring knowledge about the materials available to the attention of potential system users. Items or their surrogates may be grouped in files in some order using classification, or listed alphabetically or numerically by some physically present characteristic of each item or its surrogate. Traditional document classification groups materials by disciplines. Classification need not be disciplinary in nature; it can be based on any common characteristic of the items. As the subjects of study have diversified and multiplied, organizational schemes have changed. Because of the interplay of subjects and the speed with which scientific research turns from one line of investigation to another, most new schemes for subject search have been created for specific subjects rather than trying to provide a broad system of ordering.

Many organizations design records and *entry points,* which are searchable attributes, to meet their particular internal information needs. These may include personnel records, financial records, correspondence, statistical information—in fact, any recorded representation of any sort of information. Others make use of commercial indexes of the journal and report literature in their disciplines in order to provide access to any item that could solve a problem addressed to the system.

Typically, an indexing agency is an information system that collects all journals, reports, patents, theses, conference papers, and selected monographs deemed to contain material of interest to a defined body of readers. Indexers then assign classification numbers and index terms to a citation representing each item and may append an abstract of the item. These citations, when loaded in a machine-readable database, can be retrieved by authors' names, a combination of index terms, or other available entries. Any word or phrase in the citation can be an entry point, and it is possible to include the full text of the item itself with the citation and to make each of the text's words an entry point.

Since the user almost surely will express the topic of inquiry in his or her own words, the service must be able to relate these words to synonyms and to terms with broader, narrower, or otherwise related meaning in order to retrieve all relevant citations. For this purpose controlled word lists known as *thesauri* are developed which require continual updating as language usage changes. Complex languages have yet to been shown to be more effective than single word stems extracted from text.

These databases of specially designed information records, more and more often containing full text, are then stored in formats and data structures that can be searched by the original person with the question or by an intermediary either manually in some printed medium, or, if in machine-readable form, by software written for retrieval purposes. In all cases the product is a list of records or partial records which to some degree or other match the stated request. If we are comparing the performance of retrieval systems, or subsystems of retrieval systems, it is this level of agreement between retrieved records and query that must be measured. Value in an information retrieval system or service is normally presumed to be its ability to answer successfully questions posed to it.

1.3
Reasons for Measurement

> When you can measure what you are speaking about, and express it in numbers, you know something about it; but when you cannot measure it, when you cannot express it in numbers, your knowledge is of a meager and unsatisfactory kind: it may be the beginning of knowledge, but you have scarcely, in your

thoughts, advanced to the stage of science, whatever the matter may be. (Lord Kelvin, 1889–1894, p. 73)

This view is perhaps overstated. As Kaplan says, "Measurement surely plays a part, and a very large one; but it is by no means the only method of extending and solidifying our knowledge" (Kaplan, 1964, p. 173). Measurement, however, allows us to make statements which can be clearly understood and verified by others. We cannot expect people to agree objectively on anything that is not the product of a deductive process. Some shared observations will result in many observers making the same subjective characterization of a common observation. Such agreement is known as *intersubjective agreement,* and when it can be anticipated among a large number of observers it is the basis of most scientific communication. Measurement incorporates common standards that allow a high degree of such agreement.

If we represent a color in terms of numeric measurement of the wavelength of light, rather than as nominal values, such as red or yellow, we can count on a high degree of intersubjective agreement, and we make it possible for our reported observations to be reproduced by others with similar interests. Measurement makes precise description a possibility. Perhaps even more important, once numbers have been assigned, calculation becomes possible. The techniques of mathematics become available for prediction, explanation, and verification once measurability has been established. It is one thing to be able to say that A depends upon B. It is quite another to be able to say that A increases exponentially as B increases geometrically.

Measurement also makes possible the standardization which is a central feature of modern industrial activity. Parts for machinery can be made to fine tolerances with the use of measurement and thus can become interchangeable. We can purchase 20 ribbons said to meet the specification for a printer with a reasonable expectation that all of them will fit even if the boxes indicate different sources and times of manufacture.

1.4
Composite Measures

Many, possibly even most, measures used in the world are not the fundamental measures of physics, but consist of combinations of the basic, directly observable phenomena. A simple example is area. To compute the area of a rectangle, a right triangle, or a circle, we measure, respectively:

Length and width (also a length measure) of the rectangle, then apply the formula $A = L \cdot W$.

Length of the base and the altitude, then apply $A = (1/2) \cdot B \cdot A$.

Length of the radius, then apply $A = \pi r^2$ (where π is the constant 3.141592 . . .).

Other examples of composite measures are density, which is volume divided by mass, and electric current flow, which is the amount of electric charge passing a point in a unit of time. A composite measure is any measure defined in terms of others, normally two or more. That temperature on the Kelvin scale is $K = C - 273$ does not make K a composite. That density requires both volume (itself possibly a composite, depending on the shape involved) and mass makes it a composite measure.

In the information world we rarely deal directly with the fundamental units of physics. Some measures are so far removed from the basic units that we cannot readily identify the basic units from which they were formed. For example, relevance is an important measure in information retrieval, being concerned with the extent to which one text or expression of information need is related to another text by subject, or is useful to the person with the information need. What are the units of relevance? There are none established. It could be defined as a ratio, i.e., the ratio of the relatedness between texts X and Y, compared with the ratio of text X with itself. This stratagem gets us out of the need to have a unit of measure but gains us little else.

Another aspect of composite measures is that they permit us to combine independent measures into a composite. For example, an organization might define a measure of merit for its employees as the sum of normalized measures of experience, education, and past performance.

There is nothing wrong, in any way, with using composites, so long as the user does not lose sight of what it is that the composite measures. We should not come to believe that the composite measure of employee merit completely evaluates the person. There are other facets to human performance that this measure did not take into account.

1.5
Measurement and Human Behavior

In terms of human behavior, we may question the value of measurement as we have just described it. There is a school of thought in the behavioral sciences (and information systems are certainly both an example and a result of human behavior) which denies the valid application of quantitative methods to its subject matter, and instead suggests that qualitative description only is appropriate. What is meant by quality?

1.5 Measurement and Human Behavior

Measures of human intelligence, something we are all quite used to, most people would probably accept as being useful, if imperfect assessments of mental capacity. Yet, there is not even a universal acceptance of the meaning of intelligence, even less of a measure for it. Standardized measures of intelligence such as scholastic aptitude tests and graduate record examinations have, over the years, been good predictors of a potential student's performance in school. They do not measure persistence, integrity, "grace under pressure," or other important attributes of job success. They are, in effect, heuristic measures, strongly culturally biased. We do not know exactly why they work, but they seem to, in properly limited applications. Such tests may also be considered to be ratios of one person's performance to an ideal performance, with no other dimensions stated or implied.

1.5.1 Relative Measures

Actually, it is probably useful to consider qualities and quantities as different sorts of predicates. "Sunday was cold," versus "Sunday the high temperature was 22 degrees." The first statement expresses a personal evaluation of the temperature indicating that it was lower than the norms preferred by the speaker. It could be true at widely varying quantitative values, depending upon the speaker's norms for location and time of year and other factors, such as humidity and wind speed, which will change the speaker's perception of the temperature. Another speaker might perceive the same conditions as "cool" or even "pleasant."

The second clause is a far more abstract description of the situation. It states the highest quantitative reading taken on the day in question using a particular scale. Most humans, in most environments, will consider 22 degrees Fahrenheit to be cold. A person who sees spring come after an Antarctic winter stay may not have any such perception. If we mean 22 degrees Celsius, of course, it will be more difficult to get agreement as to the use of the qualitative predicate "cold." These qualitative predicates are shorthand ways of expressing rough estimates of a great many variables that make up a part of the state of nature as it is perceived by a particular individual at a particular location and time. These variables often include normative judgments by the speakers. They are extremely useful in everyday communication, where a delineation of a great number of quantitative variables would be incredibly boring and delay the interchange of information. Basically, when we wish to employ a scale we use quantitative predicates, and when we do not wish to use a scale, either because our knowledge is insufficient to do so or because we wish to save time and do not consider the detail necessary for communication, we use qualitative predicates.

1.5.2 Measuring Quality

We can speak of high and low quality, but we are not here referring linguistically to an unscaled predicate. Rather, this refers to an unscaled measure of the speaker's satisfaction with some item, system, or process. When something is "high quality," it conforms to, or exceeds, certain standards which are deemed to be valuable. If it is "low quality," it fails to meet these standards. This use of the word "quality" as a measure might seem to presume an ordinal scale, but there is no assurance that any two observers would agree on the relative quality of an item. Their standards may vary, as may their perceptions of the items' closeness to these standards. It seems likely that there is a large number of quantitative variables, many of whose values are estimated, which are combined using some weighting scheme that varies from observer to observer, in order to form some judgment as to quality. However, it is possible that choices can be made on the basis of a reaction to perceptions of items as wholes, rather than on some combination of the values of a set of variables.

For purposes of illustration let us consider what quality may mean in the context of learned communication, or in any information system. In an age of information overload, it is clear that we wish to collect, store, retrieve, and disseminate only high-quality information. The costs of doing otherwise will inhibit the communication process. The problem, of course, is defining quality in such a way that the definition can be used in operational decision making.

Brown, in a discussion of quality, says the following:

> What is quality? For some . . . , it is indefinable, except that they know it when they see it. For others, it is perfection. For still others, it is an acceptable error rate. I would like to disenthrall ourselves from the emotional and subjective aspects of quality and put forward a definition of quality developed by Philip B. Crosby, author of *Quality Is Free* (1979) and *Quality Without Tears* (1984). He defines quality as "conformance to requirements." (Brown, 1987, p. 3)

Indeed. But what are the requirements? Let us consider quality in an information system. What are the requirements that we may establish in order to select the best materials for a collection given the typical constraints of budget and space? Quality in learned literature seems to depend upon novelty and originality, but to only a limited extent. These are certainly qualities often attributed to high-caliber contributions to the literature, but they are hardly sufficient and may not even be necessary. Rather, what is desired is a contribution to knowledge, which is an addition to current knowledge about a topic by filling a gap in existing understanding or by the synthesis of current knowledge into a theoretical explanation which can be verified by further experimentation. The judgment as to quality is normally made by the author's peers, acting as referees, reviewers, and consumers, and they are convinced by arguments beyond originality. In the eyes of the peer group, authority, established by personal reputation and by references, is important, and so are the legitimacy of the problem addressed and the general acceptability of the methods used to address that problem. The successful author in the learned literature will spend considerable time relating the current work to past efforts and approaches. Too much originality is suspect simply because it is not convincing.

On the other hand, it is considered important to provide evidence that overturns expectations or to suggest new methods which will have broad application. If this is not so, the work may possibly be labeled trivial and redundant. Quality appears in large measure to be judged upon rhetorical grounds.

Since judgments as to quality are made by peers in the learned communication system, the information professional needs some way of attaining peer evaluation prior to selecting documents for entry into an information system, prior to selecting documents for removal from an information system, and for ranking documents which have been assembled as a response to a query. Ideally we would like some quantitative measure of quality, some concrete statement of requirements, so that we might be able to state, with some hope of objectivity, that one item embodies more quality than another. However, since quality is apparently not an objective characteristic of a document but rather a perception of a document formed by those with the same interests and expertise as its author, the study of the document is not likely to reveal its quality to the nonexpert. Thus it would appear that the quantification of such expert opinion is the best hope for the information professional. Another possibility is an automated expert system peer evaluation technique.

It may be useful to consider quality in information-bearing units (documents) as distinct from value, a distinction made by Orr (1973). In this context, quality implies potential or capability, while value connotes the presence of measurable beneficial effects. Consider the work of Gregor Mendel, a mid–nineteenth century Augustinian monk who is credited today as the father of genetics. Mendel's study of pea plants led to results that were published in the *Proceedings of the Natural History Society of Brno* but were not recognized until 31 years later as the explanation of how natural selection could result in the production of a superior animal or plant rather than an average one and thus clarify the theory of evolution. Mendel's paper was certainly high-quality work, but it was not valuable work when it was published. Its value arose at a later date when its benefit to those trying to work out the details of the evolutionary process became clear.

We might consider quality to be *intrinsic* to a document and value to involve not the document but the measure of worth that is placed upon its availability by a user of a collection, or the mean value placed on its availability by all actual or even potential users of a collection. By an intrinsic quality we mean something that is inherent or built into the entity of which it is a part. The opposite case would be that of an *extrinsic* quality, where the characteristic is assigned to the entity from the outside and may be considered incidental to the entity itself.

The concept of quality is similar to that of "relevance" in the evaluation of answer sets in relation to queries in an information retrieval system. A document may be very similar as to topic to a query and yet not be of use to a particular patron's information need. This may be so if that patron is already aware of the document, or of the information it contains, or perhaps cannot understand it sufficiently for it to have any meaning and therefore value. Its value may change for this patron as exposure to other information sources allows the patron to gain understanding and to fit the information of the previously not relevant document into his or her understanding of the topic (Boyce, 1982).

Unfortunately, this analysis does not help us very much with the choice of documents for information systems. Since it is the patrons who must be pleased in order to count an information retrieval operation successful, it is value, and not quality in Orr's sense, that must be considered in the acquisition of documents. The separation of value from quality simply seems to be the separation of extrinsic quality from intrinsic quality. The usefulness of intrinsic quality, by definition, is that it is objectively observable in the document; its weakness is that it is insufficient to make collection management judgments. The strength of extrinsic quality, by definition, is that it is the expression of the patron's current and future requirements. Its weakness is that it is impossible to measure from examining the document alone. For example, if we choose documents on information systems based upon the high quality of their illustrations, we will have used an intrinsic quality criterion for selection. On the other hand, if extrinsic quality for our users will involve a strong emphasis on measurement, we would have to anticipate this if we are to use it for selection.

There are other issues in the measurement of human behavior aside from the issue of quality. However, most of the attempts to apply measurement to human behavior involve judgments that are not highly intersubjective, let alone objective. When we attempt to measure skill, experience, reliability, or intelligence of the individual, we are in the realm of the intangible. How do we measure experience? The fact that a person has ten years experience in teaching the principles of measurement may mean that the person has had ten full years of new and interesting situations that have contributed to his or her growth and learning. It may, of course, mean that the individual had but one year of such conditions reiterated ten times. The simple count of years does not fully reflect the growth of learning that may have taken place.

1.5.3 The Measurement of Human Behavior and Skills

The measurement of skills is no less difficult to carry out. Consider the use of standardized tests to measure verbal and analytical skills which are commonly used as admission criteria by institutions of higher education. These certainly reflect the skill level of those who take them, since the skills are directly tested. Doing word associations and problems in mathematics certainly demonstrates the ability to utilize such skills. It does predict the success of a student in a given educational program which emphasizes such skills. Some educational programs may not require such skills, however, and many other factors are involved.

There are many dangers associated with such tests. This is particularly so when an assumption is made that what is being tested is intelligence. Gould (1981, p. 24) makes this point clearly when he says, "What craniometry [measurement of skull size] was for the nineteenth century, intelligence testing has become for the twentieth, when it assumes that intelligence (or at least a dominant part of it) is a single, innate, heritable, and measurable thing." The fact that something is being measured, and that the something has been given a name, does not imply that what most people would consider to be the definition of the name is that which is being measured. This is most particularly true when we speak of abstract concepts, theoretical constructs with no physical existence, as if they were physical entities. If we define intelligence as that which is measured by the Binet IQ test, then, of course, the test measures intelligence. If we do so, however, we cannot apply the results to any other more common usages of the word intelligence. It is clear that Binet would never have claimed that his scale was anything but a rough empirical guide for the identification of children in need of special assistance.

If we move to more complex skill situations the status is even less clear. Can we test for the skills necessary to repair a transmission on a BMW or for the ability to do reference work at the desk in a public library without causing disruption in a real situation? In such instances the only real indication of such skill is its demonstration under realistic conditions. It seems doubtful that operational testing may be economically feasible in many cases in the real world.

Human reliability can certainly be measured. If it is feasible to observe and record actual human practice in meeting some operational standard, then we can collect information on how reliably the standard is met. We can send the same document to any number of indexers and note the differences in their products. We can check the carburetor assemblies of certain individuals on a production line to see if all parts are present and properly aligned.

Human behavior certainly involves purposes, goals, values, and beliefs. These vary from person to person, environment to environment, and may be internally inconsistent, requiring a choice of one over another in certain instances. All may be in play simultaneously when decisions are made. This situation seems far too complex to meet the normal requirements of measurement, and it may be just these circumstances that lead to the use of quality predicates and a "quality measure" in the behavioral sciences. But quantitative methods clearly can be used. Their use involves a process of simplification which will slant the outcome with the assumptions placed upon the data, but will, in all probability, lead to a solution. Nonetheless, it seems prudent to include some discussion of the effect of the normative aspect of human interaction on measurement and of just what measurement may mean in discourse on values, beliefs, ethics, and aesthetics. Since these aspects of human behavior are far more subjective than observations of the physical world and, from observation of human behavior in that world, apparently determined by individual cultural experience, we will treat them under the broad metaphysical rubric of value measurement.

1.5.4 The Measurement of Values

We need to consider at least two sorts of value. These are *economic value* and *normative value*. There are many theories of value and they are far from consistent with one another. In fact, the internal consistency of some value systems is subject to question. Since internal inconsistencies make for ambiguous decision criteria, it seems fair to measure the value of a value system on the basis of internal consistency, if nothing else. It is not always so easy, however, to get the proponents of a value system to agree that such inconsistencies exist. If, however, we can identify two different rules that counsel different behavior in a single set of circumstances, it seems likely that we could assign a negative unit of measurement for each such instance. This, however, will not help us to distinguish among conflicting, but internally consistent, value systems.

1.5.4.1 Normative Values

Normative values are standards of worth which can be used to set goals, to determine courses of action, and to set constraints on behavior that might otherwise seem the easiest path to attaining such goals. This implies a hierarchy of goals in human behavior, where we proceed toward accomplishment in a straightforward manner until we find pursuit of one goal leads to conflict with the pursuit of another. We must then decide which goals are highest, which take precedence. The ranking and selection of goals depend upon values, normative standards of behavior, which are held by individuals and societies.

1.5 Measurement and Human Behavior

At the opening of this chapter we defined measurement as based upon a known standard unit. The term value is often used to indicate the number assigned to a particular entity that indicates the magnitude of some measurable attribute in terms of this standard unit. Our meaning here is different. Normative values are standards of measurement against which we can measure our behavior. We do not normally consider a need for quantitative data in this metaphysical realm. We do, however, wish to be able to use our standards of behavior, our values, to order, and even to formulate, our goals.

Nearly all information agencies wish to preserve the information in the materials that they have acquired, and many wish to preserve the physical media in which that information is to be found. All information agencies wish to make the information they acquire available to a group of users. Yet there can often be a conflict between these two goals. This conflict can be resolved only by referring to values. Is the preservation role more valuable than the service role? Should we be concerned with possession of materials or access to materials? There is no objective answer to these questions. We can affirm both goals, but not in instances where they provide conflicting solutions for a decision problem. We want secure buildings with easy accessibility. Clearly, decisions will arise where choices must be made between these goals.

The same sort of problem exists in aesthetic decisions. We might be able to afford either a Monet or a Dali for our lobby wall, but not both. Both are currently available and both are said by art experts to have considerable aesthetic appeal. The source of a measure for ranking is not readily apparent. It would appear that the decision will have to be made on the basis of which artistic style is more valued.

Such values are the product of the individual's life experience, and since such experience varies we can expect the values to vary. These values are believed to be true. Beliefs require no evidence, but can be changed over time both by evidence and by social conditioning. Often social groups form in order to stabilize and encourage sets of such values. When they do so they may set up laws and customs to regularize certain of their values and preserve them over time. It should be obvious that the values of scientific inquiry—objectivity, quantitative measurement, reproducibility, free exchange of information, and truth—constitute such a value system. Their strength, and indeed their weakness, is that they have led us to our current level of control over our environment. Whether or not this is a net positive for humanity is, of course, a value question. Ethics, the discipline which inquires into value systems, no longer claims to determine what values should be. It is rather concerned that all value systems be viewed critically prior to their use in decision making.

> The task of theoretical ethics is not to lay down static norms by which each new moral problem that arises can be decisively answered. Its task is rather to develop a method suitable for the evaluation and criticism of existing norms and for the exploration of new value possibilities, in order that when moral decisions have henceforth to be made their grounds may be more adequate and more worthy. (Wheelwright, 1959, p. 20)

We are left with the view that goal conflicts are resolved by value judgments, and that value judgments are normally made by a reliance on a social consensus learned by the individual in his or her interaction with society, rather than by any calculus of underlying quantities. Values are standards against which our goals are measured, but no clear scales are applied for this purpose.

1.5.4.2 Economic Values

Economic value is based upon the concepts of scarcity and allocation. We have limited resources, our salaries for example, and are able to allocate portions of these resources for varied purposes. This means that choices must be made. Some goods will be excluded from our shopping list in favor of others and some will receive a higher portion of our resources than others. This ranking is sometimes called *value-in-use*. The value-in-use of a graduate degree in industrial engineering can be determined for any individual by asking that person to rank the degree against other goods in terms of the resources he or she is willing to expend to get them. Thus, it is possible to apply ordinal scales of measurement to such valuation.

We might also consider *market value,* in which we express the value of a good in terms of some other good for which it might be exchanged. The price in money is the most common market value, although we could receive our price in diamonds or hours of labor. These would be different expressions of market value. The market value of a share in a corporation is the amount that it would bring if sold. This value is an interpersonal one in that it results from the consensus actions of many individuals all of whom discover it the same way, by actual sale. Transferring a share of common stock without a charge does not affect its market value, which is determined only by a sale. Such a transfer is a gift of market value, which the recipient can determine only by a sale. A ratio scale is appropriate for measuring market values.

In fact, we often use *imputed values,* which are estimates of either value-in-use or market value, since the first may not be easily obtainable and the second requires loss of the asset. We presume that the value of the engineering degree was greater than the time, effort, and money expended to earn it. But the recipient, upon becoming unemployable, may not agree with this imputation of value. We may impute a value to our stock holdings based on previous sales, but we may not actually realize this value.

Not only are such estimates difficult to make with accuracy, they are not stable over time. The market will fluctuate and so will our personal opinions. While economic value is preferable to normative value for the purpose of measurement, in that it can be scaled successfully, we must realize that the unit of measurement in common use, the currency unit, is not a constant unit. The dollar, the pound, the yen, the franc, and all currencies vary over time in terms of their buying power. The ruler is highly elastic. If well-controlled index numbers, allowing us to speak in terms of constant currency units, are not in place, currency values radically misstate value despite their scalability (Hall, 1962, p. 258).

It is important to note that all forms of economic value are empirical concepts that require choices in actual situations. Not only do we have difficulty finding normative value systems based upon anything but consensus, we find that economic values occur only in real situations where choices are apparent. The theory of economic value is based upon behavior, it does not provide guidelines for behavior.

If we must make a general statement on the measurement of values, it is that it will be a matter of empirical choice where we consider the effects of the decision on ourselves and those around us. Certainly the modern British and North American systems of government find their philosophical underpinnings in the work of Jeremy Bentham and John Stuart Mill. For them value, which they termed utility, should be assigned to those actions which lead to happiness. "By utility is meant that property in any object, whereby it tends to produce benefit, advantage, pleasure, good, or happiness. . . . to the party whose interest is considered: if that party be the community in general, then the happiness of the community: if a particular individual, then the happiness of that individual" (Bentham, 1962, p. 34). This means that humankind should and will act in its own self-interest as long as that self-interest does not interfere with the rights of others to pursue happiness as well. The value of an action is measured by its likelihood of bringing happiness to the individual and the community.

1.6
Summary

We have seen that measurement is the process of acquiring quantitative data about the physical world. Such data make exact communication possible. Quantitative data are normally collected only after broad qualitative statements have been made which provide a certain direction and purpose to their collection. We have broadly characterized information systems in this way as a prolog to our discussion of measurement in their context.

The measurement of information systems involves the measurement of human behavior and the effectiveness of processes designed by humans. The measurement of human behavior inposes a great many obstacles. It involves individual values which are difficult to capture and may not be stable over time. Such measurement, even if not exact, can tell us a great deal about human behavior.

In later chapters we will discuss the utility or value of an item of information as it relates to an individual's statement of information need, or state of knowledge. Such values are personal and subjective, and yet an information system charged with supplying materials that will meet individual needs must simulate these judgments of value as closely as possible. Such system judgments are of value because the final user of information has not yet had the opportunity to indicate value in use, market value, or even to supply a solicted ranking of the available possibilities.

References

Bentham, Jeremy. (1962). An introduction to the principles of morals and legislation. In *Utilitarianism: On Liberty: Essay on Bentham* by John S. Mill. New York: The New American Library.

Boyce, Bert R. (1982). Beyond topicality, a two stage view of relevance and the retrieval process. *Information Processing and Management,* 18(3), 105–109.

Brown, Rowland C. W. (1987). Quality and OCLC. *OCLC Newsletter,* p. 3, (July/August).

Crosby, Philip B. (1979). *Quality Is Free: the Art of Making Quality Certain.* New York: McGraw-Hill.

Gould, Stephen Jay. (1981). *The Mismeasure of Man.* New York: W. W. Norton & Company.

Hall, Arthur D. (1962). *A Methodology for Systems Engineering.* Princeton, NJ: D. Van Nostrand.

Kaplan, Abraham. (1964). *The Conduct of Inquiry: Methodology for Behavioral Science.* San Francisco: Chandler Publishing Company.

Kelvin, William Thomson. (1889–1894). *Popular Lectures and Addresses.* London: Macmillan, Vol. I.

Kraft, Donald H. (1985). Advances in information retrieval: where is that /#*&@ record. *Advances in Computers,* 24, 277–318.

New Encyclopaedia Britannica. (1989). Measurement. Vol. 7, pp. 991–992. Metric system. Vol. 8, p. 73. Chicago: Encyclopaedia Britannica, Inc.

Orr, R.M. (1973). Measuring the goodness of library services: a general framework for considering quantitative measures. *Journal of Documentation,* 29(3), 315–332.

Salton, Gerard and Michael J. McGill. (1983). *Introduction to Modern Information Retrieval.* New York: McGraw-Hill.

Wheelwright, Philip. (1959). *A Critical Introduction to Ethics,* 3rd edition. Indianapolis: The Odyssey Press.

2

Methods of Measurement

2.1
Direct Observation

The most obvious method of acquiring quantitative data about the physical world, through the comparison of entities of interest and a known standard unit, is by direct observation. Such observation is the foundation of Western science. As Russell says, "Scientific method, although in its more refined forms it may seem complicated, is in essence remarkably simple. It consists in observing such facts as will enable the observer to discover general laws governing facts of the kind in question" (Russell, 1931, p. 13). But what counts as direct observation is not that clear. Russell, in a later chapter, goes on to question the very act of direct observation.

Seeing a friend, for example, is described as seeing a succession of colors moving across a fixed background which, by means of a conditioned reflex, bring to your mind the friend's name. Reflected from the atoms of your friend, light quanta from the sun enter your eye and produce a current in the optic nerve which produces the event in your brain you will term "seeing your friend." Such observation is "direct" in only a rather strange sense and only relative to other possibly even less direct observations. "We do not, therefore, ever see what we think we see. Is there any reason to think that what we think we see exists, although we do not see it? . . . Is there any way of proving that there are occurrences other than those that you yourself experience?" (Russell, 1931, p. 80). This is essentially Berkeley's classic position that only thoughts exist, allowing him to consider a physical universe that exists only as God's thoughts.

A modern scientist may only claim to search for laws and theories that connect his or her sensations, and not anything physical, but the ideas so established are interrelated with the work of other scientists and validated by the latters' opinions. This would seem to argue for the usefulness of other scientists, if not their existence. Whether or not there is an external world, we certainly may have sensory experiences and we may compare these experiences one with the other. We can assign numbers to these sensations according to some rule. If we use a rule that incorporates some physical standard, a meter stick say, we assume that our observations will be very similar to those of any other observer who uses the same physical standard. Direct measurement by observation seems to depend upon the assumption of an external physical world, an assumption which is very difficult to prove but without which we would have a great deal of difficulty with Western science as we know it.

What we seem to mean by direct observation is that statements can be made concerning our sensations using terms whose application is easily and directly verifiable by multiple observers. A high degree of intersubjective agreement (by which is meant verification by multiple observers) is considered evidence of objectivity.

Suppose we wish to determine the weight of an irregular object. Using a balance and a known standard gram weight, we may compare the two by observing the position of the balance pointer on its scale. If nine out of ten observers concur that the pointer indicates a balance, we will say we have objective evidence that the object weighs a gram. The fact that we do not have complete agreement about the observation is quite normal. We will discuss this problem at greater length in Chapter 3. If we can establish direct observability and a standard of some sort, measurement is possible. Measurement may also be possible when direct observability cannot be established.

2.2
Indirect Observation

If we allow inference to play a role in our observations, they are no longer direct. This would normally mean that we establish a term (attribute value) to represent a concept that is difficult to observe and then assume a connection between it and some directly observable phenomenon. When the phenomenon is encountered the concept is inferred. A planet, say, is inferred to be orbiting a distant star on the basis of periodic changes in observed radiated light from that star. The planet is not seen, yet it is observed indirectly. We can use a meter stick or calipers to make direct measurements of length. Is measurement possible in instances of indirect observation? Certainly it is.

The classical case is that of Hiero's crown (Heath, 1920). This king of Sicily was suspicious that his crown makers might not have used pure gold in the production of his new symbol of office. The king was advised that if he knew the volume of his crown, a bar of pure gold of equal volume could be prepared, and the two weighed in a balance. Unfortunately, the crown had been designed for aesthetics and not for easy computation of volume. Its shape could be described only as irregular in all of its dimensions. It could, of course, be melted and reformed into a shape from which volume could be geometrically calculated, but this would have been *destructive measurement* of the worst kind. Destructive measurement is any measurement technique which results in a serious reduction of the utility of the object measured.

Archimedes' solution was to suggest immersing the crown in a vessel filled to the brim with water, capture the resulting overflow, and by transferring it to a vessel in which volume could easily be calculated, determine the volume of the crown. Such indirect measurement is still carried out today using a device called a *pycnometer*. For a marvelously enjoyable discussion of the parallels between crown measurement and information retrieval effectiveness measurement, the reader is directed to an essay by Cooper (1978).

A great deal of modern measurement is indirect. Composite measures, like density in the case of a crown, must often be obtained indirectly. Temperature can be measured by first measuring the pressure of the air, since pressure and temperature are known to be directly related. The measurement of electrical current is based upon the fact that a current passing through a conductor produces a magnetic field and that this field will exert a force on other currents near it. Thus we can observe the movement of one conductor, when a current is passed through an adjacent one, and use that movement as a measure of the force of interaction, which, in turn, allows the calculation of a measure of the current. A great many measuring devices are now designed to produce an electrical signal which can be processed and utilized with a great deal of flexibility by machines. When a measurement of a quantity is impossible or inconvenient or needs to be utilized by some other device, transducers are often used. A transducer is an apparatus which converts one form of energy to another. A thermocouple, for example, transforms heat to an electrical signal; a photoelectric cell, light to an electrical signal.

As we will see, much of the observation of human behavior is indirect.

2.3
Opinion Measurement

When we wish to study the processes and activities that humans carry out, we can observe and record human behavior. There are, however, some attendant problems. There is considerable reason to expect that human behavior is affected by the knowledge that a subject is being observed. Persons aware they are under observation may well behave differently—for example, the way they believe they are expected to behave, rather than the manner in which they normally behave. This is called the Hawthorne effect, because a study of worker behavior in terms of quality control inspections at the Hawthorne plant of Western Electric found that workers responded to being studied as well as to other control variables such as lighting.

> In essence the Hawthorne effect is the result of an observer's presence upon the subject of the observation. The person observed will not perform in a typical manner for some time, if ever, because of the influence of the observer. There is no way to tell how this factor will affect the person; they may become very nervous and do very badly; they may work harder than they ever do when observed; or the presence of the observer may be viewed as a threat of some kind and the person will respond with the type of performance felt to be most likely to cancel the danger. (Evans, 1976, p. 26)

For example, several commentators have expressed great concern that current practice allows television news coverage of exit polls on the east coast of the United States to be broadcast before the close of voting booths on the west coast, which could influence the vote on the west coast. This argues for the use of unobtrusive data-gathering mechanisms. Unfortunately, these are often unethical, immoral, or illegal.

The fact that we observe more of a certain behavior today than was observed in previous years may imply only that we are doing more effective observation, not that the behavior is increasing over time. Many facets of behavior that might be quite valuable for study as responses to conditions are harmful to the subject in some way, hence are avoided. The effects of mass stimuli such as thermonuclear war are difficult to duplicate in the laboratory, and difficult to be prepared for in advance if we wish to observe the behavior that follows in the real world. Thus knowledge is normally gained from observing the effects after a natural or unplanned occurrence. The observation of such "social experiments" or "nature's experiments" has the benefit of great potential for observable effect and scale, but also has the disadvantage of a lack of controls.

Maintenance of control is possible in such situations, but often at a price we do not wish to pay. We can conceal our observation or mislead our subjects into a belief that we are observing behavior A when, in fact, we are observing behavior B. We can pay them to accept pain or deprivation. These techniques are certainly used, but they bring uncomfortable moral questions into our experimental designs. For this reason, we sometimes solicit opinions *about* behavior when measuring *actual* behavior becomes too difficult, although, as with observation, solicitation of opinion can also influence those opinions.

2.3.1 Surveys and Questionnaires

In information systems, aside from technical questions concerning the physical operations and design of a system, we are interested in what people *need* in the way of information resources, what they *believe they need* in the way of information resources, how they go about *finding* and *using* these resources, how they *evaluate* particular resources as relevant or not relevant to their needs, and what will *produce satisfaction* as a response to our efforts. These questions are not easily answered from direct observation of subjects seeking information. They are more concerned with the subjects' opinions, their feelings, beliefs, and thought processes. Such information cannot be directly observed. However, the subject's expression of these things can be observed, recorded, and studied. The instrument for the collection of such data is the *questionnaire* or, when more carefully and systematically structured, the *survey* or *poll*.

The questionnaire is the means by which data are consistently gathered for use in surveys and polls. However, the use of a questionnaire is insufficient to demonstrate the presence of either a survey or a poll. The questionnaire may be only a list of questions. A good questionnaire will solicit the required information with questions that are correctly structured and precisely worded, with terms defined, and it will have a positive motivational effect on the respondent by appearing to be highly interesting, easy to comprehend, and requiring only a minimum investment of time and effort for completion. If the researcher and the participant have different interpretations of the question, the data will have little value. It has been common in information retrieval experiments to ask judges whether or not a paper was relevant to a particular request without firm agreement on what was meant by relevance. This point will be discussed again in Chapter 13. The possibility of feedback at the time the questionnaire is administered may overcome the possible ambiguity.

Questionnaires are normally administered in person by an investigator (a flexible and effective but very expensive method), by telephone (a less costly and less effective method), and by mail (which is relatively inexpensive but where response rates tend to be low). An excellent source on the design and use of questionnaires is Dillman (1978).

Marsh (1982, p. 9) defines the survey "as an inquiry which involves the collection of systematic data across a sample of cases, and the statistical analysis of the results." More specifically, she requires measurement of variables over a series of cases and analysis to determine the existence of patterns. This is what Royse (1991, p. 103) calls an *explanatory survey*. He also allows for what he terms *descriptive surveys* and *exploratory surveys*. The former provide summary data for a known population and the latter provide initial information to assist in the planning of more rigorous studies. However, such studies, because of their lack of rigor, could easily be termed questionnaire applications and not surveys at all. It is really the random selection of cases for study and the statistical procedures for analysis that make a survey study something more than a questionnaire study. Not surprisingly, a good survey study will need to make use of a good questionnaire. However, it is not uncommon to hear a good questionnaire referred to as a survey, when what is meant is rather a survey instrument.

Such instruments are quite appropriate in a setting where conducting an experiment poses some difficulty. If we construct a survey that indicates the attitudes a population has toward other people prior to a thermonuclear war and then resurvey the survivors after the "social experiment," we may well gain information on changing attitudes. In order to test a hypothesis which might explain our observations of the real world, we must use either survey or experimental methods. Since we can hardly set up a thermonuclear war in order to analyze its effect on a particular variable, we must simply gather data on that variable, form our hypothesis, and be prepared to gather data once again after the stimulus of interest occurs. This is not the same thing as the random allocation of subjects to control and test groups as an experimental methodology would require. We cannot be sure that a change in attitude that covaries, for example, with the number of explosions to which we have been exposed has not been the result of some third variable which causes the variance in both. In an experimental setting the investigator would control the number of explosions and thus could be confident in the meaningfulness of any discovered relationship.

> In other words, in survey research the process of testing causal hypotheses, central to any theory-building endeavor, is a very indirect process of drawing inferences from already existing variance in populations by a rigorous process of comparison. In practice, one of the major strategies of the survey researcher is to control for other variables that she thinks might realistically be held also to produce an effect, but she never gets round the purist's objection that she has not definitely established a causal relationship. . . . any relationship which one finds may be explained by the operation of another unmeasured factor. (Marsh, 1982, p. 7)

Since information agencies are concerned with meeting the needs of their clients, needs assessment is a key element for any information system. There are several strategies for the assessment of needs, but the survey is a most common technique (Nickens et al., 1980, p. 3; McKillip, 1987). Survey research is frequently found in the measurement of the needs of the users and potential users of information systems, and in the measurement of the success of these systems in their responses to these needs.

The opinion poll is quite similar to the survey, but its purpose is not that of scientific inquiry but rather the prediction of attitudes and feelings that a population will have concerning various topics, events, and personalities. The technique is used extensively in politics and in marketing. If we are concerned about how a population views our product, or with how many of a population are likely to vote for a particular candidate, opinion polling is quite effective. In effect the respondent is being asked to make a choice at the time of the poll, that he or she may later make on election day, or on his or her next shopping trip to the hardware store. Assuming a truthful response, and no change in opinion until the actual choice is made, such polls should be quite effective as long as the sampling procedure that is in use truly reflects the population under review. Thus, much of the work on effective polling concentrates on good sampling techniques, and polls have become more and more accurate as these techniques have improved. As long as a sample is random, it is sample size that determines the range of error. A sample of 2000 can be expected to provide a margin of error of about 3% in either direction, however large the population of interest may be. Naturally the questionnaire must be a good one that does not instill a bias and that is clear and impartial. The would-be respondents must be knowledgeable and accessible when polled.

2.3.2 Comparison to Standards and Norms

Once it has been determined what can be usefully observed and whether or not experimental or survey techniques are the appropriate approach, standards and norms must be defined so that a scale of measurement can be utilized and meaningful statements made concerning variations in observed values.

This usually means that we must have a qualitative hypothesis that allows us to choose certain variables that can be observed and on which data can be accumulated. When data are accumulated, variable values can be associated by co-occurrence with success and failure, as they are intuitively viewed. Such values become standards. Suppose we speculate that physical size will predict athletic success. If successful linemen in a professional football league weigh more than 250 pounds and are taller than 6 feet, we are probably willing to establish these values as standards and will not consider a person for the position who does not meet the standards. We may find that students with less than a 3.0 undergraduate grade point average are generally not successful in graduate education. We may then require a standard to be met as a condition of entry into a graduate program. Measurement and standards together allow us to make decisions on an objective basis.

Normally, we would like to have several measurable criteria and allow high scores in one to balance low scores in another. Thus, we might want to measure the prospective lineman's speed or the student's score on a standardized test. In both cases, we might also want to consider the intangible attribute of persistence under adversity.

The fact that something can be easily observed and measured does not necessarily imply that such activity has value. As Russell says:

> At the period when I received what was in those days called an education, psychology was still, to all intents and purposes, a branch of philosophy . . .

there existed a form of psychology which made use of laboratories and attempted to be very scientific. . . . You showed a man a picture of a dog, and said: "What's that?" You then carefully measured how long it took him to say "dog"; in this way much valuable information was amassed. But strange to say, in spite of the apparatus of measurement, it turned out that there was nothing to do with this valuable information except to forget it . . . scientifically-minded psychologists looked about for something measurable connected with their subject matter. They were wrong, however, in thinking that time intervals were the appropriate thing to measure: this position, as it turned out, is occupied by the saliva of dogs. (Russell, 1931, p. 174)

The point is simply this. Facts, meaningful observations, can be collected only with a working hypothesis in mind. Facts do not speak for themselves. We observe with certain expectations and it is deviation from these expectations that sparks our interest.

2.4
Summary

We have seen that measurement is not all that clearly objective, since the act of observation is itself not so clearly objective. We must settle for a high degree of intersubjective agreement on observations. This observation must be of useful variables that actually bear upon what we are trying to learn or establish. In some cases we must observe one attribute, whose variation reflects that of some other attribute, not so easily observed. Opinions are not directly observable and must be solicted carefully.

The maintenance of controls on variables in the social sciences is not an easy matter and the choice of variables that can be both observed and controlled greatly limits what can be chosen to support or invalidate an hypothesis. The choice must be made on the basis of the hypothesis, however. Observability and controllability are not sufficient.

References

Cooper, W. S. (1978). A perspective on the measurement of retrieval effectiveness. *Drexel Library Quarterly,* 14(2), 25–39.
Dillman, Don A. (1978). *Mail and Telephone Surveys,* New York: John Wiley & Sons.
Evans, G. Edward. (1976). *Management Techniques for Librarians.* New York: Academic Press.
Heath, T. L. (1920). *Archimedes.* New York: Macmillan.
Marsh, Catherine. (1982). *The Survey Method.* London: George Allen & Unwin.
McKillip, Jack. (1987). *Need Analysis for the Human Services and Education.* Newbury Park, CA: Sage Publications Inc.
Nickens, John M., A. J. Purga, and P. P. Noriega. (1980). *Research Methods for Needs Assesment.* Washington: University Press of America, Inc., 3.
Royse, David. (1991). *Research Methods in Social Work,* Chicage: Nelson-Hall.
Russell, Bertrand. (1931). *The Scientific Outlook.* New York: W. W. Norton & Company, Inc.

3

Accuracy and Reliability of Measures

3.1
Measurement of Measurement Devices

We can now discuss with some clarity the problems of practical measurement and the approaches to overcoming them. Even when we are concerned with measurement based upon direct observation, problems exist. It is important to understand that no measurement can be repeated with fidelity. We can easily use the same instrument to measure the same object at two different times and get different readings. Bragg (1974, p. 4) gives seven factors which will cause a simple micrometer, a device for making precise linear distance measurements, typically of the diameter of an object, to provide different readings on the same object. They are: operator changes, room temperature, dirt on the workpiece measured, tension on the spindle, zeroing error, misreading of the dial, and interpolation errors. If we are taking and recording measurements from different items, using different instruments, we may add actual variations in the items and instruments as sources of variation in our observations. As Bragg says, "variability is fundamental to all measurement systems."

There are also theoretical issues which menace consistent measurement, although they have little practical effect in everyday measurement problems. Consider what is known as Heisenberg's uncertainty relation.

> Heisenberg's remarkable discovery was that there are limits beyond which we cannot measure accurately, at the same time, the processes of nature. These limits are not imposed by the clumsy nature of our measuring devices or the extremely small size of the entities that we attempt to measure, but rather by the very way that nature presents itself to us. In other words, there exists an ambiguity barrier beyond which we can never pass without venturing into the realm of uncertainty. (Zukav, 1979, p. 111)

> It is a fundamental rule of quantum mechanics that *in principle* it is impossible to measure precisely certain pairs of properties, including position/momentum, simultaneously. There is no absolute truth at the quantum level . . . in the everyday world, the same uncertainty relation applies, but . . . the amount of uncertainty involved is only a tiny fraction . . . we can measure the position and momentum of a pool ball as we like, by tracking it as it rolls across a table, and the natural uncertainty of something comparable to 10^{-27} in either position or momentum won't show up in any practical way. (Gribbin, 1984, p. 120)

Nonetheless, unaccounted variables will always have influences on our observations, and we should realize that if what we measure influences the instrument of measurement (as it must if we are to observe a result), then it follows that the instrument may influence that which is measured. Such measurement is *intrusive* in nature. As Bragg (1974, p. 5) points out, a thermometer placed in a cup of coffee will cool the coffee.

Most measurement devices are transducers. They transfer one type of energy to another. The thermometer has thermal energy for an input and mechanical energy for an output. Unwanted input (noise), time lags (consider how quickly a mercury thermometer may register an increase in temperature), and other factors as well may result in poor transfers of energy for the measurement required. It is even possible to use one measuring device indirectly to measure a phenomenon for which it was not designed. This may or may not lead to error.

It may be possible to compensate for sources of error if they are systematic, but they will have some effect. We need to be able to operate in a measurement environment that is less than exact and still have confidence in our results. There is no such thing as exact measurement. There is the possibility of setting limits within which a measurement may be determined to fall. We need sufficient measurement technology to carry out the task at hand. This will require technical standards of measurement which will need to be met for any individual problem. In a sense, we are talking now about measuring the effectiveness of measurement systems. There is a more or less standard terminology useful in discussions of this area. Three generally descriptive terms are *resolution, precision,* and *accuracy* (Sydenham, 1979, p. 46).

3.1.1 Resolution

Resolution is the finest interval of an instrument's measurement scale that can be distinguished by an observer. Magnifying glasses and amplifiers can be used to increase resolution. It is necessary that an instrument's scale be fine enough to make readings sufficient for a problem. This does not imply that precision and accuracy will be adequate.

3.1.2 Precision

Precision, as used in measurement theory, is an expression of how well a measurement process repeats each time the same measurement is made. (In information science *precision* is a specific attribute. See Section 13.2.) It is assumed when determining precision that the parameter being measured remains fixed and that the variation in values observed is due to the process of measurement itself. In order to measure precision we must have sufficient resolution to observe its occurrence. A series of observations may all be incorrect, but if they are very close to one another they will be precise. Normally the time period in which the observations are made is quite short. When we view the scattering of values over longer periods of time the term *reproducibility* is often used for the same concept. If we are constantly using the same equipment and are not concerned about comparing results with measurements done elsewhere, resolution and precision will be sufficient to observe experimental variations.

3.1.3 Accuracy

If the values resulting from a measurement process are to be compared with measurements from other processes, we must also be concerned with accuracy. Accuracy expresses how well a value, or a measure of central tendency of a series of values, agrees with a value which has been set as a standard. Accuracy is achieved through *calibration*.

3.1.4 Calibration

Calibration is the checking of an instrument of measurement against a known standard on a regular basis to warrant its accuracy. It is rare that we can use a primary standard. As we pointed out in Chapter 1, such standards now rarely exist in physical terms, but rather are expressed in terms of naturally occurring constants. Calibration of instruments is most usually done with secondary standards, which may themselves have been calibrated with the primary standard. It is generally thought that a secondary standard should possess an accuracy at least ten times that of the instrument to be calibrated (Sirohi and Rada, 1983, p. 2). The calibration curve which is produced by plotting input values (known values of the standard in use) against output values (the corresponding readings of the instrument of measurement) should be linear. In practice, linearity *tolerances* are set at a percentage of the scale above and below the ideal curve, and calibration is assumed if the actual curve does not break these bounds.

3.2
Tolerance

Tolerance is not only basic to calibration, it is also basic to the act of measurement itself. When we carry out a measurement in order to see whether or not some item meets the standards we require, we must take into account the knowledge that nothing will ever precisely meet our standard. Even assuming an instrument brings no imprecision or lack of accuracy to measurement, that which is measured will certainly exhibit variations. Temperatures change, material expands and contracts, and if we are producing different instances of the same class of thing, a printer ribbon, a search of a database, or a hard disk drive unit, we cannot expect the product to have exactly the same measurement readings in each instance even though we try very hard to control the variables which might cause such variation.

We may demand very fine requirements be met, but we must always allow some margin of deviation from the precise measurement specified. The specification of this margin of deviation is the setting of tolerances, and the margin itself is the tolerance. Tolerances may be unilateral or bilateral. For purposes of quality control in manufacturing, if the surface of a part is not to come in contact with anything during its use, then tolerances on either side (bilateral) are acceptable. Unilateral tolerances are used to encourage deviations to occur in only one direction. Although we cannot prevent deviation, we can cause process parameters to be set to move error in the desired direction. If fit is significant to proper overall performance, then unilateral tolerances can be used, with smaller than nominal size being permissible but not larger than nominal. This would be based upon the reasoning that a slightly larger than nominal part will not fit, whereas a slightly smaller one will do so.

On the other hand, if the goal is not getting the most parts that fit on the first run but rather eliminating wastage of material, a unilateral tolerance in the other direction could be used. This would encourage errors to lead to parts too large for fit, which could then be remachined to reduce their size to within tolerance. A part cut too small would be all wastage because material could not be added back. Unilateral tolerance setting depends upon process goals.

This concept applies to measures of other sorts. Whenever we wish to minimize deviation in one direction, unilateral tolerances are used, since they encourage those who have some control over the process to ensure errors are in the proper direction. If we are searching a database we may accept a large number of less than useful records in order to be sure we are collecting the largest possible number of those we would find useful. We might also set our unilateral tolerances in the other direction in order not to have to view a large number of less than useful records, if we felt no compelling need to find every useful record.

Whether tolerance is bilateral, or in either direction, the size of the permissible tolerance is also a matter for consideration. The range of tolerance limits will be chosen as the result of a trade-off negotiation between cost and certainty of meeting the desired performance. The smaller the tolerance the more likely performance will meet expectations, but the more difficulty and expense will be involved in meeting the tolerances. If you are doing the work you will be glad to have a large margin of error. If you are using the product you will be glad to have a small margin of error.

3.3
Summary: What, Me Measure?

In our discussion of information systems in Chapter 1 we outlined the purposes and goals of such systems. This was an important activity, because if we wish to apply measurement techniques to information systems, we must first determine what variable quantitative information it might be that would assist us in understanding and operating information systems. We wish to be sure, as Russell (1931, p. 174) might say, that we are doing the equivalent of measuring the saliva of dogs, rather than the time period it takes for a person to say dog after seeing a picture of such an animal. What we measure, and to what purpose we measure it, is far more important than the device used.

There is the legend of the physics professor who asked on a final examination how one could use a barometer to measure the height of a tall building. Clearly, the professor wanted the students to discuss its use to measure the air pressure at the bottom of the building and compare it to the pressure at the top and to use the difference to calculate the building's height. One student instead discussed several other options, neglecting to mention air pressure at all. As the folklore goes, the student suggested that he could drop the barometer from the top of the building and time its fall, thereby allowing him to calculate the height indirectly. The student also suggested that he could offer the superintendent of the building a lovely barometer in return for information on the building's height. The tradition is that the student flunked the test but the dean overruled that grade because the student proved a solid knowledge of physics as well as a sense of humor on an imprecise test question.

References

Bragg, Gordon M. (1974). *Principles of Experimentation and Measurement.* Englewood Cliffs, NJ: Prentice-Hall, Inc.
Gribbin, John. (1984). *In Search of Schrodinger's Cat: Quantum Physics and Reality.* Toronto: Bantam Books.

Russell, Bertrand. (1931). *The Scientific Outlook*. New York: W. W. Norton & Company, Inc.

Sirohi, R. S. and H. C. Rada Krishna. (1983). *Mechanical Measurement*. New York: John Wiley & Sons.

Sydenham, P. H. (1979). *Measuring Instruments: Tools of Knowledge and Control*. Stevenage, U.K.: Peter Peregrinus Ltd.

Zukav, Gary. (1979). *The Dancing Wu Li Masters*. New York: Bantam Books.

4

Sets and Scales

4.1
Sets

Many measures, and the scales used to measure them, are based on considering sets of objects—such as words or records—as aggregates. Here, we introduce some of the basic concepts of sets and operations on them. A set is a collection of objects that are distinct from one another. *Set membership* is defined by either a list (Bert, Charlie, and Don) or a rule (the authors of this book).

4.1.1 Set Definitions

The set of all possible entities under consideration is called the *universal set* or *universe of discourse* and is sometimes symbolized by **X**, although other symbols may be used, depending on context. The universe of discourse when discussing playing cards as used in bridge or poker is the set of 52 cards; when discussing voting patterns it is the set of registered voters. Playing cards are often used to illustrate statistical concepts because the card deck is generally well understood and simple in form, yet allows for enough variation to illustrate the concepts.

This population is a collection of the following 52 elements:

{$A♠,2♠, \ldots ,10♠,J♠,Q♠,K♠,$
$A♥,2♥, \ldots ,10♥,J♥,Q♥,K♥,$
$A♦,2♦, \ldots ,10♦,J♦,Q♦,K♦,$
$A♣,2♣, \ldots ,10♣,J♣,Q♣,K♣$},

where we view the ace as 1 and the jack, queen, and king as 11, 12, and 13, respectively. The symbols ♠, ♥, ♦, and ♣ indicate spades, hearts, diamonds, and clubs, respectively, and spades and clubs are normally black and hearts and diamonds red.

More specific to information science, we consider *entities,* objects or concepts about which we have information; *attributes* or *fields* which describe an entity; and *values* of attributes, which are the specific instances or occurrences of attributes. Then we consider sets of attribute values called *records* and sets of records called *files*. A *file* is a set of records, where normally all the record entities have something in common, such as all the books in a given library, all the employees of a firm, or all the accounts in a bank. Examples of an entity are a book, an employee, or a bank account. Examples of attributes are a book's title, an employee's date of birth, or the bank account's balance. Values might be *Measurement in Information Science,* 22 Feb 1976, or $500.42.

4.1.2 Basic Set Operations

There are certain operations on sets that are of frequent interest to information systems. These are the operations of *Boolean algebra.* If A and B represent sets, then we define:

A∪B or A + B *Union of sets A and B;* the logical sum, or the set of elements in either A or B or both.

A⊕B *Exclusive union;* the union less the intersection, i.e., all items which are in set A or Set B but *not* in both. The operation is called *exclusive or.*

A∩B or A·B *Intersection of sets A and B;* the logical product, or the set of elements that are in both A and B.

A~B or A-B *Difference of sets A and B;* the logical difference, or the set of elements that are in A but are *not* also in B.

| A | or m *Magnitude of a set;* the number of elements in set A. In a database context, this may be the number of records in a file or the number of terms in a record.

-A, ~A or A′ *Complement of a set* or *negation of a set;* the elements of the universal set or universe of discourse that are *not* in A, i.e., **X** − A.

4.1.3 Characteristics of Set Operations

The operation *union* is *associative* and *commutative,* as is addition in arithmetic, meaning that any number of sets may be combined by *union* in any order. Associativity means that

$$(A \cup B) \cup C = A \cup (B \cup C)$$

Commutativity means that

$$A \cup B = B \cup A$$

4.2 The Concept of Scale

so that pairs of sets may be grouped and the order of appearance in an expression can be reversed or rotated.

Intersection is associative and commutative like union, so that any number of sets may be so combined in any order. *Disjoint* sets are sets whose intersection is the empty set. These may also be called *mutually exclusive,* since an element occurring in one precludes it from occurring in the other. Consider, for example, the intersection of the set of all spades in a card deck with the set of all red cards. The sets are disjoint; the intersection is empty.

The complement of the set, R, of red cards, those elements of D that are not in R, is the set of black cards:

$$R' = \{A\spadesuit, 2\spadesuit, \ldots .K\spadesuit, A\clubsuit, 2\clubsuit, \ldots .K\clubsuit\}.$$

The union of a set with its complement, R∪R', is the universe of discourse, since everything is either in that set or not in that set. The intersection of a set with its complement, R∩R', is the empty set, since nothing is both in a set and not in it.

It is also true that

$$R \cap (H \cup P) = (R \cap H) \cup (R \cap P)$$
and
$$R \cup (H \cap P) = (R \cup H) \cap (R \cup P)$$

Thus, both intersection and union follow the distributive law, as does multiplication in arithmetic. Moreover,

$$(H \cup P)' = H' \cap P'$$
and
$$(H \cap P)' = H' \cup P'$$

These relationships are known as DeMorgan's laws (DeMorgan, 1847; Quine, 1950, p. 53).

4.2
The Concept of Scale

Let us return to the idea, presented in Chapter 1, of finding a rule that will assign a useful correspondence between numerals and the objects of our consideration. The rule will state the relationship among the numerals and the objects. It is certainly not always true that the relationships so specified coincide with the normal relationships among the numbers themselves. Manipulation of the numerical symbols will reveal relationships among the objects, but what constitutes permissible manipulation will depend upon the original rule. When we use the Fahrenheit scale of temperature, if it is 60 degrees in Baton Rouge and 30 degrees in Toronto, we cannot assume that it is twice as warm in Baton Rouge as in Toronto even though 60 is twice 30.

The *scale* is the logical structure of the assignment rule. It tells us what operations on the numbers assigned for measurement will give us significant results concerning whatever it is we are measuring. Scales range from *nominal*, which essentially gives only a name to an attribute, rather than a numeric value, to *ratio*, which provides numbers that are amenable to mathematical computation. An intervening type scale is *ordinal*, which tells only which of two values is greater but allows for little computation based on the values. The scales will be reviewed in increasing order of the power of the mathematics that can be used with them.

4.3
Nominal Scales

It is possible that numbers are assigned only as symbolic names or codes. Suppose that we use a program that generates eight-digit random numbers and assigns one of these to each purchase request that we place for a computer. We can then refer to that purchase request throughout the acquisition process by that number, and perhaps we can for some purposes refer to the computer ordered by that number, but we cannot say that PR number 8990501 was generated before or after 9908501. The numbers are not additive. Their sum does not refer to any computer at all. These numbers are discrete and qualitative. They imply no order of the items. Such a use of notation defines a *nominal* scale.

We might consider telephone numbers and social security numbers if we doubt the usefulness of nominal scales in the manipulation of large files. We would not wish to identify southern Louisiana or southern Ontario by a textual description in order to make a telephone call. Whether the use of a nominal scale is really characterization of some attribute of an object in a quantitative manner is perhaps open to question. The numbers assigned have no characteristics of quantities beyond identity and difference. There is no reason to assume that area code 504 has more or less of any measurable attribute than area code 416. Thus, although it is of great utility in some cases, the usefulness of a nominal scale in measurement is at best severely limited.

Dewey classification numbers for library shelves are one example of the same sort of nominal scale. The number only implies a likeness of the materials assigned to it. We may file the 800s before the 900s, but this is a convenience to assist in finding the materials. There is no implication that history is in any sense greater than literature or that it is preceded by literature in any real sense. In fact, numerals are often assigned for classificatory purposes with taxonomies being implied by the assignment. The decimal nature of the code does have some ordering value. As we shall see in Section 4.4.3, the structure it imposes upon the subjects may be more than nominal.

4.4
Ordinal Scales

To be able to discuss useful scales of measurement we must first consider the concept of order. An *order* can be precisely defined. It is a relationship which has certain characteristics among the members of a well-defined set of items. Relations can be symmetric, asymmetric, antisymmetric, or nonsymmetric. To be an order relation, the relation must first be *asymmetrical*. This means that it can hold in only one direction when viewed relative to two members of the set.

4.4.1 The Concept of Ordering

Consider a set of eight people who are members of an extended family group and who are present in a room at a particular location. We will designate each individual by a letter, A through H. For asymmetry to hold between A and B, A must be in a relation with B and B cannot be in the same relation with A. Consider the relation "is the father of." If A is the father of B, then it can hardly be that B is the father of A. Fatherhood is an asymmetrical relationship.

Cousin is a *symmetrical* relationship. If C is a cousin of D, then D is a cousin of C. A relationship such as "not younger than" is *antisymmetric*. If C is not younger than D, and D is not younger than C, then C and D are the same age. There are *nonsymmetrical* relationships as well. That E is in fear of F does not imply that F is in fear of E or that F is not in fear of E. Either may be the case.

While asymmetry is necessary for an order relation, it is not sufficient. Such a relation must also be *transitive*. This means that if it holds between two members and between the second of these and a third, then it also holds between the first and the third. If A is the ancestor of D and D is the ancestor of H, then A is the ancestor of H. "Is an ancestor of" is transitive. Following the reasoning of the previous paragraph, it should be apparent that fatherhood is intransitive and "is in fear of" is nontransitive.

Any relation that is both transitive and asymmetric is one that establishes an order on the set in question. If every two members are in the relation in one direction or the other, the order is said to be *complete*. If the relation does not apply to some of the members then the order is said to be *partial*. Suppose that we set each of the members to complete a crossword puzzle and hand it in. They can then be ordered by the relation "is a faster puzzle solver." In fact, we can have them form a line with the first to complete first, the second, second, and so on. This will be a complete order. We can now assign numerals as a *measure* of puzzle solution speed. If A completed the task before C we must assign A a lower numeral, designating a lower number, than the numeral assigned to C. If we assigned a higher numeral to A we would be expressing the relation "is a slower puzzle solver." The numbers assigned say nothing about the magnitude of puzzle solution speed, however. The difference between the first to complete and the second could be ten minutes and between the second and the third ten seconds, but this magnitude would not be expressed in the notational order we have assigned. To indicate "is a slower puzzle solver" we could assign the sequence of numbers (17,15,13,11,9,7,5,4) to indicate the order, or the sequence (9,8,7,6,5,4,3,2), or even the alphabetical sequence (h,g,f,e,d,c,b,a). We could reverse the sequences to indicate the relation "is a faster puzzle solver."

4.4.2 Equivalence Relations

It is possible that two puzzle solvers may complete the puzzle at exactly the same time. Their puzzle-solving relationship is symmetric and transitive. We would have to assign them the same numeral to indicate that they held the same relative position to the remaining members of the set. These members are said to be in an *equivalence* relationship and the order we have established is now a *weak* order, since more than one member may hold the same position. All puzzle solvers who complete their puzzle in the same time are said to be members of the same *equivalence class*. If, however, we consider that it is the equivalence classes that are ordered, including those with only one member, the order remains *strong*. Asymmetry is used for strong ordering, and antisymmetry can be used for weak ordering. Suppose that four puzzle solvers (A,B,C,D) solve the puzzle in ten minutes, that three other solvers (E,F,G) complete it in five minutes, and that the other (H) solves it in twelve minutes. We can consider these three sets of solvers to be in three equivalent classes, the five-minute solvers, the ten-minute solvers, and the twelve-minute solvers. It does not matter how many finish in five minutes, ten minutes, or twelve minutes. The three classes are strongly ordered, and we can say that the set has been partitioned.

4.4.3 A Basis for Ordering

It is important to understand that we have imposed an order upon the items; it was not there in itself. We searched among the relations that could apply, choosing one of interest and deciding whether or not it would define an order. Many relationships exist in any set of items, and many of these will be order relations. To speak of the natural order of a set of items is to assume that some particular relation found among the items has some particular status which must lead to its choice. It may be instructive to look briefly again at the case of the library shelf classification which appears ordinal but in fact is nominal.

It would appear that a library classification scheme is a weak order with some items in the same classes and all classes strongly ordered. However, we should remember that while assignment of items to classes may exhibit a high degree of intersubjective agreement (most catalogers will assign the same item to the same class), the order of the classes rarely reflects any relation in the items. A nominal scale is in use for assignment, and the ordinal scale which is used to place the items on the shelf is inherent only in the notation. The more or less arbitrary ordering decisions made by the designer of the scheme assign classes to notation. The shelf order thus established is a convenience, but since the order is not inherent in the documents, but rather imposed externally, only a nominal scale of measurement is available for any discussion of the books relative to one another. While, using Dewey, religion is in the 200s and science in the 500s, there is no implication that religion is less than science or that it precedes science.

There is in a sense an exception to the rule that class numbers are nominal. The number of levels in the assigned code—or to simplify, its length—often signifies specificity. Certainly the code 4.4.1 in this chapter indicates a level of specificity greater than the code 4.4. In the Dewey scheme 600 is Technology, 610 Medical Science, 612.1 Blood and Circulation, and 612.11 Blood. Clearly a decimal notation has the potential for indicating specificity by its length, but it does so only if the topics it represents are consistently so assigned. A notation that expresses the structure of a classification scheme is called *expressive*. Unfortunately, this cannot be counted upon in library classifications. A scheme cannot be both expressive and hospitable to changes. If we have more than ten subclasses of a class, or if new subclasses are added over time, the expressiveness of the decimal notation will break down. Dewey used 620 for Engineering in his first edition and broke down engineering into eight subclasses without electrical engineering. It was later added as 621.3, apparently from the notation, though not in any real modern sense, a subclass of mechanical engineering. Other new subclasses had been added to fill the high 620s (Foskett, 1977, p. 171). The section notation utilized in this book is expressive and thus exhibits ordinal characteristics in its implication of increasing topical specificity by increasing length.

Now we may see how order allows us to set out useful scales of measurement.

4.5
Interval Scales

If we are concerned only with order, the assignment of symbols that provide an order will be sufficient. The assignment of (2,3,4,5,6,7,8,9) to our eight puzzle solvers has been shown to be an example of an *ordinal* scale. If, however, we have concern with how much faster A solves a puzzle than does B, we are concerned with the distance or closeness between two elements of our set. This will require the use of an *interval* or *cardinal* scale, where the numbers representing elements also indicate the magnitude of distance between the ordered items.

In an interval scale all that is required is a point of origin and a unit of measurement. In effect, the assignment of any two numbers to any two items establishes the complete scale giving a point of origin and a unit of measurement. If we assign zero to the freezing point of water and one to the boiling point, we have a temperature scale with its origin at either point and a defined unit running in one direction. We may then use the fractions between zero and one for measures if that is our area of interest, or we may use the *cardinality* of the units above or below if that is more useful. By cardinality we mean the number of elements in a given mathematical set. If we call such a unit the bf unit (boiling to freezing unit), we may measure the boiling point of gold in bf units and have a relatively small number. Celsius, a common temperature scale of this sort, assigns 0 to the freezing point of water and 100 to the boiling point.

We cannot perform arithmetical operations on the numbers assigned. Four degrees is not twice as hot as two degrees on either the Celsius or the Fahrenheit scale, both of which are interval scales. Adding one degree to three degrees gives four degrees, but the result is not four times hotter than one degree. As we shall see, scales are possible which will allow arithmetic operations.

4.6
Ratio Scales

Consider, for a moment, differences in temperature rather than the temperatures themselves. Interestingly, the differences in temperature do not have arithmetical restrictions. The difference between five degrees Cel-

4.6 Ratio Scales

sius and ten degrees Celsius is one half that between five degrees and fifteen degrees. This is because for differences the point of origin is no longer arbitrary. Zero degrees difference represents no difference.

If we have a meaningful fixed origin or zero point and equal but arbitrary intervals, we have a ratio scale. If we use the Kelvin scale to measure temperature, where zero represents the coldest possible temperature at which molecular motion ceases, then our zero point is no longer arbitrary. We can now multiply any measure by a constant, since this changes only the size of the unit. For example, we could define the BMK scale of temperature where a BMK degree is 0.8 times a Kelvin degree. Thus 500 degrees Kelvin is 400 degrees BMK. The advantage of the ratio scale is that we may now use the full range of mathematical operations on our assigned numbers with meaning.

Figure 4.1 illustrates the effect of scale choice on the numerical values assigned to the boiling and freezing points of water (BPw, FPw) and of gold (BPG, WPG). The actual temperatures are, of course, invariant.

Another example of a ratio scale is length. If we have a piece of lumber 5 feet in length, it is twice as long as a board 2.5 feet in length. Moreover,

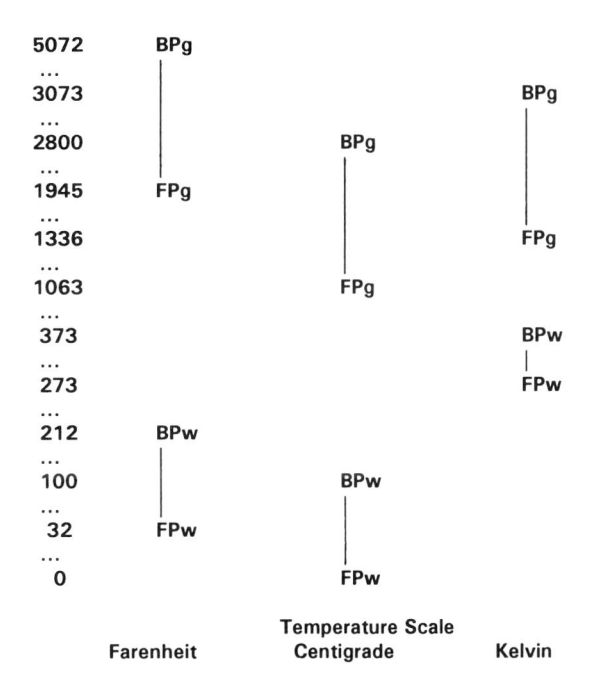

Figure 4.1
Different unit scales. This chart shows the various scales of temperature, Farenheit, Centigrade, and Kelvin. We note the boiling points (BPw) and freezing points (FPw) of water plus the boiling points (BPg) and freezing points (FPg) of gold on all three scales.

if we glue a 2-foot board and a 3-foot board together, they produce a 5-foot board. If southern Louisiana gets 1 foot of rainfall while southern Ontario gets 1 inch of rain, we can say that it is 12 times as wet in Baton Rouge as in Toronto.

For this reason measurement using ratio scale is sometimes known as *extensive* measurement. It is not the only choice available to us, despite its commonality. We can devise any sort of scale we wish by mapping our items of interest into some abstract space. If we have some reason, see some benefit, in using a scale other than the ratio scale, we may certainly do so. It is the power of mathematics, however, that leads us to search for ratio scales. If we can establish such a scale, this power is available to us. Ordinal and interval scales are used because they are steps on the way to ratio scales, and all the requirements for a ratio scale cannot always be established. It is possible also to speak of a *difference scale,* where the unit is meaningful but the origin is arbitrary. In the Roman calendar a year is the time necessary for the earth to circle the sun. The unit is meaningful. The origin is an estimate of the birth year of Jesus and is somewhat arbitrary. A calendar would be equally valid with another historical event marking the year of origin. If both the origin and the unit are fixed and meaningful we have an *absolute scale,* such as the Kelvin temperature scale.

4.7
Summary

In this chapter we have introduced several concepts that will be needed for understanding the following chapters. The ideas of sets, scales, order, and equivalence are basic concepts in the collection, structuring, reduction, and manipulation of data to be used for measurement.

References

Adler, Irving. (1966). *Probability and Statistics for Everyman.* New York: New American Library, 16–32.
DeMorgan, A. (1847). *Formal Logic.* London: unknown publisher.
Foskett, A. C. (1977). *The Subject Approach to Information.* London: Clive Bingley.
Quine, Willard Van Orden (1950). *Methods of Logic.* New York: Henry Holt & Co.

Two

Mathematical and Statistical Concepts

5

Statistical Measures—Description by Reduction

5.1
Introduction

This chapter and the next are brief introductions to a most complex and detailed topic, statistical analysis. It seems necessary to introduce these concepts in order to have a meaningful discussion of practical measurement. On the other hand, the topic is a very large and detailed one and our treatment is necessarily brief, selective, and elementary. Many textbooks, of which those cited here are but a sample, are available to provide a more complete introduction and understanding of the topic, including Christensen (1992), De Santo and Totoro (1992), and Salvia (1990).

The purpose of statistical analysis is threefold: (1) data reduction or abstraction, representing the characteristics of a set of data with a small amount of data; (2) comparison of sets of data and drawing inferences from differences or their lack; (3) and determining the nature of the mathematical relationship among variables.

In this chapter, we deal with methods of reducing data to a meaningful level. If we collect large sets of unorganized numbers which in some sense describe a phenomenon of interest, we need to summarize these numbers into measures which reflect something meaningful. This is the concern of *descriptive statistics*.

Then, we need to be able to state with some certainty whether the differences we observe are meaningful and reflect the actual situation or whether they are the result of chance in the selection of our observations. This is known as *inferential statistics*.

Finally, we may wish to know if some relationship exists between two or among several sets of observations. If we can consistently see that sets of data vary in some relationship to one another, we can then predict what might happen to one observation when we know what has happened to the other. This identification of relationships is the key to experimental statistics and is known as correlation.

We very rarely can observe all the possible occurrences of some phenomenon of interest. We must begin with a selection of observations called a sample and attempt to learn what we can from such limited observations. To understand the process involved we need to look at the concept of the sample.

5.2
Sample Spaces

Let us begin with a discussion of what it is that we sample. In any experimental activity there are a certain population of items or events under study and a certain number of outcomes that are of interest. It is important that we accurately define the population. We cannot properly draw a sample from a population whose bounds are not known and well understood. Suppose we have a population, D, of the 52 regular playing cards and are interested in the first card dealt after the deck is randomly ordered by shuffling. The cards make up the population and we may say that we have a sample space of 52 possible outcomes. This space can be viewed, as in Chapter 4, as a collection of the 52 elements:

{A♠,2♠, . . . ,10♠,J♠,Q♠,K♠,A♥,2♥, . . . ,10♥,J♥,Q♥,K♥, A♦,2♦, . . . ,10♦,J♦,Q♦,K♦,A♣,2♣, . . . ,10♣,J♣,Q♣,K♣},

where, for ordering purposes, the ace has the value 1 and the jack, queen, and king have the values 11, 12, and 13, respectively.

A sample space is not based solely on the elements of the collection under consideration. It also depends on our interest in and classification of the elements. If we are interested only in the suit of the first card dealt, then the sample space set need have only four elements: {♠, ♥, ♦, ♣}. If we are interested only in the color of the first card dealt, or whether the number assigned to it is odd or even, then the spaces have but two elements in their respective collections: {black and red} or {odd and even}. It is wasteful of resources to choose a sample space classification too fine for a given experiment. But to choose a space with too gross a classification greatly limits the questions that can be asked after the data are recorded. If we record the suit drawn, we may later address color questions, but not questions as to number. If we record color only, we cannot later address either suit or number.

A sample space must also take into account all possible outcomes given the classification in place and must not contain multiple classes which could apply to the same outcome. {red, heart, club} would not be a sample space,

5.2 Sample Spaces

since both red and heart would apply to the same 13 possible outcomes. It would also not qualify, since 13 outcomes (A♠ . . . K♠) could not be classified.

A sample space can be infinite. Suppose, for instance, we were asked to choose a real number between 0 and 1. In this case there is an infinite number of real numbers in the sample space. A more interesting, but not so obvious, example occurs in the possible number of repetitions of replacement, shuffle, and deal that will be required for the card dealt to be the ace of spades. Suppose that we shuffle the deck and turn over the top card. If it is an ace of spades we will stop. If it is not, we will repeat the process. The sample space is the number of shuffles required to obtain the ace of spades from the top. The sample space then consists of the positive integers, 1, 2, . . . , to infinity. We can repeat this experiment of repeated shuffles so that every time we find an ace of spades we can record some number of shuffles between one and infinity.

5.2.1 Probabilities of Events

The probability of occurrence of an event, or simply the *probability of an event,* is the number of possible ways that outcome could occur, divided by the total number of possible outcomes. In cards, for example, there are four aces in a deck. If we draw a single card at random, there are four ways this card could be an ace: A♠, A♥, A♦, and A♣. There are, however, 52 possible outcomes of a single-card draw. Hence, the probability of an ace is 4/52 = 1/13. Symbolically:

$$p(A) = \text{Number of aces}/\text{Number of Cards} = 4/52$$

The *conditional probability of an event* is the probability of occurrence of the event *given that some other event has previously occurred.* For example, if we are to draw two cards without replacing the first one, and if the first card was an ace, what is the probability of the second being an ace? We use the symbol $p(X \mid Y)$ to mean the probability of event X, given that event Y has occurred. Then, the probability of an A, given that an A has already been drawn, is

$$p(A \mid A) = 3/51$$

because there are only three aces and 51 cards are left after the first draw was an ace.

We can look at the probability of drawing an ace as the first and second cards as the *joint probability* of the two events: drawing one ace and then another. The probability of the first card being an ace is 4/52, of the second 3/51 because there is one less card in the deck and one less ace in the deck when the second card is drawn. The joint probability of the two events is then $4/52 \times 3/51 = 1/221$. Thus, the joint probability can be calculated using the conditional probability as $p(A \cap A) = p(A \mid A) \cdot p(A)$. Another notation for joint probability is $p(A, A)$.

There are two important laws involving conditional probability. Suppose one of m possible outcomes can occur. There are 13 differently numbered cards that can occur in a standard card deck. Imagine that a card with a particular number, say a king, will be drawn, and we wish to calculate the probability of a different but related event, say that the card will be a heart. Let Y be the related event and X_1, X_2, X_3, . . . ,X_m be the m initial outcomes. We are considering $p(Y \mid X_i)$, the probability that Y will occur given that X_i has occurred.

Consider the probability of a king being drawn as the top card from a shuffled deck. This can be expressed as the probability of a king given that a spade has been drawn, plus the probability of a king given that a heart has been drawn, plus the probability of a king given that a diamond has been drawn, plus the probability of a king given that a club has been drawn, i.e.,

$$p(K) = p(K \mid \spadesuit) \cdot p(\spadesuit) + p(K \mid \heartsuit) \cdot p(\heartsuit) + p(K \mid \diamondsuit) \cdot p(\diamondsuit) + p(K \mid \clubsuit) \cdot p(\clubsuit)$$

This is the *law of total probability*, which states that $p(K)$, the probability that the event K (a king being drawn in our example) will occur at all, is equal to the summation over m (number of suits) of all the products of the probabilities $p(K \mid X_i)$ times the probabilities $p(X_i)$. The probability that the event K will occur is the probability that K will occur given X_1 times the probability that X_1 will occur, plus the probability that K will occur given X_2 times the probability that X_2 will occur, and so on over all m initial outcomes (in our example, m is 4 and the X's are the suits). Thus, we have

$$p(K) = \Sigma \, p(K \mid X_i) \cdot p(X_i)$$

where the sum is over $i = 1, 2, \ldots, m$.

If we wish to calculate the likelihood that outcome X_i previously occurred, given that some event Y is known to have occurred, we have a situation that is more or less the reverse of the previous one. We wish to find $p(X_i \mid Y)$. Bayes' law states that

$$p(X_i \mid Y) = p(X_i \cap Y)/p(Y) = P(Y \mid X_i) \cdot p(X_i)/p(Y)$$

Using the total probability law,

$$p(X_i \mid Y) = p(Y \mid X_i) p(X_i) / [p(Y \mid X_1) p(X_1) \\ + p(Y \mid X_2) p(X_2) + \cdots + p(Y \mid X_m) p(X_m)]$$

5.2 Sample Spaces

In our previous example this would permit us to calculate the likelihood that a card drawn is a king given that it is a heart. Thus, we have

$$p(X_j \mid Y) = \frac{p(Y \mid X_j)p(X_j)}{\Sigma\, p(Y \mid X_i)p(X_i)}$$

where the sum is over $i = 1, 2, \ldots, m$ (Kachigan, 1982, pp. 476–482).

Sometimes the probability of X_i given Y is very difficult to discover but we can use Bayes' law to calculate it using the more discernible probability of Y given X_i. Consider a case where we need the probability that a traveler visiting Baton Rouge came from Toronto (X_1), as opposed to the probability that the traveler came from some other city (X_2), given that the travel time was three hours (Y). Bayes' law as just stated will give us this probability, if we can find the likelihood of an arrival coming from Toronto, the likelihood that a trip from Toronto to Baton Rouge took three hours, and the likelihood that a trip from any other city to Baton Rouge would take three hours.

Given two events, A and B, we denote the probability of both A and B occurring as $p(A \cap B)$. Then, if

$$p(A \cap B) = p(A)p(B)$$

A and B are *independent events*. This equation is the definition of statistical independence and leads to

$$p(A \mid B) = p(A)$$

and

$$p(B \mid A) = p(B)$$

We cannot always deal with as well defined and limited a population as a deck of 52 cards. Often we must deal with larger and more complex populations, while still setting up a sample spaces and observing and recording outcomes that occur within them. We presume that we can estimate the probability of occurrence of outcomes for a whole population by studying only a portion of it.

5.2.2 Statistical Samples

A *population* is a set of entities we wish to consider for some purpose. This purpose will determine how we identify the membership of the set and how we define the variables that will make up our sample space. If we wish to study the people employed in the information industry, we must first determine who these people might be. This is often a far from trivial task. We might list a set of job titles and define our population as all those individuals who hold such jobs. If we are concerned with the people who work in a particular building, or the documents filed in a particular set of cabinets, the population is more easily specified. When the population is too large to study economically, we may choose a *random sample,* one where every possible sample of a specified size has an equal chance of being selected; i.e., any member of the population has an equal chance to be in the sample. This is often accomplished essentially by a blind draw from a shuffled population. We could deal 13 cards from a well-shuffled deck to attain a 25% random sample of the deck. *Inferential statistics* (see Chapter 6) then allows us to make statements about the whole deck based upon our observations of the sample.

It should be clear that our interest at any given time is limited to certain characteristics of a population. We may, for example, be interested in the suit of the cards or in the frequency of occurrence of certain outcomes of an experiment which we have defined in terms of our sample space for that characteristic. For the characteristic *suit* these are spades, hearts, diamonds, and clubs. Our concern is with the frequency with which each possible outcome occurs in the sample space. An example would be a determination of how often a heart would be drawn. With sufficient draws from the population we should find that about one quarter of the draws are hearts, since one quarter of the population is hearts. If we are drawing from a random sample we should achieve the same result. This is because nearly one quarter of our random sample should be hearts, and thus the frequency of occurrence should be the same.

5.3
Frequency Measures

We will be concerned with certain characteristics of the population and the sample that represents it. These characteristics will have certain possible values that make up the sample space for our observations. Once we have chosen the characteristics of interest and determined their sample space, the characteristics may be called *random variables.* A random variable is a variable that may take on different values that are stochastic; i.e., they depend upon the result of some experiment or the outcome of some event. For example, the random variable h could represent the number of hits a particular batter gets in one game of baseball. Randomness enters the picture because we cannot predict with perfect accuracy how many hits the batter will get (assuming a fair game). A variable may have a small sample space, such as {male, female} or {bound document, unbound document}. Such a space is useful for gross divisions of the population; or it may be a characteris-

5.3 Frequency Measures

tic that can be measured (compared with a known standard unit and represented as a number of occurrences of that unit). A measurable variable x will have a *range* from 0 (or some other minimal number if a ratio scale is not in effect) to some maximal number n. The variable may be *discrete*, that is, take only certain defined values within its range, so that the range is finite. Alternatively, it may be *continuous*, meaning it may take any possible value within its range, so that the number of possible values of the random variable within the range is infinite. The weight of a file cabinet is a continuous variable, because only the efficacy of the measuring device limits the exactitude of the fraction of a unit that can be assigned. The number of file cabinets in a file room is a discrete variable, because there can be no partial file cabinets and the sample space is thus limited to the integers in the range.

We may wish to limit the sample space of a measurable variable by assigning *class intervals*. We might classify the weight of a file cabinet as either 0 to 50 pounds, 51 to 100 pounds, 101 to 150 pounds, or 151 to 200 pounds. We might classify the number of file cabinets as either 0, 1 to 10, 11 to 20, 21 to 32, 33 to 45, or 46 to 50. If such a grouping does not destroy the accuracy needed, it simplifies the data significantly and may lead to a more clear presentation of results. It also simplifies the observational accuracy required for continuous variables except when observations appear to fall on the class limits of the interval. One of the goals of statistical analysis is to summarize data by reducing the volume of data while retaining the information that is critical. Often the observations are made as accurately as possible and the class intervals are determined after data collection to facilitate ease of representation.

5.3.1 Frequency Distributions

The number of times that a particular value or class interval for a variable is observed is the *frequency of observation*. A *frequency table* is a set of class intervals, each paired with a frequency of observation. If x is a value of a discrete random variable or represents a class interval, then we can define a function of x, $f(x)$, specifying the frequency of occurrence of x, which is called a *frequency function*. In general terms, the count of how frequently each value in the sample space of a variable occurs over a set of objects in a population or sample is known as a *frequency distribution*. Normally, the distribution is arranged in either increasing or decreasing order based upon the value of the variable.

Consider an example of filled file cabinet weights in a given department of a great university. Let x be a weight and $f(x)$ be the number of file cabinets which have weight x. These weights are measured in *stone*, a British unit of measurement equal to 14 pounds. The frequency distribution of weights is displayed in Table 5.1.

Table 5.1
Cabinet Weight Frequency[a]

x	freq (x)
30	1
32	1
40	3
41	1
43	1
44	1
47	1
54	2
60	1
	n = 12

[a] The left-hand column shows weights of file cabinets, the right-hand column the number of cabinets having each listed weight.

A frequency distribution simplifies the data, allowing us to determine quickly the range of the data and where they cluster. The cardinality of the frequency is a measure of the magnitude of this clustering. We may wish to consider the *relative frequency*, the frequency of observation of each variable divided by the total number of observations and expressed as a percentage. This allows a statement such as "15% of the file cabinets in the entire university currently weigh between 30 and 32 stone." This seems more easily understood than the technically similar statement "18,598 of the 123,987 file cabinets weigh between 30 and 32 stone." The magnitudes of the clusterings are thus expressed by a measure that is comparable to other clusterings of different occurrences. We could thus make a meaningful statement, "15% of our file cabinets weigh between 30 and 32 stones while 40% of yours weigh in the same range." This allows us to express the fact that 39,940 of your 99,852 file cabinets are in the same weight range as 18,598 of our 123,987 with single values that are comparable.

We may also find *cumulative frequencies* to be useful. Here, we assume the distribution is arranged in increasing order upon the value of the variable. For the measure associated with a particular element of the sample space, we assign the frequency of all observations that have occurred up to and including that particular element, rather than the frequency of observations of that element. This permits us to make a statement such as "5 of our department's file cabinets weigh no more than 40 stone." The highest measure will be associated with the total number of observations in such a scale. Cumulative frequencies can also be expressed as percentages by dividing them by the total number of observations, giving us, for example, the fact that 42% of our 12 file cabinets weigh no more than 40 stone. This would provide a measure known as *cumulative relative frequency*. Table 5.2 shows the data of Table 5.1 with the frequencies cumulated.

Table 5.2
Cumulative Frequencies[a]

x	$f(x)$	cum$f(x)$	cum%
30	1	1	.08
32	1	2	.17
40	3	5	.42
41	1	6	.50
43	1	7	.58
44	1	8	.67
47	1	9	.75
54	2	11	.92
60	1	12	1.00
	$n = 12$		

[a] This shows the same data as Table 5.1, but with frequencies and percentages cumulated.

5.3.2 Graphical Portrayals

Frequency distributions are most commonly displayed graphically as *histograms* or as *frequency polygons*. A histogram is a bar chart where the horizontal axis shows the elements of the sample space ranked in increasing order and the vertical axis indicates the frequency of occurrence of the element. Using the same vertical and horizontal scales, a frequency polygon is constructed by connecting the midpoints of the tops of what would have been the bars of the histogram with straight lines. If we consider that we might use infinitely fine class intervals as elements in the sample space, the bars of the histogram would become infinitely thin and the line of the frequency polygon would approach a smooth curve. This then becomes a continuous frequency distribution, which is theoretical in nature because we could not empirically create an infinite number of points representing an infinite number of observations. The vertical axis value y would then be a continuous function of the horizontal value x. Since the whole area under the curve represents 100% of the observed values, the area under the curve between any two values of x will be a measure of the relative frequency of that range of values. Polygrams and histograms are illustrated in Figures 5.1 and 5.2.

Since it is often useful to view relationships that do not produce histograms that are straight lines in a way that makes them appear linear, plots often make use of logarithms on one or both axes. The well-known algebraic formula for a straight line in Cartesian coordinates is $y = ax + b$. If the relation between variables is actually the curvilinear $y = ka^x$, and if we take the logarithm of both sides, we would produce $\log y = x \log a + \log k$. This is in the linear form given above and will plot as a straight line. If we use paper that is called *semilogarithmic*, where

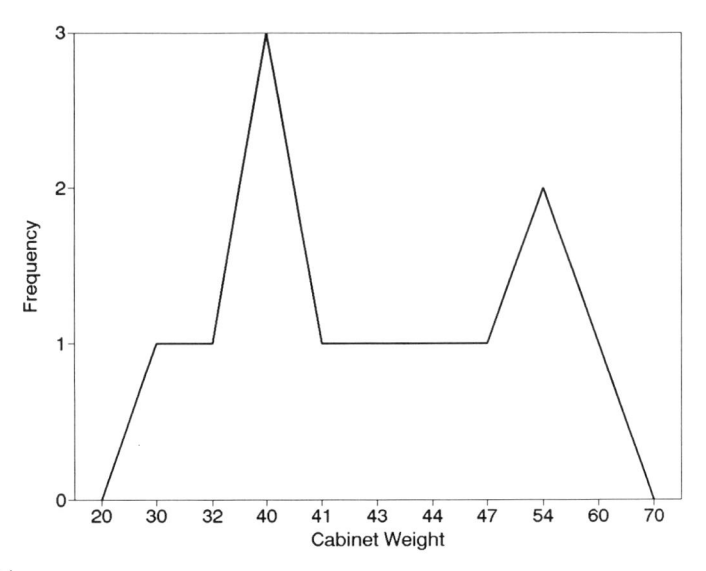

Figure 5.1
Frequency polygon. This shows a polygon, or line graph, for the data of Table 5.1. The x axis represents values of the variable, in this case cabinet weights, and the y axis the frequency of occurrence of a weight value.

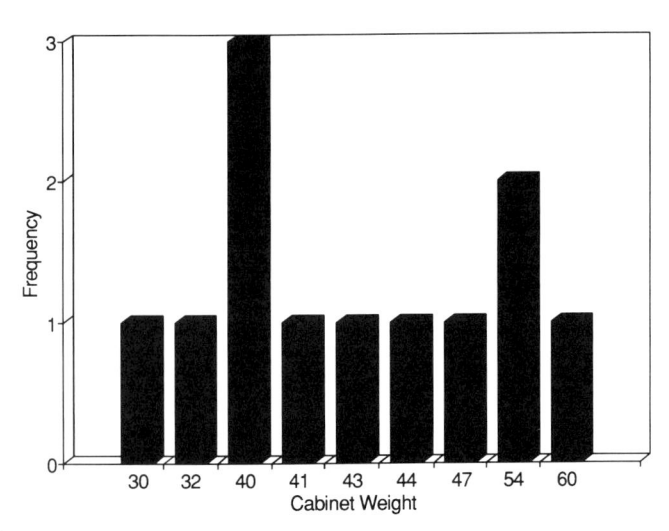

Figure 5.2
Frequency histogram. This shows the same data as Figure 5.1, but presented here as a histogram or bar graph.

5.3 Frequency Measures

the lines on one axis are distributed in a logarithmic manner and those on the other conventionally, we can directly plot x and y as a straight line representing a curvilinear one, as shown in Figure 5.3.

Some of the more commonly used discrete probability distributions are the binomial, Poisson, negative binomial, uniform, and hypergeometric distributions. Some of the more commonly used continuous probability distributions are the uniform, normal, lognormal, chi-square, student's t, f, negative exponential, and gamma distributions. Detailed descriptions of many of these are to be found in Kraft and Boyce (1991, p. 105).

The most common form for a frequency polygon is a symmetrical bell-shaped curve known as the *normal distribution*. Other distributions certainly occur. Frequency polygons with the shape of J's or U's are not uncommon, and there are uniform distributions which produce a straight line parallel to the horizontal axis. Also common is the asymmetrical bell or skewed distribution, which falls somewhere between the normal and the J polygon. These are shown in Figure 5.4.

The normal distribution, however, is ubiquitous in frequency distribution data and its characteristics are basic to statistical analysis.

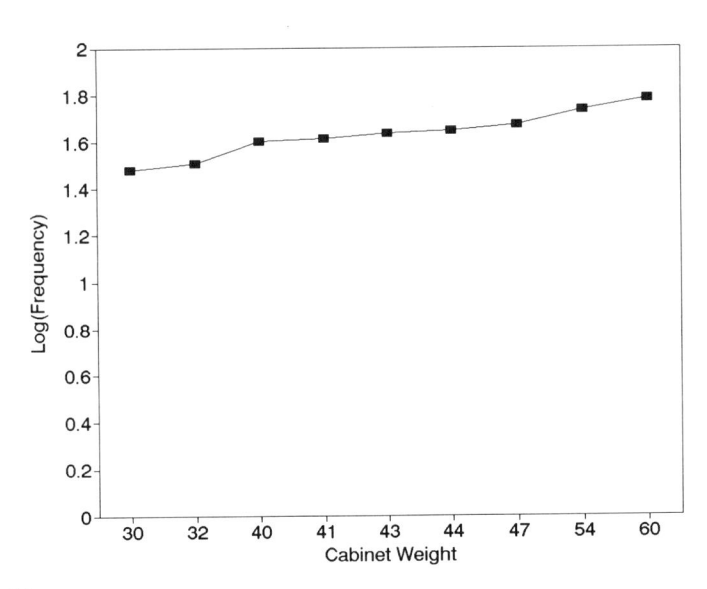

Figure 5.3
Polygram of logarithmic data. This shows the data of Table 5.1 in which the y axis shows the logarithms of the frequencies, making the graph nearly a straight line.

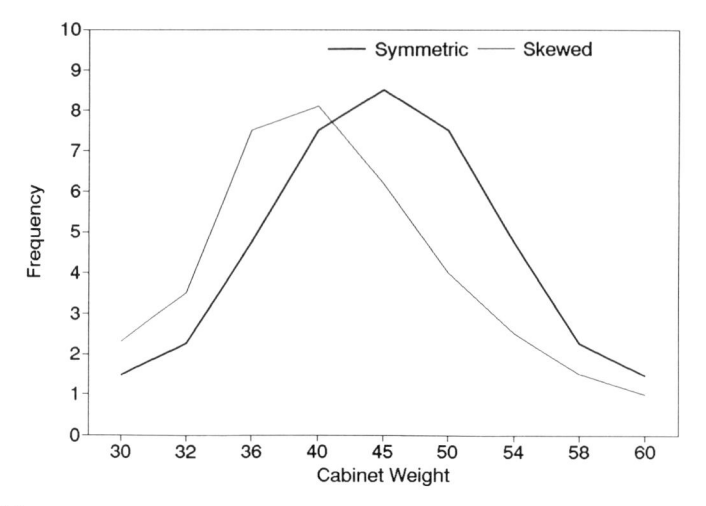

Figure 5.4
A normal frequency distribution. This shows the typical bell-like shape of a symmetric normal frequency distribution and a skewed normal distribution.

5.3.3 Measures of Central Tendency

A frequency distribution is a summarization of the data on collected observations, but we can go even farther and attempt to represent the whole distribution with a single value that measures the location of the most dense clustering of observations. One obvious measure is simply to use that value which is most frequently observed as the measure of centrality.

mode Mode; the value of a distribution that occurs most frequently.

To calculate the mode it is necessary only to rank the data in a weak order and observe the equivalence class with the most members. This element of the sample space has the highest frequency. If the data are grouped in the sample space, the midpoint of the interval with the highest frequency of observation is used. The mode does not have many useful mathematical properties but it is easily obtained. It also provides a check on the homogeneity of the objects in the population under observation. A *bimodal* distribution, one with two distinct modes, could be an indication that there are two distinct populations which differ substantially as to the variable under observation and are being incorrectly considered together.

If we arrange the data in a weak order and ignore the equivalence classes so that each observation is counted while counting up or down the order exactly one half the number of observations, we will reach the middle value of the distribution. Should the number of observations be even, there will be two middle values; if odd, there will be but one. In the former

5.3 Frequency Measures

case the theoretical value midway between the two is used. Thus, for any distribution we have

> *median*   Median; the middle value of a distribution, the value where one half the observations precede and one half follow.

In grouped data the median may be determined by interpolation within the interval where the cumulative relative frequency reaches 50%. It is a measure of centrality which is unaffected by atypical values that are found in the extremes of the distribution. The median is often encountered in the reporting of social statistics, such as the the median income of professors in Louisiana. Like the mode, however, it does not have properties suitable for robust mathematical analysis.

Another measure of central tendency is

> $\bar{x}$ *or* μ Mean or average; the sum of the values of a set of observations divided by the number of observations. The mean of a frequency distribution of the variable x is usually designated μ (Greek mu) if we are dealing with a complete population or $\bar{x}$ ("x bar") if this is a sample.

The mean is a measure whose value is affected by every observation. It can be thought of as the center of gravity of a distribution. Outlying values which are atypical of the distribution will affect the mean and move it toward the tail of a skewed distribution. If the mean and median are nearly equal, the distribution will be *symmetrical*. If the mean is higher than the median the distribution is skewed right; that is, it has several outlying values to the right side of the mode. If the mean is lower than the median the distribution is skewed left; that is, it has several outlying values to the left side of the mode. In a known symmetrical distribution, the mean will vary the least of the three as we analyze repeated samples of the same size. Thus, for a symmetrical distribution, it is the most accurate measure of central tendency.

Consider the data of Table 5.1. The mode is 40, the median is 42, and the mean is 43.75, as illustrated in Figure 5.5.

Performing an arithmetic operation on the mean of a distribution changes the mean just as would performing the same operation on each observation. For example, suppose we wish to convert the mean of a set of Fahrenheit temperatures to Celsius. We need not convert every individual value. We merely convert the Fahrenheit mean to Celsius to obtain the Celsius mean. The conversion is accomplished by use of the formula $C = (F - 32) \cdot (5/9)$, where F is a Fahrenheit temperature and C is a Celsius temperature.

The mean we have just discussed is the *arithmetic mean*. There are two other ways to define a mean:

> $\bar{x}_g$ *Geometric mean;* the nth root of the product of n observed values.

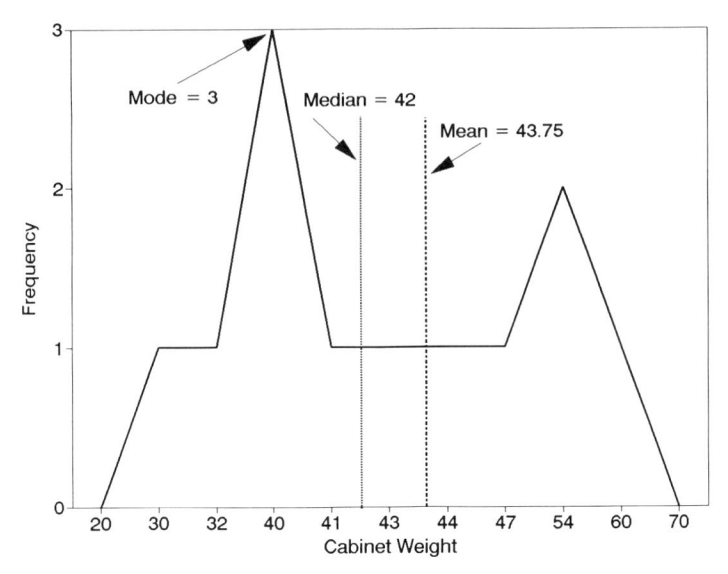

Figure 5.5
Graphic example of mode, median, and mean. Using the data from Table 5.1, the mode is the most frequent value, the median the value such that half of other values are greater and half less, and the mean is the arithmetic average.

The geometric mean is sometimes used to produce an average of percentages, ratios, and rates. For example, if a user population increases by 10% over a decade, the annual increase is not the arithmetic mean of 10%/10 = 1% (Rao, 1983, p. 38). The geometric mean can be used as a measure of location at various times, such as when the observations are products of a series of independent random variables.

$\bar{x}_h$ *Harmonic mean;* the number of observed values, n, divided by the sum of the reciprocals of all these values.

The harmonic mean, which is not all that commonly used, is less than or equal to the geometric mean, which is less than or equal to the arithmetic mean. One application for the harmonic mean is calculating an average rate of speed for a vehicle when a series of different rates for a given distance is known. Another, more important one is that of providing a compromise value when sample sizes are unequal but the statistical procedures under consideration require equal sample sizes.

Using the data from Table 5.1, the geometric mean is 42.93, the harmonic mean 42.11.

5.3 Frequency Measures

5.3.4 Dispersion Measures

In order to characterize a distribution, we are interested not only in the location of the centrality of its frequencies of observations but also in the dispersion of those observations, the degree to which they differ among themselves. For example, consider the case of the statistician who believed that he could wade across a specific bayou because it had an average depth of 6 inches. However, the actual depth was 2 inches except for one unfortunately located hole that was 7 feet deep.

We must consider measures of dispersion or variation. A quick but crude measure is the range.

range   Range; the difference between the value of the highest and lowest observations in a distribution.

$$range = x_{max} - x_{min}$$

A statement of the mean and the range gives us a picture of the breadth of a distribution as well as its center of gravity. Like the median, however, the range does not take into account the value of all observations. The observations could be very close to the mean except for two outliers on each side. This would result in a wide range even though most of the observations approximated the mean. The observations could, on the other hand, be evenly distributed across the same range with the same mean.

A range is sometimes divided into four equal subranges called *quartiles* by marking three points on the range from left to right or from the lowest to highest value. The first point can be found by dividing $n + 1$ by 4 and choosing the value in that position in the range. The second point will be an equal number of values to the right, and the third, an equal number of values to the right of the second. Another way to partition the range is to use 99 such points constructed with 100 as the divisor of $n + 1$. The range is now broken up into *percentiles*. Such a division allows us to indicate simply a rough idea of the relative position of a particular observation. Another common approach is division into ten groups, called *deciles*. A general term for such divisions is *n-tile*.

Actually, a sensible measure of variation that utilized all observations could be constructed by discovering how far each observation was from the mean, its *deviation*, and finding the centrality of these differences. Unfortunately, since the sum of the values of the deviations will always be zero, so will their average. A possibility is to treat the deviations as absolute values, ignoring their signs, while finding the mean of their differences from the mean. This gives

mad   Mean absolute deviation or *MAD*; the mean of the absolute values of deviations of all observations from the mean. The use of absolute values limits the mathematical operations that may be used on the mad.

We can avoid some mathematical difficulties by getting rid of the signs in another way, by squaring the deviations of each of the observations from the mean and adding them together. Dividing this sum by the number of observations defines:

σ^2 or s^2 *Variance;* usually represented by the use of the lowercase Greek letter σ^2 (sigma squared) for the population or s^2 for the sample variance.

$$\sigma^2 = \Sigma \frac{(x_i - \mu)^2}{n} \qquad s^2 = \Sigma \frac{(x_i - \bar{x})^2}{n-1}$$

The variance in a random sample of observations will underestimate the variance of the population sampled. Thus, when estimating the variance of a population using observations from a sample, the number of observations is reduced by one (to $n - 1$) prior to being divided into the sum of the squared deviations. This is not necessary when the purpose of the measure is only to characterize the data available and not to approximate the variance of some larger population of which it is a sample.

A related measure of dispersion is a central value of the deviations in the distribution and is known as

σ or s *Standard deviation;* represented by the letter σ or s, or sometimes as the root mean square or *RMS*. Clearly, the higher the standard deviation, the more the observations vary about the mean.

If we were using meters as a unit of measurement in our recording of observations, the unit of deviation would also have been meters. The variance would be in square meters. Since squaring the deviations has changed their unit of measure, the original unit can be recovered by taking the square root of the variance. Again, using the data from Table 5.1, the variance is 78.39 and the standard deviation 8.85.

Now, to provide a measure of relative variation, we define:

coevar *Coefficient of variation;* the ratio of the standard deviation to the mean, used to measure the relative deviation.

We can generalize from the definition of variance to the following. Instead of squaring the deviation of the difference of each observation from the mean and calculating an average as we do for variance, we raise the differences to the rth power and calculate their average. This gives the rth moment about the mean. Mathematically, the rth moment is $\Sigma(x_i - \mu)^r/n$. If r is 2, we have the formula for the variance.

An *r* of 3 yields

coesk Coefficient of skewness; calculated as the third moment. It measures the symmetry of the probability distribution.

$$coesk = \Sigma(x_i - \mu)^3/n$$

A zero value of the coefficient of skewness means that the distribution is symmetric about the mean; i.e., the mean equals the median equals the mode. If *coesk* is negative, then the distribution is skewed to the left; i.e., the mean is less than the median, which is less than the mode. If the coefficient is positive, then the distribution is skewed to the right; i.e., the mean is greater than the median, which is greater than the mode.

An *r* of 4 gives

coekur Coefficient of kurtosis; the fourth moment which measures the pointedness of the peak of the probability distribution.

$$coekur = \Sigma(x_i - \mu)^4/n$$

5.3.5 Using the Standard Deviation as a Measure

Remembering that the relative frequency of occurrence of values in any interval is measured by the area under the curve in that interval, and using the standard deviation as a measure of the distance from the mean, we can determine the the percentage of observations within a standard deviation of the mean. If the distribution is normal, 66% of the observations will fall within one standard deviation of the mean in either direction. Within two standard deviations we would expect over 95%, and within three standard deviations 99% of the observations. This means that the standard deviation is approximately one sixth of the range. Neither the standard deviation nor the variance changes if a constant is added to each observed value, but if each observed value is multiplied by a constant the standard deviation is also multiplied by that constant and the variance by the square of the constant.

To illustrate how the various scales defined in Chapter 4 help to select the type of central tendency and dispersion measures to use, consider the following rules. If we have a nominal scale, the best central tendency measure is the mode and no dispersion measure is possible. If we have an ordinal scale, we can use the median for central tendency and the range for dispersion. Only if the scale is interval or ratio does it make sense to use the mean for meauring central tendency and the variance for dispersion.

5.3.6 The Law of Large Numbers

The *law of large numbers* establishes the value of the mean as representative of a distribution when samples are large. In order to understand the importance of this law, let us start with some basics. Let us assume that we have a random variable x with a mean μ and a variance of σ^2. Then the probability of the absolute value of the difference between x and μ being greater than some constant k standard deviations is less than or equal to $1/k^2$,

$$p(|x - \mu| > k\sigma) < 1/k^2$$

This relationship is known as *Chebyshev's inequality*. It shows that the likelihood of a value of x being more than any given number, k, of standard deviations away from the mean grows smaller as k increases.

Now, suppose that we conduct a series of n independent experiments that each have one of two possible outcomes. For convenience we will term one outcome success and one failure. Let x be the number of trials that result in success, and let p be the probability that any one of the trials results in success. Then, the mean $\mu = np$ and the variance $\sigma^2 = np(1 - p)$. Now let y be the random variable $(x/n - p)$. The law of large numbers says that the probability that the variable y exceeds any given small amount goes to zero as n increases. The ratio of x to n approaches p as n gets larger, or, in notation-free language, the more observations you consider, the better the probability of success will be reflected by those observations.

For example, suppose we have a deck of cards with some number of aces (not necessarily four; the deck may be modified from the standard discussed earlier). In other words, suppose that there are A aces in a deck of M cards. If we draw a card at random, look at it to see if it is an ace (success) or not an ace (failure), and then replace the card in the deck, the probability of any draw being an ace is $p = A/M$. If we draw n cards at random and note x aces, we are more confident that the ratio x/n approximates p as n increases. If we have 5 aces after 65 draws we are more confident that the ratio of aces to all cards is 1 to 13 than we would be if we had 2 aces after 26 draws. If there are 52 cards and we are confident the ratio is 1 to 13, we will conclude that there are indeed four aces present. What has been demonstrated is that the mean becomes more representative as sample size increases. Does this seem obvious? Yes, but isn't it nice to know that there is a formal proof of this assumption?

5.3.7 The Poisson Distribution

If the sample mean and the sample variance are approximately equal, $\bar{x} = s^2$, this is an indication that the probability of a particular observation occurring might conform to a *Poisson distribution*. It is applicable to frequency distributions of times between occurrences of accidents, defects, or rare events in general. In such cases, the time when a certain event occurs is not dependent on when it last occurred; hence the occurrences are independent. To be more specific, if the occurrences of an event are independent of each other, and if the probability of the event is proportional to the size of the time interval in which it is observed, and if a small interval exists with a low probability of occurring more than once, then the Poisson distribution describes the intervals between events. If this is true, we may assume that the pattern of occurrence of observations is random because this is always so for a Poisson distribution. If not, then there is an indication that there may be some cause and effect at work which we might be able to identify.

5.3.8 The z Score

We are now in a position to say a bit more concerning the measurement of skills than we were in the first chapter. If we ask a series of questions on examinations that require the demonstration of skills that are of interest to us as potential employers and administer this examination to a number of subjects, we will collect observations of their scores which will form a frequency distribution. If we know the mean and standard deviation of the distribution we can clearly interpret an individual score. Since the standard deviation and the observed deviation of each score from the mean are expressed in the same units, their ratio is dimensionless, hence independent of the units used.

z z *score;* the deviation of an observation from the mean divided by the standard deviation, expressed in number of standard deviations by which the observation differs from the mean.

If the standard deviation is 10 and a score is 20 points above the mean, it is two standard deviations above the mean. This means that less than 3% of those taking the exam would be expected to score higher. If the standard deviation was 20, the score of 20 would be one standard deviation above the mean, or 16% would be expected to obtain a higher score. The z score is a powerful composite measure which incorporates the mean, standard deviation, and the observed score in one value.

But statistics is not just about data reduction. All measured observation is subject to error. We want to know if the differences we observe are meaningful or due to chance. We also want to know how precise our measurements really are. Statistics provides us with a the means to make statements about our certainty of the results of measurement. It also allows us to test whether two variables covary, i.e., whether some systematic relationship exists between them. This is the topic of the next chapter.

5.4
Summary

The purpose of descriptive statistical analysis is to reduce data both to manageable quantities and to meaningful aggregations. If we collect large sets of unorganized numbers which, in some sense, describe a phenomenon of interest, we need to summarize them into measures which reflect something meaningful. We very rarely can observe all the possible occurrences of interest. We must begin with a selection of observations called a sample and attempt to learn what we can from such limited observations. In this chapter we have outlined the rationale for sampling and have described the basic statistical techniques for data reduction.

References

Christensen, Howard B. (1992). *Introduction to Statistics: A Calculus-Based Approach*. Philadelphia: Saunders Publishing.
De Santo, Carmine and Michael Totoro. (1992). *An Introduction to Statistics*. Whittier Publications, Inc.
Kachigan, S. K. (1982). *Statistical Analysis: An Interdisciplinary Introduction to Univariate & Multivariate Methods*. New York: Radius Press.
Kraft, Donald H. and Bert R. Boyce. (1991). *Operations Research for Libraries and Information Agencies*. San Diego: Academic Press.
Rao, I. K. R. (1983). *Quantitative Methods for Library and Information Science*. New York: John Wiley & Sons.
Salvia, Anthony A. (1990). *An Introduction to Statistics*. Philadelphia: Saunders Publishing.

6

Statistical Tests and Correlation

6.1
Errors and Confidence

The defining characteristics of a population, the measures that allow us to characterize its frequency distribution for a variable, are known as parameters. In inferential statistics we attempt to estimate these parameters from like measures of a sample of the population which are called *statistics*. The mean and standard deviation of a sample are statistics that serve as estimates of the mean and standard deviation parameters of the population the sample represents. If we measure a sample of the variable *time to answer a question while interacting with a computer* and produce a frequency distribution of such times, we can use the sample mean to estimate the mean of the complete population of all question interaction times. We must use a sample because we have not timed past interactions and do not wish to time every future interaction.

If we want to know the breaking strength of printer ribbons coming off an assembly line, we cannot test each one, since the test is destructive. We must test a sample and estimate the mean for the population. In fact, with many populations we can never know the exact mean. As another example, suppose that we wish to determine the favorite candidate in a gubernatorial election at a given moment in time. Even if we make the incredible assumption that it is physically and financially possible to poll the entire adult population of a state (even a small state), it is certainly not possible to do so in one moment in time. Since opinions change in time, often quickly, we are compelled to poll a properly chosen sample and use the sample statistics to infer whom the population considers as a suitable governor. Since we do not know our population mean, we can never know exactly how close our sample statistic is to that population mean. If, however, we know that the population mean probably lies between two values, we can state how confident we are that it falls within that range.

If we choose a very large interval we can be relatively sure that the mean will be found within it. As we decrease the size of the interval our

67

confidence that it contains the mean declines. Thus, confidence depends upon the size of the interval and the associated probability that the mean falls within it. Since a statistic is an estimate of a parameter, any statistic plus or minus some unknown amount of error will predict its associated parameter. We cannot know the error that differentiates any sample mean from its parameter, but we can attach a probability to errors of a certain size if we know the shape, mean, and standard deviation of a distribution of those errors.

Adding a constant, in this case the mean, to the error will not change the standard deviation or the shape of the distribution. Thus, it can be shown that the standard deviation of sampling errors is equal to the *standard error of the mean*, i.e., the standard deviation of the distribution of the means of an infinite number of samples of the population. The shape of the sampling distribution of the mean is approximately normal if the sample size is large enough, and therefore the shape of the distribution of sampling errors is normal. Because 95% of the observations are within 1.96 standard deviations from the mean, this implies that we are 95% certain that the population mean is in an interval 1.96 standard errors above or below the sample mean.

This is a statement of what is known as the *central limit theorem*. It demonstrates that we can know the characteristics of the distribution of the means of samples drawn from a population. Consider a random sample of size n taken from a population with a mean μ and variance σ^2. Letting $\bar{x}$ be the sample mean, we will define a random variable z to be the difference between the sample mean and the population mean, measured in terms of the number of sample deviation units by which they differ:

$$z = \frac{\sqrt{n} \cdot (\bar{x} - \mu)}{\sigma}$$

z is a random variable, since $\bar{x}$ is a function of random variables. This z variable is related to the z score of 5.3.8. The central limit theorem states that, as n (the sample size) increases, z becomes normally distributed with a mean of 0 and a variance of 1. Because of the central limit theorem and the confidence it gives that z is normally distributed, the confidence intervals and hypotheses testing discussed earlier are possible.

We can use this concept to set a *confidence interval* about a sample mean. Suppose we have a sample of 144 printer ribbons which break at a mean force of 100 grams. Looking at the records of past tests, we see that the standard deviation of the force required to break a ribbon is 10 grams. The standard error of the mean is then $10/\sqrt{144} = 0.8333$. The population mean of the force required to break a ribbon is now estimated at 95% confidence by using the product of 0.8333 and the 1.96 standard error as the size of the interval above and below the mean. In other words, we can say that we are 95% confident that this batch of ribbons will break when a force exerted upon them is in the range between 101.633 (100 + 0.8333 · 1.96) grams and 98.37 (100 − 0.8333 · 1.96) grams. Thus, we can define:

> *confint* Confidence interval; the distance on either side of a sample mean in which the population mean is likely to fall, with probability equal to a set amount.

$$confint = \bar{x} \pm 1.96 \cdot sem$$
$$= \bar{x} \pm 1.96 \cdot \sigma/\sqrt{n}$$

We will have set some standard, say 90 grams, which depends upon the stresses to which our ribbons are normally subjected. Since the break point interval's lower bound is higher than our standard, we will feel confident that our current run of ribbons will not cause our customers serious problems. For 99% certainty we would follow exactly the same procedure but use 2.58 rather than 1.96 in order to reflect the number of standard deviations within which 99% of observations lie. The interval now exceeds 10 grams, 5.06 on either side of our 100-gram sample mean break point. However, the lower bound is still well above our 90-gram standard and we will be satisfied with our manufacturing process. The destructive measurement of a small sample of our production run has given us confidence that our customers will not complain about our ribbon's strength.

6.2
Testing of Hypotheses

Such direct estimation of parameters using confidence intervals about a statistic is most important in measurement of continued performance. However, another sort of parameter estimation is also of great value. Here, rather than wishing to know with a stated confidence a range of a parameter of the population, we wish to discredit, or alternatively support, some speculation that we make about such a parameter. Such a guess about the nature of a parameter is an hypothesis. The determination of the probability of the truth or falsity of such a parameter is *hypotheses testing*.

We might look at the printer ribbon break point problem in this way. If we speculate that the average ribbon will break at 100 grams, we have a working hypothesis. We would normally call this the null hypothesis and use the notation H_0: μ is equal to 100 grams (where μ is the mean of the distribution of break points of the population). This is null in the sense that the hypothesis states that no difference exists between the two values. In order to cover the other possibilities we would need an alternative hypothesis, H_1: μ is not equal to 100 grams. Of course, we could be speculating that any parameter of the population equaled any value, and the converse. The "μ" and the "100 grams" are arbitrary examples that fit our ribbon problem. This is also true of the "not equal" relation.

We may not really care if our ribbon breaks *above* 100 grams. It will, after all, break at *some* point. We are very concerned that it not break below. Thus we would be interested in a hypotheses set where H_0: μ is less than or equal to 100 grams and H_1: μ is greater than or equal to 100 grams. If we can reject the null hypothesis we will feel quite safe. In some cases we will not believe that a change in one direction is possible. If, as a cost-saving measure, we decrease the thickness of the ribbon by four microns we will assume that it might be weaker and that the break point has not increased. We might then use a truncated hypotheses set of H_0: μ is equal to 100 grams and H_1: μ is less than 100 grams.

How do we test the hypothesis that μ is equal to 100 grams? Let us now suppose that the 144 printer ribbons in the sample break at a mean force of 101 grams. Looking at the records of past tests, we see that the standard deviation of the force required to break a ribbon is 10 grams (we could use the sample mean divided by the square root of the sample size as an estimate). The standard error of the mean is then $10/\sqrt{144} = 0.8333$. Expressing our observed sample mean, 101 grams, in standard error units (z = difference in sample and hypothesized means divided by the standard error) we find $z = (101 - 100)/.8333$ or 1.2. This shows that our sample mean of 101 deviates from our hypothesized mean by 1.2 standard errors.

How likely is it that we would get such a deviation if our hypothesis was correct? Something less likely than 0.05, or 1 in 20, is normally considered unlikely. The standard of 0.01, 1 in 100, is also commonly used. Such a standard should be set before the test is carried out and is known as the *significance level*. It is usually expressed in notation as the Greek letter alpha, e.g., $\alpha = 0.01$.

If we have an exhaustive hypothesis set, then the probability of an unlikely outcome will be distributed in both tails of the distribution, a *two-tailed test*. If we have a truncated hypotheses set, a *one-tailed test*, where the probability of an unlikely outcome will be considered to be in only one side of the distribution, will be utilized.

For example, if we wish to see if the salaries of recent graduates from Canadian universities differ significantly from the salaries of recent graduates from United States universities, after factoring in the appropriate currency exchange rate, we would have the hypothesis that the mean salaries are the same; that is, the difference between the average salaries is zero. This would imply a two-tailed test, because the alternatives include both the case in which Canadian salaries exceed U.S. salaries and the opposite case. What makes this a two-tailed test is that the difference can vary either on the positive side or on the negative side, so that we must consider both possibilities. Since the original hypothesis dictates that the difference in salaries has a middle value (zero), we can reject that hypothesis by having the difference be either too large (positive) or too small (negative).

On the other hand, if we change the original hypothesis to state that U.S. university graduates have salaries that are larger than those of Canadians, this could be restated as: the difference between the mean U.S. salary and the mean Canadian salary is positive. This calls for a one-tailed test because there is but one alternative, that U.S. salaries exceed Canadian salaries. Here, the original hypothesis specifies that the difference in salaries is positive, so that we can reject that hypothesis only by finding that the difference is too small (zero or negative).

On the distribution for a two-tailed test, with $1/2\ \alpha$ in each tail, a deviation greater than 1.96 standard errors will occur 5% of the time. With an α of 0.01 (a likelihood of occurrence of 1%), a deviation greater than 2.58 standard errors is required for rejection. Thus we see that with a two-tailed test, our hypothesis that the population mean is equal to 100 for the printer ribbon example is supported. This is the case because the average breaking strength for the sample was but 1.2 standard deviations away from the hypothesized population mean, and it would take a deviation greater than 1.96 standard errors to reject our hypothesis. We can therefore accept 100 as a population mean.

If we are doing an experiment where a one-tailed test is appropriate, a z value greater than 1.65 will be required to reject at a significance level of 5%, and if $\alpha = 0.01$ a value greater than 2.33 will be necessary. Again, our z value of 1.2 allows us to accept our hypothesis that the population mean is less than or equal to 100. It is quite likely that mean break point has not deviated from 100 despite our cost-saving procedure.

We thus see that statistics as a discipline gives us the capability of determining measures of whole populations of items or events from the use of relatively small samples from these populations. If we can demonstrate that the observations of one variable vary in the same manner as those of another, we can establish the mathematical relationship between the variables. Such a relationship will allow us to measure one variable and make an indirect inference about another based upon our observation of the first. If one variable is relatively easier to observe and measure than the other, we would want to seek to establish the mathematical nature of this relationship so that we may rely upon our observations of the easily measured variable. This is what experimental statistics is all about, and we are now led to a discussion of correlation, the third use of statistics.

6.3
Measures of Association

As we have seen in the first chapter, the nature of the items under observation and our ranges of interest in their behavior decide our rules of measurement. We want to be able to assign numbers to certain aspects of physical items and to the frequency of occurrence of certain results when a procedure is carried out. It is this latter sort of measurement that is of most interest in information systems. We can measure the dimensions of a library with a meter stick, but these dimensions will tell us very little about the effectiveness of the service that the library resident in that space provides. The age and number of items in the collection of materials might tell us more. We might consider that the number of materials circulated would measure the service in some way, or perhaps the number of reference questions successfully answered.

But what constitutes good performance? What are the standards and norms with which we might compare our counts? When we speak of the length of a wall in meters, how can we know what is an excellent or poor length, an acceptable or unacceptable length? A good length is one which leads to the achievement of the goals of the system that resides within the measured space. Thus, if we want to talk about a useful length, we must first agree upon a measure of the fulfillment of system goals and then measure the system's performance, while at the same time keeping track of changes in wall length that occur over time as we measure performance.

If, by way of illustration, we decide that the number of reference questions answered in a day is a measure of success, we may measure our walls every day, count our reference questions every day, and attempt to determine if changes in the count occur in a pattern which is similar in occurrence to the changes in wall length. Thus, if our wall length never changes and our count of questions never changes, we may assume that there is a relationship (albeit a tenuous and possibly humorous one) between the two measures. If the count changes but not the length, we may begin to doubt our assumption of a relationship between the two. Or, suppose changes in the amount of beer consumed by students are observed at a time when changes are noted in the salaries of faculty members at a great university. If we can show that a change in beer consumption is any function of a change in faculty salaries, we will assume a relationship between these two phenomena. It should be obvious that correlation does not imply causality; asking students to drink more beer may not result in large raises for the faculty; both measures should be seen as indicators of the local economy. In addition, constant wall lengths should not be seen as the cause of the lack of increase in reference questions asked.

6.3.1 Measures of Correlation

Statistical measurement is concerned not only with single values representing large distributions of data and with the measurement of errors and confidence, but also with the possibility of using observable variations in easily obtained data to make estimates about less easily obtained data. If we can show a relationship between variables such that when one changes, the other changes in a predictable fashion, the observation of the first becomes an indirect measurement of the second. Such relationships can be either experimental or correlational.

If they are experimental, we control the values of one variable and, while changing them, observe the changes in the other variable. We might provide different levels of information service to researchers and observe any differences in their productivity. We would need to be able to measure both service level and productivity effectively. It would also be wise to see that no other variable that might influence productivity was allowed to vary during our observations. If this is done effectively, we can interpret the results as *causal* in nature. If we can be sure that no other variables are affecting our number of daily reference questions in the example in the previous section, and we systematically change the wall length and find a corresponding change in the number of reference questions, we will be willing to impute a causal relationship where wall length influences the number of reference questions.

If the values are not controlled but simply observed as they vary together in a natural environment, then the analysis is correlational. Just as with one-tailed and two-tailed tests, where the distinction depends not so much on the data but upon the formulation of the hypothesis, the distinction between experiment and correlation depends on whether or not we meaningfully assign values to one of the variables, or whether we assign them in an unbiased random fashion as presumably they would occur naturally. A *contingency table* can be used to show how frequently observations with values of one variable occur along with values of a second variable in order to test the relationship between the two values; a chi-square distribution is often used to test this *covariation*.

6.3.1.1 The Chi-square Statistic

Consider a contingency table for male and female users and nonusers of a computerized information system, as given in Table 6.1. In order to see if usage is correlated with gender, we first calculate expected numbers for the table. Since half of the sample population of 100 people consists of males, we expect half of the 34 users to be male and half to be female, i.e., 17 users for each gender. And, in like manner, we expect half of the 66

Table 6.1
Contingency Table Showing (Hypothetical) Covariation of Gender and Usage of an Information System

Gender	Use by Users	Nonusers	Total
Males	10	40	50
Females	24	26	50
Total	34	66	100

nonusers to be male and half to be female, i.e., 33 nonusers for each gender. We then calculate:

χ^2 *Chi-square;* the squared difference between the expected and observed number of occurrences in each cell in the table, divided by the expected number and summed over all cells.

$$\chi^2 = \Sigma_{i,j}(O_{ij} - E_{ij})^2 / E_{ij}$$

χ^2 (Rao, 1983, pp. 149–153) is a measure of the extent to which two distributions are different, in this case the expected distribution and the observed one. For our example, we get $\chi^2 = 8.7344$.

We now introduce a parameter called *degrees of freedom*:

df Degrees of freedom.
$df = (r - 1) \cdot (c - 1)$, where r and c are the numbers of rows and columns, respectively.

The number of degrees of freedom influences the test value, χ^2, used to measure independence between distributions. The parameter $n - 1$, 1 less than the sample size, frequently appears in statistical tests of significance. There is no obvious reason why it is called *degrees of freedom* in this case, but we can illustrate its use. The parameter *df* registers the number of observances that can vary, once the sample statistics have been specified. For example, if we have n observations of a random variable, x, and have calculated the sample mean $\bar{x}$, we have $n - 1$ degrees of freedom because, if we know $\bar{x}$ and $n - 1$ of the x values, the last (or nth) observation must be such as to ensure the proper value of $\bar{x}$.

The last element for each distribution of values is thus determined when the mean and other parameters are known, and thus only one value is not free to vary. If there are multiple variables, as in the preceding example of use and gender, each will have its domain as a row or column. One element of each of these rows or columns is determined when the mean (or for that matter, the sum) of the row or column is known. The others are free to vary. Thus, the product of the number of rows, less 1, and the number of columns, less 1, indicates the number of cells free to vary. This, then, is called the number of degrees of freedom.

For the preceding example, consider a contingency table for male and female users and nonusers of a computerized information system, as shown in Table 6.1. In order to see if usage is correlated with gender, we first calculate expected numbers for the table. Since half the sample were male, half of the 34 users are expected to be male. Similarly, half of the 66 nonusers can be expected to be male. Then, calculate χ^2, in this case 8.7344. The number of degrees of freedom, df, is $(2 - 1) \cdot (2 - 1) = 1$. A table of chi-square statistical values for $df = 1$ yields 3.814, so we must reject the null hypothesis, for these hypothetical data, that gender and usage are independent. Such a table may be found in Kachigan (1982, p. 570), most other statistics books, and any edition of the *Handbook of Chemistry and Physics*.

6.3.1.2 The Correlation Coefficient

The covariation may occur in a number of ways or not at all. If no relationship can be found, if high and low values are as likely as not to be paired with one another throughout the range of observations, then we would say that the variables were *orthogonal* or *statistically independent*. If high values are associated with high, and low with low, and if the two variables are plotted on Cartesian coordinates, the curve connecting the x and y pairs would rise toward the right and we would have a positive association. Conversely, if high values are associated with low, the curve would fall toward the right, and we would have a negative association. We might expect the annual earnings of a business to be positively correlated with its sales and negatively correlated with its salary and wages budget. It is also possible that the relationship may be other than *monotonic*; that is, its graph may not maintain a constant direction but rather move from positive to negative, negative to positive, or even cyclically back and forth.

Plotting the covarying observations is a powerful technique that will lead to useful measures of association. Such a plot is known as a *scatter diagram*. If we plot the number of books acquired by a university library against the annual university operating budget over time, we should expect that the two increase together, yielding a *positive correlation*.

On the other hand, if we plot the number of uses of journal volumes against their age in years, we might expect that the uses would decline as the age increased (indicating a *negative correlation*), and, in fact, we would find a scattering of points around a theoretical line descending from the left (high use on the y axis) to the right (high age in years on the x axis). If this line is approximately straight, the relation is said to be linear, and the *product moment coefficient* will measure the relation between the variables.

r or *ρ*   *Pearson's correlation coefficient*; a measure of the mathematical similarity of two distributions.

$$r = \Sigma(x_i - \bar{x}) \cdot (y_i - \bar{y})/(n-1)s_x s_y$$

where x_i represents the *i*th *x* value and y_i represents the *i*th *y* value, $\bar{x}$ represents the sample mean of the *x*'s and $\bar{y}$ represents the sample mean of the *y*'s, s_x represents the sample standard deviation of the *x*'s and s_y represents the sample standard deviation of the *y*'s, and *n* is the number of sample pairs (x_i, y_i). This statistic, also known as *Pearson's correlation coefficient,* is traditionally called *r* for sample data and is an estimate of *ρ* (Greek rho), the coefficient for the population.

The range of *r* is [−1,1].

A coefficient of 0 indicates no statistical relationship, +1 indicates an exact positive correlation, and −1 an exact negative correlation. It should be noted that

$$r = \Sigma\, z_{xi} \cdot z_{yi}/(n-1)$$

i.e., the sum of the products of the *z* scores for *x* and *y* divided by the degrees of freedom. There are other correlation coefficients that are useful when assumptions for the product moment coefficient do not hold. There are rank coefficients for ordinal data, a contingency coefficient for nominal data, the correlation ratio for curvilinear data, multiple correlation coefficients when more than two variables are involved, and others for many special cases. (For further details the reader is referred to Hollander and Wolfe, 1973 and to Overall and Klett, 1973.)

The square of the correlation coefficient, r^2, is an indicator of the strength of the correlation. To be more specific, it signifies the proportion of the variance in the first variable attributable to or predictable by the second variable.

6.3.2 Regression

Consider again two variables that seem to be linearly related. Sometimes we need to investigate not only if variables are related but also the nature of the relationship. If we can assume a specific linear function, although there are advanced methods for nonlinear functions, we can model the relationship as

$$y = f(x) = ax + b$$

We then need to find the values of parameters *a* and *b* that would describe a line that best characterizes the relationship between observed values of *x* and y. This process is called *linear regression*. Use of the *least squares* method allows us to calculate the best a and b parameter values in order to fit a line to the data. The least squares method finds the a and b values that minimize the sum of the squared differences between each of the observed y values and the corresponding computed y value, calculated as $(ax + b)$ for each observed x value. This means to minimize $\Sigma(y_i - \bar{y}_i)^2$, where $\bar{y}_i = ax_i + b$. If $\bar{x}$ is the mean x value, $\bar{y}$ is the mean y value, and n is the sample size, then (Rao, 1983, pp. 104–108):

$$b = [\Sigma x_i y_i - n \cdot \bar{x} \cdot \bar{y}]/[\Sigma x_i^2 - n \cdot \bar{x}^2] \quad \text{and} \quad a = \bar{y} - b\bar{x}$$

We note that if a is positive, we have a positive correlation; if negative, we have a negative correlation. If a is not statistically different from zero, we have no correlation between the variables x and y. Thus, regression not only indicates that a relationship exists, it describes the nature of the relationship. In addition, regression can help specify the accuracy of the regression function. In *multiple regression*, we try to find parameters for a function of multiple *independent variables* $(x_1, x_2, \ldots)$ to predict values of the *dependent variable* y, and we can predict the relative contribution of each of the independent variables in explaining the variation of the dependent variable y. Incidentally, methods used when the function is curvilinear come under the heading of *nonlinear regression*.

Expanding on the theme of measuring the relationships among a set of variables, we can attempt to look at the variation of the dependent variable and see how it correlates with the variation of the independent variables. This branch of statistical analysis is called *analysis of variance*. If we cannot assume a specific functional form for the regression equation, or if we prefer not to, there are some statistical tests that do not assume a specific function; these are called *nonparametric statistics,* about which more can be found in Hollander and Wolfe (1973), to which the following page references refer. Some of the more well-known nonparametric tests include the Spearman and Kendall rank correlations to test whether two rank orderings are similar (p. 194), the Kolmogorov-Smirnoff test to see if a sample fits a given population (pp. 219–228), and the Mann-Whitney test of the difference between two samples' positions on an ordinal scale (p. 71). For additional information about these statistical issues, the reader should see Egghe and Rousseau (1990, Chap. 1).

6.3.3 Correlation and Regression in Information Science

We conclude our discussion of correlation with an example of its use in information science research. In 1989 Wallace and Boyce investigated the relationships among library holdings of journals, as indicated by holdings counts from the OCLC database, and citation figures from the *Journal*

Citation Reports section of *Science Citation Index* and *Social Sciences Citation Index,* with sales figures from *Ulrich's International Periodicals Directory*. Their hypothesis was that journals held by large numbers of libraries would have high scores on the other measures and that the distributions of sales, gross citations, and impact factors would be strongly correlated with holdings. The possible substitution of quickly accessible holdings for the citation measures would simplify management data collection and allow the inference that replacing current more or less subjective collection development practices with more objective ones would not necessarily change the resulting collections.

Since a holdings figure, a count of total citations, and an impact factor (total citations to a journal/total papers published by that journal) were available for each journal, and a sales figure for a larger portion, Pearson's correlation coefficients were calculated between each distribution and the holdings distribution. Although the coefficients varied considerably as to strength over the eight subjects, the combined sample, and a systematic sample, significant correlations of widely varying strength were found between holdings and the citation measures of six of the eight subjects and for the systematic and combined sample. A significant correlation was also found between sales and holdings in five of the eight subjects and both the combined and systematic sample.

They concluded that a relationship exists but that it cannot be considered valid when a sample cuts across subjects. Since many of the correlations, while significant, were quite weak, we might suspect that libraries are not consistently including journals that will be the most highly cited. Alternatively, if collective decision making on journal selection does measure quality, then we might well be suspicious of citation-based indicators of quality.

Larson (1991) used a regression model to show trends in subject searching over time in an online library catalogue. Plotting numbers of subject searches against time in days since the beginning of the data collection period, he was able to calculate the parameters *a* and *b,* where the sign of *a* would show whether or not subject search was declining and the magnitude would indicate the rate of change. He was able to show a consistent rate of decline in the use of subject search techniques in the catalogue, over time. He was also able to show a corresponding increase in the use of keyword searching.

6.4
Summary

We can see that in all likelihood, within a high confidence interval, we can accept the hypothesis that statistics is a good and useful but sometime vexing tool. Statistics allows us to compute measures that characterize large volumes of data in a manner that can be understood. We can also make inferences about large populations from small samples. We can measure the extent of our confidence that our sample data measure the characteristics of the population we wish to measure. If we can show that two variables are correlated, we can measure one and use it to estimate the other, thus measuring indirectly. If one variable is particularly difficult to measure, this can have significant value.

References

Egghe, L. and R. Rousseau. (1990). *Introduction to Informetrics*. Amsterdam: Elsevier.
Hollander, Myles and Douglas A. Wolfe. (1973). *Nonparametric Statistical Methods*. New York: John Wiley & Sons.
Kachigan, S. K. (1982). *Statistical Analysis: An Interdisciplinary Introduction to Univariate & Multivariate Methods*. New York: Radius Press.
Larson, Ray R. (1991). The decline of subject searching: long-term trends and patterns of index use in an online catalog. *Journal of the American Society of Information Science*, 42(3), 197–215.
Overall, J. E. and C. Klett (1973). *Applied Multivariate Analysis*. New York: McGraw Hill.
Rao, I. K. R. (1983). *Quantitative Methods for Library and Information Science*. New York: John Wiley & Sons.
Wallace, Danny P. and Bert R. Boyce. (1989). Holdings as a measure of journal value. *Library and Information Science Research*, 11(1), 59–71.

7

Clustering, Similarity, and Set Membership Measures

7.1
Classification

It is a characteristic of human thought to group like things together into classes and then treat the classes as if they fully represented the individual elements which, in the aggregate, make up the class. If we considered every individual we observe as a totally unique entity, we would not be able to make any generalizations or do any prediction. If we believe all snakes are dangerous to humans, we are unlikely to step knowingly in the path of a snake. In fact, not all snakes are dangerous to humans, but many are, and the rule leads to behavior that avoids danger even though it clearly discriminates against harmless snakes. Using the nonpejorative sense of the word, the rule fails to discriminate between harmless and other than harmless snakes.

Classification is a basic human activity which allows us to understand our observations and make predictions based upon past experience. The classic Aristotelian class is a set which is defined by either its stipulated members or a rule specifying a set of necessary and sufficient properties. The set of all men in Louisiana with green eyes constitutes such a class. All members will be male, reside in Louisiana, and have green eyes. Such a class is *monothetic,* which means that each member has all the properties that define the class (van Rijsbergen, 1979, pp. 43–44). However, everyday classification is not so definite. It is *polythetic,* by which we mean that each member possesses a large number but not necessarily all of the properties that define the class. Some threshold of properties present will cause us to assign membership. When we see dark clouds, notice that the wind strength has increased, and hear distant thunder, we class these observations together as precursors of a storm and predict rain. If we have a pain in our throat, our nose is running, and we are sneezing, we class these symptoms together as those of the common cold and assume we will be ill, but not too ill, for several days. There are other symptoms of both storms and colds, and those mentioned need not all be present for the storm or cold to occur.

This form of classification assigns individuals to the class based on the presence of an adequate number of characteristics of the class and then assumes that all individuals so assigned have all the characteristics of the class and will behave as the class is expected to behave. All practical classification is discriminatory in this sense. Classification on the basis of a few prominent characteristics can be used to make totally unjustified predictions. Racial and sexual characteristics can be used to impute behavior patterns that are entirely unjustified when applied to all individuals so classified. Classification is a powerful and dangerous process that is nonetheless basic to human thought. It underlies Western science and has made the human race technologically powerful. At the same time, it has often led to tragic social consequences.

In this chapter our concern is with methods of grouping things together. We want to understand how we can decide in a more or less objective manner that one item is in some way close enough to another that they may be classified together. This will normally involve some sort of measurement of the theoretical distance between the items under consideration based upon a subset of their characteristics. If information systems are designed to answer questions, we would like to characterize the records in our files in such a way that the groupings make it easier to answer the questions. We may also wish to so classify our users and their questions to be better able to control the process.

Like descriptive statistics, classification is clearly a data reduction technique. We wish to deal with vast collections of individual elements and we can do so only by generalization. In this chapter we review several such techniques.

7.2
Data Aggregation

In statistics we often deal with nominally scaled qualitative variables. We can use race, religion, political party, education level, and so forth to characterize our sample. In other words, we make broad classifications based upon easily recognized characteristics and then look for relationships with quantitative variables. However, it is also possible to use analysis techniques to define the boundaries between classes of elements using the quantitative variables. This process is *discriminant analysis*.

7.2.1 Discriminant Analysis

The idea in discriminant analysis is to use quantitative predictor variables to forecast the value of a qualitative criterion variable, after identifying the predictor variables that are related to the criterion variable. Morrison (1974) provides a useful description of the technique. For example, we may wish to predict sex from an array of values of quantitative variables that describe a person's physical characteristics. The process is, in effect, the same as a regression analysis except that the criterion variable is not continuous and may be only nominal in scale. Each item to be classified is scored according to a *discriminant function*. This function is the weighted sum of the values of the predictor variables that are to be used. If x_i is one of k predictor variables and w_i its assigned weight, then the discriminator function, D, is

D Discriminator function; used to separate entities according to values of a set of predictor variables.

$$D = w_1 x_1 + w_2 x_2 + \cdots + w_k x_k$$

The variables and their weights are determined by using the characteristics of known class members. A cutoff score is then used to discriminate between classes if the qualitative variable is binary. If the qualitative variable has more than two values and if we are creating multiple classes, we will need multiple discriminant functions. One will serve to separate the first class from the aggregation, another to separate the second from the remaining aggregation, and so on. This implies one less discriminant function than the desired number of classes, or the same number as that of the discriminating variables if this value is smaller.

The number of functions should be that necessary to describe the variance. Thus it is possible that not all the implied functions will be necessary. They may appear to account mathematically for some small portion of the variance in the data due to errors of sampling, but not really exist in the population. A test of the significance of the discriminating information not already accounted for by previous functions will allow us to decide if enough information remains to utilize another function. *Wilk's lambda* (Klotz and Johnson, 1983, p. 462) provides such a measure.

Λ Wilk's lambda; an inverse measure of the discrimination power in the variables not yet removed.

$$\Lambda = t_{11}^2 \cdot t_{22}^2 \cdots \cdots t_{pp}^2$$

where the t_{ii} are diagonal elements of the quantitative variables matrix.

The greater the value of Λ, the less information remains for an additional function. Using chi-square to test Λ, we can identify when the next function has no significant variance to explain.

In this way, we can decide that if D is meaningful and exceeds a certain threshold, then this set of predictor variable values implies a value for a qualitative variable. If height and weight and muscle mass exceed certain limits, we may conclude that the subject is male rather than female. There will always be error in this sort of classification process. We can change the weights, or the cutoff value, in order to allow more correct items into a group. This will have the unfortunate effect of incorrectly allowing too many entities into the group. Trade-offs must be made based upon the relative costs of error in either direction. Functions and cutoffs should always be validated with a fresh data sample. It is here that the power of the analysis will become known, since the original data will have supplied chance relationships that are built into the analysis.

We can, of course, limit the number of needed predictor variables by finding intercorrelations and redundancies among them. One method of doing so is *factor analysis*.

7.2.2 Factor Analysis

In discriminate analysis we began with knowledge of the classes into which we wished objects to fall and attempted to determine predictors that would allow us to assign new objects to classes. If we have no real knowledge of classes in advance of the analysis, we may try to reduce the data by identifying the relationships that exist among the variables we have recorded. This is done in *factor analysis* by determining which variables are correlated and removing redundancy from them by forming a small set of independent derived variables or factors that represent them. In a sense we are classifying similar variables or considering them as representatives of some underlying factor.

This process allows us to choose a representative variable in a factor to represent a whole factor and thus reduce the amount of data that would need to be collected in future studies. The knowledge that certain information should be considered together will improve our understanding of the phenomena under consideration and may allow us to concentrate in areas that have the most effect on the classification process. If we consider the items as a set of values of multiple random variables, they can be clustered together using these techniques. Homogeneous groups can thus be identified. Harman (1967) provides an excellent overall review of the topic.

The process itself involves the creation of a correlation matrix of variables. This is a display of the correlation coefficients that exist between all possible pairs of variables. Using matrix algebra the correlation matrix is transformed into a factor matrix, where the rows represent the variables and the columns the derived factors. The cells contain *factor loadings* which indicate the correlation of each variable with each factor and vary from +1 to −1. The high loads in a factor column indicate the variables that contribute strongly to this factor. Each of the factors will also have a *factor score* for each observation. This is a weighted combination of the observed scores on each variable in the factor.

An *eigenvalue,* a concept from linear algebra (Hadley, 1961), is used in factor analysis to measure the relative amount of variance accounted for by a factor. In this case, it is calculated as the percent of variance accounted for by a factor divided by the percent of variance accounted for by the average factor. If we have five variables, each will on average account for 20% of the variance. If a factor accounts for 50% of the variance it will have an eigenvalue of 50/20 or 2.5. An eigenvalue of 1 represents a factor that accounts for exactly the average variance for the data. Thus the eigenvalue is a measure of the variance accounted for by a factor in average variance units. In order to determine how many factors to derive from our data, as a rule of thumb, we may wish to create enough factors so that any additional ones would account for less variance than the average variable. There would be no data reduction if the factor accounted for less variance than an original variable. We would then not include factors whose eigenvalue was less than one.

An initial question is always how many factors would be useful. We might begin with the number of variables equal to the number of factors. This is known as *principal components analysis.* The factor analysis algorithm will typically extract the factor accounting for the most variance first, but by looking at the eigenvalues we can easily select those factors which contribute more than the average variance. Once we have selected a number of factors, we may wish to get an impression of which variables really define the factors so that we can discover their meaning. Since most of the variables will provide high factor loadings on the first factor, this may not be obvious. If we could redefine the factors so that there were few medium-sized loadings, we could more easily identify the high-load variables in our factors.

The procedure for doing this is *factor rotation.* There are actually several procedures, but their purpose is to redefine the factors so that their meaning, in terms of the underlying variables, is more obvious. After rotation we can assign a descriptive name to each factor based upon the high-loading variables in that factor. At the completion of the procedure we have classed our variables and given names to the classes. Clearly the naming process is less than objective, but it is often very useful in interpretation.

Factor analysis is a technique for clustering variables and thus could come under the broad heading of cluster analysis. However, the expression *cluster analysis* is more normally used to describe techniques for classifying together, not variables, but the objects whose characteristics we observed in order to measure the values of our variables.

7.2.3 Clustering

The concern in clustering is not with what characteristics of records can be considered together, as it was in factor analysis, but rather which records can be classed together in terms of common characteristics. We could, for example, use factor analysis to determine if common citations and common index terms occurring in a set of documents fell in the same factor and could thus be substituted one for the other. In cluster analysis we are concerned with using these characteristics to classify the documents themselves into like groups.

In discriminant analysis we were interested in classifying objects into classes (binary variables) provided prior to the analysis. In cluster analysis we are searching for object classes implicit in the data, not necessarily previously identified. This is done by measuring a set of variables over all our objects and then defining a measure of similarity between each pair of objects. The result is the conversion of an object-variable matrix into an object-object matrix where the cells contain the values of the similarity measure. We then construct an algorithm which will create classes based upon these pairwise similarities. The best classes are those that have little within-cluster variation but large between-cluster variation. They will thus represent great discrimination among the various clusters and great homogeneity of class membership. We will review in general terms measures of similarity and the techniques available to create clusters from them. Since these techniques have considerable application in information systems, we will discuss some of the specific applications in that milieu.

7.2.3.1 Measures of Distance and Similarity

Similarity and distance may be considered to be complementary terms in the context of cluster analysis. We are creating an object space where the objects are separated by distance or difference. This distance is then a measure of *dissimilarity*. The minimization of distance will be the maximization of similarity. Thus we must always be sure we are aware whether a large value of a particular measure is indicating similarity or dissimilarity.

Euclidean distance is an obvious measure. If we consider the value of two variables on two objects, we can plot the difference between the values on Cartesian coordinates, with the point of origin representing one object and the second located by plotting the differences in values on the x and y axes and finding the location of the intersection point. The Euclidean distance is then the length of the hypotenuse, running from the origin, object one, to the intersection point, object two. Although actual values of variables can be used to determine the coordinates of any object, O_j, relative to any other object, O_i, the use of z scores will eliminate the effect of unequal variances.

Since we will be dealing with $n > 2$ variables in most cases, the distance from O_i to O_j can be expressed using a general form of the Pythagorean theorem:

$D(O_i, O_j)$ *Object distance;* the distance from one object to another measured in terms of values of various dimensions.

$$D(O_i, O_j) = [(x_j - x_i)^2 + (y_j - y_i)^2 + \cdots + (n_j - n_i)^2]^{1/2}$$

where i and j indicate the objects (documents, typically) whose distance is to be measured and $x, y, \ldots n$ are the dimensions in n-space.

For a second possibility, in a sort of inverse factor analysis, we can invert a correlation matrix so that instead of the correlations representing a relationship between variables they represent a relationship between the objects that were observed. Objects that are highly correlated are similar, and the correlation coefficient is a measure of that similarity.

If the variables are binary, it is possible simply to count the number of variables on which two objects have the same value, whether that value is one or zero. These counts would normally be divided by the total number of variables to provide a similarity index, which is the percentage of the variables on which the objects agree. In files of information records where the number of binary variables is large, it is a common practice to ignore variables with a zero value when calculating the similarity measure. If records are our objects and keywords our binary variables, then only a small number of keywords will be assigned to each document and use of unassigned words would result in little additional information.

7.2.3.2 Record or Text Similarity Measures

At the document level, again there can be both semantic and statistical meanings of relatedness. Two texts that are related in subject matter can be related by assignment of a common or similar subject classification term, or by the selection of a common or similar set of subject descriptors. Statistical similarity is generally defined in terms of the similarity of word frequency distributions; i.e., two texts are similar if they use approximately the same set of words and with approximately the same relative frequencies. Salton (1983, pp. 202–203) and van Rijsbergen (1979, p. 30) list several *similarity measures* for texts or documents:

$SIM1(T_1, T_2)$ *Dice's coefficient;* twice the ratio of the number of co-occurrences to total number of occurrences of either value.

$$SIM1(T_1, T_2) = \frac{2[\Sigma(f_{i,k}) \bigcirc (f_{j,k})]}{\Sigma f_{i,k} + \Sigma f_{j,k}}$$

where T_1 and T_2 represent texts 1 and 2; $f_{i,k}$ represents the frequency of occurrence of term (value) k in text i; $(f_{i,k}) \bigcirc (f_{j,k})$ is the number of

7.2 Data Aggregation

co-occurrences of term k in text i and text j; and m is the magnitude of the database.

If each value occurred in each record, without the factor of 2, the denominator would be twice the numerator, but the 2 normalizes the range to [0,1].

A second measure is

SIM2 (T_1, T_2) *Jaccard's coefficient;* reduces the denominator of *SIM1* by the number of occurrences in common, hence it is a ratio of co-occurrences to non-cooccurrences, rather than to total occurrences. Range is [0,1].

$$SIM2(T_1, T_2) = \frac{\Sigma(f_{i,k}) \bigcirc (f_{j,k})}{\Sigma(f_{i,k} + \Sigma f_{j,k} - \Sigma(f_{i,k}) \bigcirc (f_{j,k})}$$

Think of a Euclidean space of n dimensions, one dimension for each attribute value being used in the measurement. If the attribute used is a word in a text, then n is the number of different words used or potentially used throughout a set of texts in a database. The n words constitute the vocabulary. A text is represented by a vector in this space. The value of each dimension may be the frequency of occurrence of that value in a given text, or it may be 1 if the value occurs in the text, 0 otherwise. This is called the *vector space model* of a set of texts or records. Based on this model, a third measure of similarity is:

SIM3(T_1, T_2) *Cosine coefficient;* measuring the angle between two vectors in the vector space model of a text. Its range is [0,1].

$$SIM3(T_1, T_2) = \frac{\Sigma(f_{i,k}) \bigcirc (f_{j,k})}{[\Sigma(f_{i,k})^2 + \Sigma(f_{j,k})^2]^{1/2}}$$

Summation, in all cases, is over the number of dimensions or possible terms, i.e., $k = 1$ to n.

The cosine coefficient is then the cosine of the angle between the vectors. The smaller the angle, the more similar the texts, in terms of vocabulary used. Texts with identical vocabularies will have a subtended angle of 0, whose cosine is 1. Texts with no values in common would have the n-dimensional spatial equivalent of a right angle between them, with cosine 0.

Still another measure is

SIM4(T_1, T_2) *Overlap measure;* the ratio of the number of terms in common to the number of terms in the text with the smaller number of terms. Its range is [0,1].

$$SIM4(T_1, T_2) = \frac{\Sigma(f_{i,k}) \bigcirc (f_{j,k})}{MIN(\Sigma(f_{i,k}), \Sigma(f_{j,k}))}$$

There is no *right* similarity measure. Experimentation may tell which is best for a particular application. But the measure of closeness, here, is entirely a statistical one. If two texts use the same vocabulary, they are close by all three definitions but *not* necessarily by the judgment of every reader. Take, for example, a text deemed by a reader to be highly relevant to that person's need, scramble the words so their order is random, and these measures do not change, but the relevance or value of the revised text will surely change.

The cosine coefficient has become very popular for the nearness of a record to another record or to a question that has been represented in the same manner. Keywords, or assigned index terms, are typically used for the binary variables, but any common characteristic which might lead to useful clusters could be used. References and citations, or portions of them, are likely choices for documents from the learned literature. It is also possible to use weights for a term rather than just a binary value. A common method of calculating such weights, inverse document frequency, is discussed in Section 8.8.2.

We see that there is a relationship between similarity/dissimilarity measures and the idea of distance. If a similarity coefficient meets the proper criteria it is certainly a distance. The first of these criteria is that the measure be greater than or equal to zero. Distances are not negative. Second, the measure between an object and itself must be zero. No object has a positive distance from itself. Third, symmetry is required. If an object is a given distance from a second object, then the second object must be that same distance from the first. Finally, if the measure is a true distance it must meet the *triangle inequality*. The measure from object one to object two must be less than or equal to the measure from object one to object three plus the measure from object two to object three. A measure that meets these three requirements is a true distance or metric.

Clearly, Euclidean distance is a true distance. Some similarity measures are distances; other similarity measures are quasi-distances, that is, measures which fail to meet one or more of the requirements for a distance (usually the failure is to meet the triangle inequality). Once we have established our similarity measures we must choose a technique to form classes and complete the cluster analysis.

7.2.3.3 Clustering Techniques

We wish our clusters to be equivalence classes on some relation generated from an interobject similarity matrix. We might, for example, wish to cluster documents based upon common citations, authors, index terms, or words in the text. Clearly, there will need to be some cutoff value for the similarity coefficient above which our objects are considered to be in the same class. If we set this value high there will be a large number of

7.2 Data Aggregation

small classes. At some high value all classes will be single-member classes and there will be an equal number of classes and records. If we set the cutoff value low there will be a small number of large classes. At some low value there will be one large class. The number of classes is a problem of resolution or of focus. The solution to the problem depends upon our reasons for creating the classification and our perception of a useful class size for a given problem. The other problem is the choice of a clustering method.

For information retrieval a classification needs several characteristics to be judged useful. Since files are large, grow continually, and are regularly searched, they need to be compact and both easily searched and easily updated. We would not wish the clusters produced to be radically altered by the addition of new objects, nor would we wish that the initial ordering of objects affect their clusters.

If we have a matrix of correlation coefficients between objects we may use the factor analysis algorithm. The factor matrix will now consist of objects, rather than variables, loading on factors which might better be called, in this application, cluster dimensions. We then assign objects to the clusters upon which they load highly. This method is little used with documents at the present time.

Graph theoretic methods are also a possibility. One example of their application is to cluster documents using citation statistics, so documents cited by common documents, or citing common documents, are clustered together. These methods have also been used to study the sociology of various branches of science. Using an object, object similarity matrix we can create a graph where objects are nodes and a link is defined by an arbitrarily high enough cell value between objects. Strings, connected sequences sometimes called walks, are then formed from a selected starting point. These could be considered classes, or we could insist that the class be a maximal complete subgraph, one with all its node pairs connected. Such multiple link classes are often known as *cliques*. This more stringent requirement will reduce the size and increase the number of classes.

Single-link algorithms create connected component subgraphs (i.e., classes or clusters) for any cutoff value of a similarity coefficient. For an object to belong to a cluster it need have only one link to any other member of that cluster. As the cutoff value is increased fewer and fewer cells of the matrix exceed it, and fewer and fewer objects cluster together. Therefore varying this threshold value will cause classes to group together or break apart. If we begin with a low threshold and one large class and then systematically increase the threshold and recompute the classes, we will create the levels of a hierarchical classification. For retrieval purposes this is an excellent classification method because, with the proper cutoff value, we can retrieve all members of the class best matching the query as an answer to a question.

Given n objects, however, it will require on the order of n^2 operations to complete the classification. Single-link methods are expensive.

Most common clustering algorithms use a similarity function to measure the closeness of the objects. Many utilize iteration and the assignment of arbitrary parameters like cluster size and number to determine the outcome. These methods require only on the order of $n \log n$ operations to create and thus are in common use. They do not tend to be stable when updated, however. Quite often the initial class representatives are more or less arbitrarily chosen, initial assignments are made, and in additional passes through the data a cleanup takes place so that the clusters meet the initial parameters.

A *single-pass* algorithm (where only one pass through the data is required for the operation) is possible, where the first object becomes the center of the first cluster, and if the second does not cluster with it, it in turn becomes the center of the second cluster, and so on until the file is exhausted. Normally the assignment of a new object to a class causes its center to be recomputed to reflect mean values over all objects assigned. Such classifications are dependent upon the initial order of the objects processed.

In a cluster analysis, depending upon the number of objects to be classified and upon their diversity, as already noted, a large number of dimensions may be needed to represent the existing data in an accurate fashion. In factor analysis we create factors which represent in an abstract manner each of the underlying dimensions of our variables. We shall now introduce *multidimensional scaling* with which we attempt the same sort of data reduction in order to decrease the complexity of the object space.

7.3
Multidimensional Scaling

The goal of multidimensional scaling (MDS) is to reduce object space to two or three dimensions so that it may be easily understood and in fact graphed. As Schiffman et al. (1981, p. 3) say in their excellent introduction to the subject, "Multidimensional Scaling is simply a useful mathematical tool that enables us to represent the similarities of objects spatially as in a map."

In simple scaling we are representing the relationships between pairs of objects visually as points on a line relative to one another. The relationship between two points can be shown in one dimension, and if their relationship is a distance from the origin where the triangle inequality holds, multiple points can be so graphed. A ruler is an example of such a graph.

If the triangle inequality does not hold—say, for example, that the quasi-distance from A to B is 1, from A to C 3, and from B to C 1—then we cannot graph in one dimension but must go to two dimensions, e.g.,

7.3 Multidimensional Scaling

a 1,1,3 triangle, to represent the relationship. As the number of objects increases the necessary dimensions increase, if the relationships are not true distances. As we have already seen, it is possible that we may here require multiple dimensions because we have multiple relationship criteria between our objects.

When we consider a point in n-dimensional space and wish to place it on a scale relative to other points in the same space, we must consider what sort of order relation we are discussing. When we are dealing with one dimension, we may place points on a line to the right of an origin point indicating that they are larger than the origin point. This is a one-dimensional concept of scaling. In n-space, being to the right of another point does not exactly represent being larger than the point to the left, because "larger than" involves distances in several dimensions. We need some rule to combine the various differences so that we can consider them as one dimension. Euclidean distance is certainly a possibility, but so is the so-called *taxi-cab distance*, which moves from the origin to a point along lines parallel to the axes as we would need to travel on city streets. In two dimensions, this means not using diagonal distances but only the legs of right triangles.

$td_{i,j}$ *Taxi-cab distance;* the distance is the sum of the various distances p over the number of segments required.

$$td_{i,j} = \Sigma \mid x_{ip} - x_{jp} \mid$$

Another possibility is the zero metric:

$zd_{i,j}$ Zero metric; *a simplification of the taxi-cab distance.*

$$zd_{i,j} = \Sigma \mid x_{ip} - x_{jp} \mid^0$$

where

$$\mid x_{ip} - x_{jp} \mid^0 = 0 \text{ if } \mid x_{ip} - x_{jp} \mid = 0$$
$$1 \text{ if } \mid x_{ip} - x_{jp} \mid > 0$$

The idea in multidimensional scaling is to produce a two- or three-dimensional representation of an n-dimensional situation with as little loss of information as possible. In the basic process arbitrary coordinates for points equal in number to the data points are chosen such that their distances will display in the desired number of dimensions. Their distances are calculated. These distances are then ordered from smallest to greatest. The smallest is assigned as the distance for the most similar objects in the similarity matrix. The next largest is the distance for the next most similar objects, and so on. This produces a matrix of distances known as configuration distances.

Some considerable loss of accuracy of representation occurs in the process. Although the new distances may be graphed in the desired dimensions, they may have little relationship to the distances required by the data. The measure of this loss is termed *stress*. Stress decreases as the configuration distance approaches the observed distances of the objects in the space. It can be calculated from the distances in the data and the configuration distances (Ven, 1980).

stress Stress; loss of accuracy in multidimensional scaling.

$$stress = [\Sigma \mid d_{i,j} - d'_{i,j} \mid ^2 / \Sigma \mid d_{ij} - \overline{d} \mid]^{1/2}$$

where $d_{i,j}$ = the configuration distance between objects i and j, possibly the taxi-cab distance, but possibly another like measure; $d'_{i,j}$ = the target distance (observed distance in n-space) based on the data; and d = the mean of the configuration distances.

A stress of 0.15 or less is often considered satisfactory. Most algorithms vary the configuration distances to approach the observed distances and continue to iterate until improvement in the stress measure is minimal or until some set value is attained.

In effect, interobject distances that could not be accurately represented in the desired number of dimensions have been changed to the closest values that can be so represented. The objects are normally then displayed on a *perceptual map*, usually in two dimensions. The map is thus a set of coordinates where the underlying meaning of the two dimensions can be deduced only from an analysis of the distribution of objects in the four quadrants and relative to one another. A cluster analysis may be superimposed by drawing boundaries for the clusters formed. An interesting example is to be found as the frontispiece of Griffith (1980). Here authors in information science were correlated on the basis of cocitation, the resulting author-author matrix passed through a multidimensional analysis algorithm, and clusters formed of authors whose distances apart were small. Unfortunately, the underlying meaning of the remaining dimensions is unclear.

7.4
Matching Functions

In information retrieval the concept of a *matching function* allows us to compute a relationship between a record and a query. In early retrieval systems, records were deemed to match or not match. Now, we tend to be concerned with the degree to which they match. The assumption is that a function can be defined which allows us to test whether or not a record should be considered a match to a query, either by a person or a program distinct from the search and matching algorithm. Such functions are attempts to model the relation of relevance in an operational manner. A general statement of this concept is: Given any query, each record, x_i, of the database bears a relationship to it as defined by the matching function. The computation of the value of the function is an operation distinct from that of deciding which records to retrieve. That decision may be made after a set of functional values has been created. Different match functions may be used by different systems, and it is even possible to allow each user of any one system to define the function best fitting that person's needs of the moment.

In the Boolean model of information retrieval, the matching function means that sets of records containing terms specified in the query are located and assigned to a single set on a binary basis. This results in a binary division of the file into relevant and other than relevant records. Then, there is no decision about which records to retrieve, because there is no way to partition the "relevant" set. It is also possible to count those characteristics whose specifications in both the query and the record are identical and assign this count to each record as an indication of its value for retrieval. The records may then be ranked using this retrieval status value and some cutoff point used to return a ranked list of the most relevant records. (See also Section 13.4.) This method is normally called the *coordination level*. If this coordination level is normalized in some way, we have the similarity measures already discussed, which can be used to model the matching function as well.

7.5
Fuzzy Set Theory

We have discussed basic set theory in Section 4.1, where we defined set membership as follows: "A set is a collection of objects that are distinct from one another. *Set membership* is defined either by a list (Bert, Charlie, and Don) or a rule (the authors of this book)." Clearly, in this sense, an element under consideration either belongs to a set or it does not. As we pointed out in Section 7.1, the classifications used by human beings in everyday life are not always so clear-cut. Some items that we could assign to a class are more strongly associated with the class than are others. A *fuzzy set* might be a better model of the situation. A set is considered to be fuzzy when an element can belong partly to it, rather than be strictly included or not included. If we indicated membership (or full membership) with a 1 and nonmembership with a 0, fuzzy or partial membership could be indicated by a value between 0 and 1 (Smithson, 1987).

One problem that arises with the classical notion of a set is that it does not allow for ambiguity, uncertainty, vagueness, and imprecision (i.e., fuzziness). Suppose that we consider a universe of the current full-time faculty at Louisiana State University. Moreover, suppose that we want a list of all middle-aged male faculty who are overweight for a study of the effects of nutrition and diet on weight loss. If we have information on the faculty as to their gender, age, and weight, we still do not have a precise list. How much weight is considered "overweight"? Moreover, at what age does a male faculty member begin to be considered "middle aged" and, perhaps even more uncertain, at what age is he considered no longer to be "middle aged" (i.e., now he is "old")?

For the skeptical, consider another example. Suppose you are asked to gather grains of sand to form a pile of sand. You start by getting one grain of sand and placing it in the desired location. Is that grain the pile you seek? Of course not. Now, you get a second grain and place it next to the first. Do you now have the pile? Again, of course not. The question is, how many grains do you need before you do have a pile? Is 50,000 grains the boundary that makes a bunch of grains a pile, so that 49,999 is not a pile but 50,000 grains is? Clearly, an appropriate way is needed to model such imprecise situations.

Thus, instead of the notion of either being in the set under consideration or not, we generalize to the notion of partial membership. A fuzzy set is a list of each element in the universe with a number in the range [0,1] assigned to it. This number, called a membership function, indicates the degree to which this element is in the set under consideration. For example, we might consider a candidate for the study mentioned who is of age 39 to be in the set of middle-aged male professors with a degree of 0.65.

We immediately start to develop a mathematics around this notion. For example, how do we represent the normal Boolean connectives, AND, OR, and NOT in a consistent manner? Several representations have been suggested, including the minimum function for AND, the maximum function for OR, and the 1-minus function for NOT. Of course, this forces us to rethink Boolean logic. For example, if I am 0.8 middle aged, then I am $1 - 0.8 = 0.2$ not middle aged (making me either too young or too old). This leads to the notion that I am then minimum $(0.8, 0.2) = 0.2$ both middle aged and not middle aged. This is different from ordinary Boolean logic in that it violates the law of the excluded middle, which states that the truth value of anything being both x and not x for any property x is zero.

Other possible definitions for operators include the use of the product for AND and the sum minus the product for OR. There is even the notion of a fuzzy number. For example, suppose that I am about 50 years old and that you are approximately 10 years younger than I; how old are you? In addition, there are the notions of subsets or set inclusions, fuzzy relations, fuzzy logic, and possibility theory, which is the fuzzy analogy to probability theory.

There is also the notion of linguistic hedges, i.e., adverbs that modify the fuzzy adjectives. If, based on my height, I am 0.8 in the set of "tall" people, how much am I in the set of "very tall" people (concentration) or in the set of "somewhat tall" people (dilation)?

One application of recent vintage is in control theory. This consists of a series of if–then rules for controlling a system. For example, consider a mobile robot trying to navigate in a room. One rule could be that if the robot's sensors detect that the robot is moving forward toward a goal location but is too close to the wall on the robot's left, then the robot should turn slightly to the right to correct the situation, while still moving forward toward the goal. The notions of "closeness" to a wall and of turning "slightly" to the right are certainly imprecise and can be represented by fuzzy sets.

The major measurement issue associated with fuzzy sets is the assignment of the value representing the degree of set membership. In some way the membership function must be derived for each item under consideration. This is often a more or less arbitrary process. In the main information system application that will be discussed in Part IV, fuzzy operations are applied to information retrieval. Determining which documents are about a given topic in response to a user query for information is certainly an imprecise process that can be appropriately modeled using fuzzy set theory. In order to derive a membership function we can allow indexers to assign weights to the terms used to index a document. This weight would reflect the relative importance of a term in specifying what the document in question is about. If done by human indexers, this is a highly subjective process. If done by software, it normally reflects counts of word occurrences. The inverse document frequency weight described in Section 8.2.2 is an example.

7.6
Summary

We have reviewed the various ways in which data can be aggregated and combined in order to create classes for rational consideration. These techniques have use in information systems both for the organization of stores of information and for the generation of answer sets in response to stated information needs.

The remaining chapters of this book are devoted to what may be measured in information systems and to what end we might measure it. In each instance we will discuss the possibility of quantifying varying aspects of information systems, the usefulness of such an effort, and any issues of reliability that accompany the use of such measures. We begin the next chapter with the measurement of what we have termed *language phenomena*.

References

Adler, Irving. (1966). *Probability and Statistics for Everyman*. New York: New American Library, 16–32.
DeMorgan, A. (1847). *Formal Logic*. London: unknown publisher.
Griffith, B. C., ed. (1980). *Key Papers in Information Science*. Washington, DC: American Society for Information Science, vii.
Hadley, G. (1961). *Linear Algebra*. Reading, MA: Addison-Wesley.
Harman, H.H. (1967). *Modern Factor Analysis*. Chicago: The University of Chicago Press.
Klotz, Samuel and Norman L. Johnson, eds. (1983). *Encyclopedia of Statistical Sciences*, Vol. 4. New York: John Wiley & Sons.
Morrison, D. G. (1974). Discriminant analysis. In R. Ferber, ed. *Handbook of Marketing Research*. New York: McGraw-Hill.
Quine, Willard Van Orden. (1950). *Methods of Logic*. New York: Henry Holt & Co.
Salton, Gerard, and Michael J. McGill (1983). New York: McGraw Hill Book Co.
Schiffman, Susan, M. L. Reynolds and F. W. Young. (1981). *Introduction to Multidimensional Scaling*. New York: Academic Press.
Smithson, Michael. (1987). *Fuzzy Set Analysis for Behavioral and Social Sciences*. New York: Springer-Verlag.
van Rijsbergen, C. J. (1979). *Information Retrieval*, 2nd ed. London: Butterworth & Co. Limited.
Ven, A. H. G. S. van der. (1980). *Introduction to Scaling*. Chichester: John Wiley & Sons, 222–243.

Three

Measures of Information Phenomena

8
Measures of Language and Text

8.1
Informetrics

Informetrics is a term whose definition is somewhat ambiguous in the literature. It appears to have been first introduced in 1979 as a general term covering both *bibliometrics* and *scientometrics*. (Brookes, 1991) All three terms have been used loosely to mean more or less the same thing. Informetrics can be perceived in its broadest sense as "the study of the quantitative aspects of information in any form" (Brookes, 1991, p. 1991) or as "the search for regularities in data associated with the production and use of recorded information" (Bookstein et al., 1992). This implies a very broad scope indeed. Most would probably not limit the term to recorded information, the measurement of which is generally considered the realm of bibliometrics. It thus would include ephemeral communication activities such as unrecorded speech and chalkboard graphics. We might define bibliometrics as the search for measurable regularities in the production and utilization of recorded information, and informetrics as the search for measurable regularities in all communication processes.

Prior to Pritchard (1969), bibliometrics was discussed under the heading of statistical bibliography. Since scientific literatures were the primary body for study, those interested in the sociology of science saw in the approach a method useful in their research, and scientometrics was born. Scientometrics is concerned with the quantitative aspects of science as a social or economic endeavor. Science for the purpose of this definition includes both the hard and social sciences, and is sometimes considered as covering all scholarly activity. Humanistic research would be included only by a minority of regular users of the term. Since recorded communication is a part of the social aspects of science, there is an overlap with bibliometrics. Since social and economic activities involve an exchange of information, scientometrics falls within the realm of informetrics. Informetrics, however, would not be limited to the study of any particular social class or profession as is scientometrics.

Past work in informetrics has been primarily in five areas. Two of the most important are bibliometrics and scientometrics. A third is the discipline of *computational linguistics,* which is concerned with the statistical aspects of language. A large literature, known as *information theory,* also exists concerning information in Shannon's sense, as a measure of the removal of uncertainty during technical transmission (Shannon and Weaver, 1949). Finally, there is a large body of work pertaining to the measurement of closeness between questions and answers, sets of proposed and known to be correct answers, and among multiple questions or multiple answers in information retrieval systems.

In this book we discuss scientometrics in only a tangential manner. The remainder of this chapter will be devoted to measurement in the area of computational linguistics. The following chapter will cover bibliometrics and information theory. We will also devote chapters to measurement as a component of retrieval systems and to measurement of the performance of such systems.

8.2
The Measurement of Language

In formal linguistics a systematic grammar is assumed, which allows the combination of language units into well-formed expressions. In such a system predictions can be made based on the known units and the rules of which combinations will be considered well formed by a native speaker. If language can be reduced to component parts and rules for the combination of these parts, then we can expect to be able to count the occurrences of these parts and their combinations as they occur in written or spoken language. Such information can give us data on the probability of occurrence of units and their combinations and thus permit us to identify variations from the standard.

This reduction to component parts normally begins at the level of distinctive sounds made by a native speaker. These distinctive sounds are called *phonemes* (Bolinger, 1968, p. 41). In fact, phonemes are made up of combinations of distinctive sonic features that can be produced by the human vocal apparatus. If the sound produced by such a combination is not considered different by a native speaker from the sound produced by a similar but not identical combination, both combinations would be instances of a single phoneme in that language. Such variations are *allophones* of a phoneme.

Phonemes, with a vowel-like sound, alone, or in combination with consonants, make up *syllables.* Each language has an identifiable, but complex, rule structure for the formation of syllables. When meaning is attached to a syllable or combination of syllables, the result becomes a *morpheme.*

8.2 The Measurement of Language

This is not necessarily a word or *lexeme*. Prefixes like "un-" are morphemes because they are syllables with attached meaning. They are not words. Words are defined by Bolinger (1968, p. 53) as "the prefabricated units of syntax." This means that lexemes are the units we combine into sentences in order to express ideas. They are the combinations of syllables between which a pause can be inserted. This pause seems to indicate that another combination could be inserted at this point, whereas it could not within the combination that is a word. Lexemes, or words, are the smallest components of language which can stand alone and express meaning.

Phrases, combinations of words, and sentences, combinations of words and phrases, are assembled to express meaning according to rules. Such rule systems are called *grammars*. Words are classed as parts of speech, and grammars are the rules that exist in a language for the combination of parts of speech. *Syntax,* which means "putting together," is just a term for the combinatory rules in use in a language. It is primarily in use at the level of a grammar, but it can apply at any level of linguistic combination.

It thus becomes possible to measure the complexity of languages by counting the number of rules necessary for proper syntax at any of the levels discussed. However, in information systems, our interest is not in measuring the complexity of structure of a language but rather in using our knowledge of the objective characteristics of a language in order to measure something else indirectly.

8.2.1 The Measurement of Meaning

This something else is *meaning*. Morris (1946, p. 3) considers three types of meaning based on the relationship of what he calls "signs" (words or lexemes in our context) to other external factors. *Pragmatic meaning* is the relation of signs to situations and behaviors in a sociological context. For example, the phrase "Baton Rouge" stated at a airline ticket counter in Toronto could mean that we wanted a ticket to go to Baton Rouge, but the same phrase stated to a airline attendant who is announcing that the plane is about to land could mean that we want to know if we are landing in Baton Rouge. *Syntactic meaning* is the relation of signs to one another in a linguistic context; for example, the phrase "Venetian blind" is different in meaning from the phrase "blind Venetian." *Semantic meaning* is the relation of signs to their significates. For example, the semantic meaning of the term "keyboard" refers to the typewriter-like object with which the authors typed in this sentence. In information systems most of our concern is with semantics, with the determination of what words and symbols in our systems might signify.

Most linguists prefer to remove meaning from their field of study or to define it in such a way that it refers to a morpheme's relation with other morphemes in a structural model of language or perhaps as the "set of conditional probabilities of its occurrence in context with all other morphemes" (Joos, 1950). Meaning in the psychological or sociological context, pragmatic meaning, is more likely to be addressed by psychologists. Words, indeed all signs, are viewed as stimuli, and the question becomes the identification of the conditions under which such a stimulus becomes a sign for something, i.e., when it generates a thought or idea of that which it signifies. This process may be considered a mental one by those who believe in a mind–body dualism. The behaviorist might well believe that both the sign and the significant are stimuli which evoke the same response or perhaps that the sign produces, if not the response, a disposition toward making the response that the significant would have elicited. Osgood et al. (1957, p. 7) would claim that a sign stimulates a *mediation process* where the part of the response generated by the significant itself occurs along with other responses generated by previous associations of the sign with things other than the significant, and that such a process can be measured by the *semantic differential*.

The semantic differential is claimed to be a measurement of a behavior of users of signs which depends heavily on the meaning process and only slightly on other variables. The subject is given a concept to differentiate and a set of bipolar adjectival seven-step scales. A choice is made which indicates both intensity and direction within each adjective pair. Examples would be: loud.......soft or fair.......unfair. The use of such judgments allows the creation of a multidimensional semantic space in which each concept can be located. A factor analysis is utilized to produce factors upon which the signs can be rated. Using this technique we can measure the reaction of subjects to certain word combinations, to pictures, and to other stimuli. Whether this reaction is what is meant by meaning in regular discourse is not entirely clear.

Information has traditionally been stored in physical units of some sort. Examples are books, file folders, personnel data forms, financial accounts, telephone use statements, and so forth. When we have an information need we wish to be able to pass the information system an expression of that need and receive in return the proper unit or units that contain the needed information. If the units are sentences, paragraphs, or lists of data that can be restructured, we may be able to provide the exact information rather than a unit thought to contain it or a reference to such a unit.

8.2.2 Indexing

Choosing the right units involves characterizing units and information needs in a similar manner and then matching these characterizations. The

8.2 The Measurement of Language

choice of signs to represent what we shall loosely call documents is the process of *indexing*. The choice of signs and relations among them to represent questions is the processes of search strategy formulation or query or search formulation. The most common characterization of either a question or a document is a list of words. Thus the choice of words from a document to represent its meaning involves measuring the importance of each word in the document, not only in terms of how much it reflects just what the document is about, but also in terms of how well it will allow us to discriminate one document from another.

If we have a file of documents on measurement, the term *measurement* may very clearly represent what any document in the file is about. Unfortunately, since it applies to all documents, it does not allow us to discriminate among the documents in the file. How can words that discriminate and are representative of meaning be identified?

A common method of identifying the importance of a word in characterizing the meaning of the document is to count its occurrences. In such processes the word as an abstraction is called a *type,* and each occurrence of it in the document is called a *token*. We thus count the tokens of each type and rank the types in descending order. This clearly can be done within the context of a single document or across the whole file. The most useful words are those of high document frequency and low file frequency. They are both representative and discriminating. It would be possible to use a coefficient called the *inverse document frequency weight* to identify such types.

$W_{i,k}$ *Inverse document frequency weight;* a weighting of word frequencies to reflect the difference between high rate of occurrence in all (most) documents and high in only a limited set of them.

$$W_{i,k} = F_{i,k} (log_2(n) - log_2 D_k + 1 \quad (8.1)$$

where $F_{i,k}$ is the frequency of occurrence of a type k in document i, D_k is the number of documents in the file in which type k occurs at least once, and n is the number of documents in the file.

This coefficient will rank the types as needed and assign a high measure of importance to a relatively small number of words (Salton and McGill, 1983, p. 63). The discrimination value of a type can also be measured by using some similarity measure between document pairs. For such a measure we would count common occurrences of some characteristic of the documents (the common types in the document, for example) and normalize this value in some way. The average of these similarity measures would then represent the similarity of the file. By removing types and recomputing the average, we can use the difference in the average with the type and without it as a measure of the discriminating power of the type. This is effective but computationally intensive.

If we have already classified documents into satisfactory sets based upon their topicality, we can use a *discriminant coefficient* suggested by Williams (1963) to identify words whose use should allow us to distinguish among groupings. This set of terms can then be used to characterize the classes and add new documents to them. The coefficient, D_i, is defined as

D_i Discriminant coefficient; a measure of the discriminating power of words and frequencies to separate document sets by subject classes.

$$D_i = \sum_{j=1}^{J} ((p_{i,j} - \bar{p}_i)^2 / \bar{p}_i) \qquad (8.2)$$

D_i *is the coefficient for word* i, *which appears in* J *groups, where* j *is the group number,* $p_{i,j}$ *is the probability of word* i *occurring in group* j, *and* $\bar{p}_i$ *is the mean probability of word* i *across all groups.*

Using only the words with highest values of D_i to represent a group, new texts can be compared using their discriminant words and thus classes of text extended.

It is also possible to classify words using cluster analysis. We simply create a matrix of terms and documents, either weighted or binary, and then convert it to a term–term matrix where the cells reflect the number of documents that have the terms in common. On the assumption that terms that occur together often are related, we can then group the terms that exceed some value representing common occurrence into classes. Such classes could be used to expand the terms in search expressions, or to supplement the terms assigned to documents, or to create thesaurus-like controlled vocabularies.

The most frequent types are words that bear little content but are used for grammatical purposes. These are often prepositions, conjunctions, pronouns, and passive verbs, and these are normally discounted in the characterization of meaning, although pronouns might be considered as tokens of their antecedents and so counted. Terms of minimal content may be identified by the use of a *stop list*. Such a list contains all such words that are anticipated and eliminates them from consideration whenever they occur. It has also been suggested that only those words that occur in a document significantly more often than they occur in standard text should be considered. This eliminates not only the words with little content but also content-bearing words that do not exceed their normal usage.

One problem is that words with different endings but the same root—*library, libraries, librarian, librarians,* etc.—could give a bias to the word frequencies. One way around this is to *stem* or provide a count for all words with a common root, i.e., *libr* semantically or *librar*, which most computer programs could generate. There are several algorithms that can carry out the process (Lovins, 1968; Paice, 1990; Porter, 1980).

It is clearly possible to consider *phrases* made up of multiple words as the types. This will greatly increase the total number of types, since we must consider all the possible well-formed phrases which can be extracted from the text. Not every two- or three-word combination will constitute a well-formed phrase, but many will and thus will need to be searched for and counted. The token count will decrease, however, since the likelihood of a several-word combination is less than that of an individual word. If only a restricted set of words and phrases is permitted in the characterization of documents and questions, the restricted set is known as a controlled vocabulary, as opposed to *free text*. The words or phrases then become *index terms*. This many-to-one mapping is done either by humans or by software.

8.2.3 Word Association and Vocabulary Control

If words occur together in texts we can assume that they have some relationship to one another, some reason that they co-occur. The more often they co-occur the more strongly they may be considered associated. Measures of co-occurrence were described in Section 7.2.3. If we have a file of documents and form a document–term matrix where each row represents a document and each column a term which occurs in at least one of those documents, then by examining any two columns, or term vectors, we can determine in how many documents both terms occur. This value can then be used to determine a measure of similarity between the two term vectors using the measures discussed earlier. These measures may then be used to cluster the terms. The rationale for term clustering is to increase the number of items retrieved by using the whole class of terms associated with a search term rather than the term alone. The process, like stemming, is the beginning of an attempt to control vocabulary for retrieval purposes and is discussed in detail in Salton and McGill (1983, pp. 52–110).

The creation of index terms and a term association process may lead to the creation of a *controlled vocabulary,* a subset of natural language that can be used to represent documents just as can the words or phrases extracted from documents. Such languages are created, usually manually, and their terms are then assigned to documents, also usually manually. The idea is to make it possible for the searcher using the index to find material without having to think of all the possible terms or phrases by which it might naturally be described in text. Problems that arise from synonyms, homographs, word order, and context are thus considerably lessened if not eliminated.

Although a controlled vocabulary can save search time, the saving may be balanced by the effort invested in construction and maintenance of the vocabulary and by the cost of assigning the terms to the documents. It is, of course, necessary to make use of the vocabulary at the time of the search so that only controlled terms are used. This imposes an added step of translation from natural language to the search process.

Controlled vocabularies have often been tested against *free text indexing systems* in terms of their success in retrieving relevant and rejecting irrelevant documents. They have not been shown to provide any great advantage (Spark Jones and Kay, 1973, p. 29). Free text indexing systems, where terms are selected either by human review and association or, more often, by algorithmic extraction from the text itself, make no use of authority lists of index terms. The purpose of the controlled vocabulary is really not to provide better discrimination than single words or extracted words, but rather to reduce the effort required at the time of search. It may well be that metrics commonly used to evaluate such languages, those which measure the power of the system to find relevant and reject nonrelevant documents, are therefore inappropriate.

8.2.3.1 Occurrence of Attribute Values

Relationships between attribute values may be defined semantically as in "*Physics* is a branch of *science*," or statistically as in "When the word *nuclear* occurs, the word *physics* will be found in the same record 20% of the time." Here, we deal with statistical relationships.

The following expressions are concerned with the information represented within a record. Unfortunately, a wide range of terminology is used to describe the same concepts. Following linguistic terminology, a value *type* is a value symbol; a value *token* is an occurrence of a type. In the preceding sentence, the type 'a' occurs four times. The 'a' is a single type, distinct from other types such as 'of' or 'an.' There are four 'a' tokens. In our usage, we define:

$t_{i,j}$ *Term value;* the ith possible value of attribute j within the database, or a representation of term type i. Assume all author names in a database are extracted and duplicates removed. Then $t_{i,j}$ is the ith name in this list.

$t_{i,j,k}$ *Term value;* this usage, involving three subscripts, denotes an occurrence of the ith value of attribute j in a specific record, k. This notation differs from $t_{i,j}$ only in that it includes an index for record number.

$f_{i,j,k}$ *Term frequency;* the frequency of occurrence of term type i of attribute j in record k. Whereas an attribute such as *publication date* will occur only once in a record, an attribute such as *named person* may occur many times in the text of a news article.

Sometimes there may be more than one value of the attribute in a single record, as in the case of multiple authors of a book. This might necessitate a subscript on the subscript, a typographic complication we will try to avoid. Some authors use $t_{i,k}$ to designate the *frequency of occurrence* of term type i in record k (omitting explicit denotation of an attribute). This assumes there is only one attribute of interest, at least when working with frequencies, a common situation if the attribute consists of a text. But most techniques applicable to text attributes can also be used with nontext. In the general case it is necessary to specify attribute as well as value, unless the attribute intended is clearly understood.

8.2.3.2 Co-occurrence of Values

Consider the number of times two different term types co-occur; i.e. the types are both found within a single attribute or in two or more different attributes within a single record. How often, for example, does the author name (term type) BOYCE, BERT R. co-occur with KRAFT, DONALD H. or the type MEASURE with OCCURRENCE? There are several aspects of *co-occurrence* which, unfortunately, we cannot combine into a single measure. Within a single record, we can measure the strength of the co-occurrence relationship of two terms by noting their respective frequencies. This is a measure of *depth* or intensity of co-occurrence. The average frequency of co-occurrence over a range of records may also indicate depth. The number or percent of records over a range in which the two co-occur at least once measures the *breadth* of co-occurrence. If two author names almost always occur together whenever either one of them occurs, this indicates a great breadth of co-occurrence. If the probability of their co-occurring in the database is low, then the breadth is minimal. In brief, the team does not publish often, but its members do tend to work together when they work. We define the following measures, where the symbol o indicates the co-occurrence of two types:

Two measures of the statistical relationship between terms are:

$f(t_1 O t_2)$ *Frequency of co-occurrence;* the number of records in which terms or values t_1 and t_2 both occur.

$termco1(t_1,t_2)$ *Term co-occurrence1;* the frequency of co-occurrence of the terms, divided by m, the number of records in the database (its *magnitude*).

$$termco_1(t_1,t_2) = f(t_1 O t_2)/m \qquad (8.3)$$

The range of $termco_1$ is $[0,1]$.

$termco2(t_1,t_2)$ *Term co-occurrence2;* this form takes into account the relative frequencies of occurrence of the t's within a single record. More weight is given to a pair of terms that occur frequently together, multiple times in each of n records, than occur once only in each of the n records.

$$termco2(t_1,t_2) = \frac{\Sigma f(t_{1,i} \oplus t_{2,i})}{\Sigma f(t_{1,i} \cdot t_{2,i})} \qquad (8.4)$$

where ⊕ is the operation of counting the total frequency of occurrence of t_1 and t_2 in record i, the denominator is the total number of occurrence of the terms, and summation is over all records. Again, the range is [0,1].

8.2.4 Characteristics of Text

The process of ranking types for naturally occurring text by frequency of token occurrences yields a consistent distribution. Estoup (1916), Condon (1928), and Whitehorn and Zipf (1943) each independently recognized a distinct regularity in English or French natural language texts, in that they have the following characteristic. This was also pointed out by Zipf in a study of the index to *Ulysses* by James Joyce (Zipf, 1949, pp. 19–55). If the words of a text are ranked in descending order by frequency, then the relationship between the frequency (f) and rank (r) is roughly an equilateral hyperbola:

$$f \cdot r = \text{constant}$$

or

$$f = k \cdot r^{-1} \tag{8.5}$$

Note that $r = 1$ indicates the most frequent token. This form of the relationship has come to be known as Zipf's Law, even though it was first proposed by Condon. From observed data, k is only roughly a constant. In the *Ulysses* text, k varies from 20,000 to nearly 30,000.

If we take the logarithm of both sides of Eq. (8.5), the result is linear. That is, plotting the logarithms of f and r in any corpus of naturally occurring English text will yield an approximate straight line descending from left to right at about a 45-degree angle, i.e., the graph will have a slope of approximately -1. Moreover, since the constant k approximates the total number of unique types, 29,899 in *Ulysses*, it becomes a measure of the richness of the vocabulary of the author of the text in question. Note that, when the slope is -1, k gives both the number of word types and the frequency of the most frequent word.

However, Whitehorn and Zipf (1943), and later Zipf (1949, pp. 56–133) and Mandelbrot (1953), all noticed distinct deviations from the log–log straight line when the text under analysis is either in a language much more inflected than English or French or was not edited, standard English. For example, Whitehorn and Zipf noticed a distinct nonlinear segment of the frequency–rank plot of text taken from schizophrenic patients or from children.

Mandelbrot (1953) proposed a refinement to Zipf's law:

$$f = k \cdot (r + m)^b \tag{8.6}$$

8.2 The Measurement of Language

which actually fits much of the observed data better than does the original Eq. (8.5). The parameter *m* is a measure of the nonlinearity of the distribution, actually of the extent of deviation of the first point (rank = 1) from the value it would have if the distribution were linear. The exponent *b* takes values close to -1.0, but it is not a constant as originally proposed. The two parameters, *m* and *b*, are now characteristics of a frequency distribution of a text, analogous to the mean and standard deviation as characteristics of a normal distribution. There has been some preliminary work to show how these parameters can be used to characterize a language, but it is not definitive (Meadow et al., 1993).

Considering again the plot of *f* versus *r*, it will be apparent that as we reach the lower right side of the line, where the rank is high and the frequency low, we will encounter multiple types with an equal frequency of tokens. A great many words will occur only once, twice, or three times. Thus the low-frequency words, while approximating a straight line for the whole distribution, will be more accurately described by some step function. Booth (1967) describes this distribution as:

wordfreq Word frequency ratio; the ratio of the number of occurrences of any word to the number occurring once.

$$I_n/I_1 = 2/n(n + 1) \quad (8.7)$$

where I_n indicates the number of words occurring *n* times.

Yule (1944) suggests other measures of complete texts. These are used, along with Zipf's constant, to compare texts, or sets of texts, with one another.

typetoken Type-token ratio; the ratio of the number of word types appearing in a text (the number of different words used) to the number of tokens, the number of word occurrences, including repetitions.
$\bar{f}$ Mean frequency; the average frequency of occurrence of a word type in a text.

$$\bar{f} = 1/typetoken$$

K Yule's characteristic; a measure devised by Yule (1943, p. 47), somewhat similar to $\bar{f}$ but bringing the dispersion of word frequencies more into play.

$$K = 10{,}000\frac{\sigma^2 - \bar{f}}{\bar{f}} \quad (8.8)$$

where σ^2 is the standard deviation of the frequency distribution and the constant 10,000 is used to avoid small numbers. (Today, we might omit the constant and define the units as *milliyules*.)

Yule's *K* has the advantage of reflecting type-token distribution while being independent of the size of sample of text used. Since Yule was working in a precomputer era, his work was based upon samples rather than complete counts of large texts as would normally be done today.

8.3 Summary

In this chapter we have seen that regularities can be discovered in language and that these regularities can be quantified and used in the measurement of various aspects of language. Since language is the basic form of human communication over distance and time, its measurement brings some degree of objectivity into the study of information and its exchange among people. In a search for further objectivity we will now seek measurable regularities in the use of documents, the items in which language is stored and transmitted.

References

Bolinger, Dwight. (1968). *Aspects of Language*. New York: Harcourt, Brace & World, Inc.

Bookstein, Abraham, Edward O'Neil, Martin Dillon, and David Stephens. (1992). Applications of loglinear models to informetric phenomena. *Information Processing and Management*, 28(1), 75.

Booth, Andrew D. (1967). A 'law' for occurrences of words of low frequency. *Information and Control*, 10(4), 386–393.

Brookes, B. C. (1991). Biblio-, sciento-, info-metrics??? What are we talking about? In L. Egghe and R. Rousseau, eds., *Informetrics 89/90*. Amsterdam: Elsevier, 31–44.

Condon, E. U. (1928). Statistics of Vocabulary. *Science*, LXVIII (1733), 300.

Estoup, J. B. (1916). *Gammes Stenographiques*. 4th edition. Paris: Publisher not identified.

Joos, M. (1950). Description of language design. *Journal of the Acoustic Society of America*, 22(2–3), 701–708.

Lovins, J. B. (1968). Development of a stemming algorithm. *Mechanical Translation and Computational Linguistics*, 11(1), 22–30.

Mandelbrot, B. (1953). An informational theory of the statistical structure of language. In W. Jackson, ed. *Communication Theory*. London: Butterworths Scientific Publications, 486–502.

Meadow, C. T., J. Wang, and M. Stamboulie. (1993). An analysis of Zipf–Mandlebrot language measures and their application to artificial languages. *Journal of Information Science*, 19(4), 247–258.

Morris, C. W. (1946). *Signs, Language, and Behavior*. New York: Prentice Hall.

Osgood, C. E., G. J. Suci, and P. H. Tannebaum. (1957). *The Measurement of Meaning*. Urbana: The University of Illinois Press.

Paice, C. D. (1990). "Another Stemmer," *SIGIR Forum*, 24(3), 56–61.

Porter, M. F. (1980). An algorithm for suffix stripping. *Program*, 14, 130–137.

Pritchard, A. (1969). Statistical bibliography or bibliometrics? *Journal of Documentation*, 25, 348–349.

References

Salton, G. and M. J. McGill. (1983). *Introduction to Modern Information Retrieval*. New York: McGraw-Hill.

Shannon, Claude E. and Warren Weaver. (1949). *The Mathematical Theory of Communication*. Urbana: The University of Illinois Press.

Spark Jones, K. and M. Kay. (1973). *Linguistics and Information Science*. New York: Academic Press.

Whitehorn, J. C. and G. K. Zipf. (1943). Schizophrenic language, *Archives of Neurological Psychiatry*, 49, 831–851.

Williams, J. H. (1963). A discriminant method for automatically classifying documents. *Proceedings of the Fall Joint Computer Conference, 1963*. Montvale, NJ: AFIPS Press, 161–168.

Yule, G. U. (1944). *The Statistical Study of Literary Vocabulary*. Cambridge: Cambridge University Press.

Zipf, George Kingsley. (1949). *Human Behavior and the Principle of Least Effort*. Cambridge: Addison-Wesley Press.

9

Measures of Bibliographic Phenomena

9.1
Bibliometrics

What is treated in the bibliometric arena is the production and dissemination of knowledge studied operationally as the production and dissemination of the units of the media in which that knowledge is recorded for storage and distribution. Such processes are normally considered in terms of sources and items, or classes and observations, or in the linguistic terms we used above, types and tokens. Thus we might speak of words and their occurrences, papers and their citations, books and the number of times they are loaned by a library, journals and the number of times they are to be found in a subject bibliography, authors and the number of papers they publish, and other such pairings. It is possible to view such processes either *diachronically*, i.e., as a time-dependent process, or *synchronically*, at a single point of time.

Although Broadus (1987) mentions some early instances of the counting of these items, Cole and Earles (1917), Hulme (1923), and later Gross and Gross (1927) are the predecessors of Zipf (see Section 8.2.4), Lotka (see 9.6.2), and Bradford (see 9.6.1), who are the key figures in the twentieth-century development of bibliometrics. Budd (1992a, pp. 345–378) provides an excellent review of "bibliometrics as a means of investigating formal communication mechanisms and patterns," with an excellent selective review of the work in the field.

9.2
Citations

Documents can be classed together using cluster analysis techniques based upon the number of high document frequency and low file frequency words they contain in common. Other attributes, such as the references at

9.2 Citations

the end of a document, or the other documents that cite a given document, may be used in the same way as a quantitative indication of subject relatedness. By counting common references or citations or by counting common content-bearing words, we may indirectly measure from objective attributes the intersubjective relationship of common subject content. Such measurement depends upon the assumption that the content of a document is indicated by a subset of its words and by its references and citations.

> Since the terms *reference* and *citation* tend to be used interchangeably, the following example will be used to clarify their differences. Paper A contains a reference to paper P. By necessity, paper P is published prior to paper A. Paper P is cited by paper A. A contains a reference P; P has a citation from A. The number of references a paper has is measured by the number of items in its bibliographic list. The number of citations a paper has up to year t, is found by looking up the paper in a citation index from its year of publication to year t. One checks to see in how many papers it may have been cited. (Pao, 1989, p. 20)

Kessler (1963) suggests the use of common references in the bibliographies of document pairs as a measure of similarity, and common citations are put forth by Small and Griffith (1974). Citations to documents have the advantage of growing over time to reflect changing use. References are, of course, static. Such studies are dependent upon the existence of a database of broad scope in the learned literature which has a record made up of a bibliographic description of a document supplemented by bibliographic descriptions of its references. Such records can be *inverted* to produce a file of records organized by, and based on, the union of the descriptions of references. Each such record is then supplemented by descriptions of the documents that cited them.

We can use measures of similarity derived from such databases to produce maps of disciplines, or to cluster documents for the purposes of retrieval. Since the counting of citations to the work of people, journals, and institutions that sponsor research is inherent in such analysis, it becomes possible to use such counts as a measure of the relative utility of the output of these bodies. Journals, for instance, can be compared on the basis of the number of times they have been cited during a fixed period of time. In order to discount the effect of the different numbers of papers published in different journals, use of an *impact factor,* computed by dividing the number of citations to the journal by the number of papers published by the same journal in the period, is common (Garfield, 1979).

Papers, and thus journals, are cited for many reasons. Reliance on the utility of their content in the production of the citing work is but one of these. Some cited works will have been of much greater utility than others cited in the same work. We must also consider that the impact factor of a journal is greatly affected by a small number of papers. Thus the impact factor of a journal is not representative of the impact of its average paper.

In speaking of the representativeness of a journal's impact factor on its constituent articles, Seglen (1992, p. 631) states, "The skewness of the journal article distribution shows that this premise does not hold true: only a minor fraction of the articles are anywhere near the journal mean." Despite such criticisms, citation counting would seem to provide one tool for the measurement of learned productivity. Several studies (Virgo, 1977) have found strong correlations between citation counts and other methods of evaluating science.

Citation indexes, of course, were not developed to create a new means of computing document similarity. Their original and most significant use is in the search for unknown documents on a topic when at least one topical document is known. It has always been possible to move backward in time from a known topical document by checking its references for its topical ancestors. With a citation index it is possible to move forward in time to a paper's descendants, those papers which cite it. The searching of citation indexes, and their creation, *citation indexing,* is an important technique for the control and usage of the learned literature.

9.3
Growth

As sources produce items over time, clearly growth in the number of items takes place. If sources reach their individual capacity it is possible that the number of sources will grow as well. This is particularly so in the learned literature. Budd (1992b, p. 50) provides the percentage in growth of the number of papers indexed by several indexing services from 1978 to 1988. For *Biological Abstracts* the growth is 75.9%, for *Computer and Control Abstracts* 106.6%, for *Mathematical Reviews* 188.1%, while for *Chemical Abstracts* it is only 7.7%. However, it should be noted that the chemistry literature consisted of over 225,000 papers in 1978, while *Biological Abstracts* indexed less than 75,000 in the same year and the other two less than half that number. In 1988 alone the 100 Association of College and Research Libraries university libraries added over 2.3 million volumes to their collections (Molyneux, 1989, p. 25).

The typical growth curve is plotted with cumulative items on the y axis and time on the x axis.

> *growth* Growth of a population; population size at a given time t, the product of the initial size times e (Euler's number, the number whose natural logarithm is 1) to the power of mt.

$$G(t) = G(t^0)e^{mt} \tag{9.1}$$

where t^0 indicates time zero and $G(t^0)$ the initial size of a population.

9.3 Growth

In this case *m* is a constant often known as the *Malthusian parameter* and the curve produced is one of exponential growth rising to the right. This means that the current literature alone in any topic will be large enough to be difficult to assimilate fully for most scholars. Simply stated, "Because of the exponential growth of the scientific literature, the bulk of it is the most recent" (Goffman and Warren, 1980, p. 6).

This distribution is explained by a success-breeds-success principle. The thought is that the more items a source has produced, the more likely it is to produce more still. This situation has often been characterized as the *Matthew effect*.

> For whosoever hath, to him shall be given, and he shall have more abundance, but whosoever hath not, from him shall be taken away even that he hath.
> —Matthew 13:12.

Simon (1955) first portrayed this class of distribution and it was later elaborated by Price (1976) under the name *Cumulative Advantage Distribution*.

In fact, growth does not empirically increase exponentially without limits. At some point the curve becomes *logistic;* that is, it shifts from concave to convex, or if you will, its *j* shape shifts to the characteristic *s* shape of a logistic curve. Stated another way, when enough time and growth have taken place, the curve turns parallel to the *x* (time) axis and growth stops, as shown in Figure 9.1.

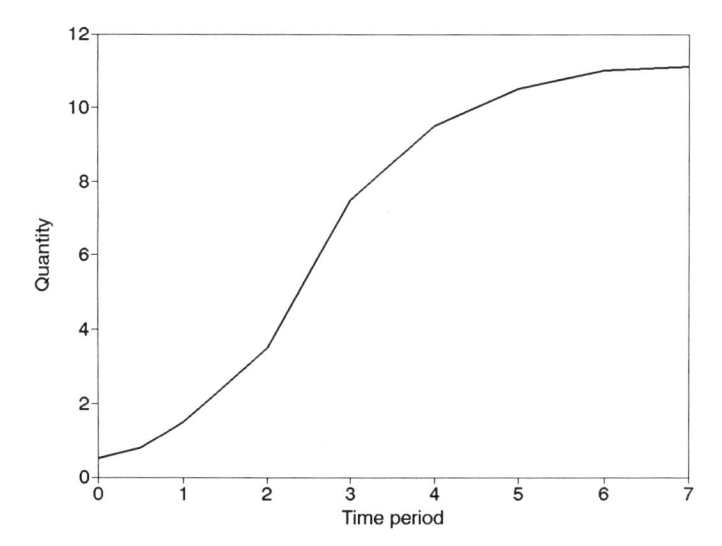

Figure 9.1
An example of a logistics curve. Growth typically starts slowly, accelerates rapidly, but does not continue to increase forever. The curve must eventually turn toward the horizontal (no growth).

If a journal has published a great number of papers on a specific problem, it is most likely that authors with something to say on that problem will send their papers to that journal, since they are well aware that the topic is published in that source and they can only be rejected for lack of quality, not the inappropriateness of the subject. Journal editors become overwhelmed with the papers on the topic in question and begin to wonder if they should not set some restrictions on the number of papers on the topic which will appear in their journal. They may set arbitrary limits, send such papers to more difficult referees, or actually suggest to referees that for this topic standards must be higher to avoid domination. The resulting higher rejection rate of such papers leads to submission to other sources and the resultant scatter. Eventually the market for new sources and the number of authors working on a problem stabilize and growth stops.

Growth of a literature is measured by counts of sources and items over time. Growth in the underlying discipline can be inferred from these counts or by looking at the number of active researchers in the discipline in successive time periods, or the rates of change in the size of this group. This technique is particularly useful in studying the historical development of a discipline.

9.4
Obsolescence

By *obsolescence* we mean the decline in utility of an information source with its increasing age. Line and Sandison (1974, p. 283) use the phrase "decline over time in validity or utility of information." This is normally measured by means of comparative circulation statistics on the local level where the source is available for loan, or by the counts of citations in order to get a more global viewpoint. Most such studies have been synchronic in nature, using a fixed period of time to count in-house uses, circulations, or citations of journals. Unfortunately, circulation studies do not recognize in-house use, which is particularly difficult to measure in most information agencies that allow free access to their materials. If we are concerned with practical library decision making, it is the local usage that would seem important.

The most mentioned measure of obsolescence is

halflife Half-life; the period of time in which half the total use for a set of items will have taken place.

If we say that the half-life of scientific journals is ten years, we are normally referring to one of two methods of obsolescence measurement. We may mean that half of all the circulations of bound volumes of such journals will be of volumes printed in the last ten years. We might also mean that half of all citations to scientific journals will be to journal volumes published in the last ten years. If we have such a measure, in some unit of time, we could make statements about one discipline using material of more recent origin than some other discipline.

Half-life is also sometimes used as a measure of the immediacy of the literature of a discipline. If we have a complete bibliography of a subject and arrange it by year of publication and accumulate the number of papers as we go backward in time, we will reach a point where the accumulation contains one half of the bibliography. The number of years we have moved backward is then the half-life of the discipline, the time it takes to produce half its literature.

The hypothesis of obsolescence is that a decline in use takes place with increasing age. There is certainly some evidence to support that position. However, it can be argued that the current literature is more utilized because there is more of it than of older literature. If the number of contributors grows commensurately with the growth of the literature, however, then this should counteract the larger size of the current literature. It seems prudent to consider growth and obsolescence together, as suggested by Line and Sandison (1974).

9.5
Scattering

As time passes and the size of an interest area grows, insufficient resources are available in the original sources to accommodate the growth. In the journal/paper example, authors being refused by the original journals try other sources, and work that has connections with other problem areas draws papers toward those sources. The sources may split, or new ones come into being as dictated by demand and the growth of interest in the subject. Thus as the number of items grows it also scatters over a wide number of sources. As an example let us consider the scatter in the schistosomiasis literature:

> The extent of the dispersion of papers (9,914) among journals (1738) was a bit surprising . . . . Although the schistosomiasis literature is apparently highly dispersed, it must be considered that 908 journals or 52 percent of the total number contained only one paper on the subject. On the other hand, about 19 journals contained almost one-third of the literature, and less than 50 journals had almost one-half the literature. Under these circumstances it would be relatively easy to obtain 50 percent of the literature. If the percentage of total articles is plotted against the percentage of total journals from which they have been obtained, it becomes obvious that almost 70 percent of the articles are found in about 10 percent of the journals; in other words, as the percent of articles is

increased, there is an exponential increase in the number of journals among which they are dispersed. (Goffman and Warren, 1980, p. 61)

We see that while there is considerable scattering there is also considerable concentration. In fact, this data is an example of the *80/20 rule,* which states that if the sources are arranged in decreasing order of productivity, the top 20% of the sources will provide 80% of the items (Trueswell, 1975). The rule was originally formulated in terms of library circulations of books but has been shown to have far broader application.

Knuth (1973) suggests that the distribution known as the Zipf distribution and the 80/20 rule could be used to order a file of computer records to minimize the expected search time for one given record. He notes that a linear file of n records, ordered by the frequency of times records are sought, and with the Zipf distribution in effect, would be about $0.5 \ln n$ times as fast as searching a random file.

To optimally generate a binary tree file structure, putting the most frequent records into the tree first so that they will be at or near the top for easy access, seems a sensible procedure. Knuth submits that since the frequencies of record use are not often known before the fact, a self-organizing file might be employed. When a record is sought and found, it is placed at the beginning of the file. Over time, the most frequently sought records will be near the beginning of the file, and the least frequently sought records will be at the end of the file. We will discuss measures of optimal file structures later in this book.

This idea of the efficiency of a push-down store file structure had been suggested by Booth (1969) several years earlier for library shelves, particularly if they are to be automated for physical retrieval. He demonstrates the efficiency of the spiral stack arrangement wherein all new additions and returns are placed at the head of the stack. In this manner, books frequently used will congregate in one, easily accessible portion of the stacks. This procedure can also lead to an automatic weeding policy.

9.6
Laws of Source Yield

If we search for instances of the 80/20 rule in the production of information-bearing items, we will certainly find them. If we reconsider the Zipf distribution of words, we will see that only a few word types provide a large percentage of the total token count. If we look once again at the journal as source and the paper as item in the schistosomiasis literature, we see an indication that journals and papers may distribute much like words in text. In fact, such regularly recurring concentrations of yield of sources ranked by their productivity have become known as the bibliometric laws. Indeed, the Zipf distribution is commonly referred to as Zipf's law. The phenomenon of concentration of papers in source journals is known as *Bradford's law*.

9.6.1 Bradford's Law

The regularity is named for S. C. Bradford, who first reported it in 1934. Beginning with a topical bibliography, we order the sources, in this case the journals, by their decreasing yield of items, in this case their number of papers on the topic under consideration.

> . . . we can then group the journals into zones by going down the ranked list. Each zone is equally productive, having the same number of relevant articles. Bradford, having followed this procedure, found that each successive zone needed an increasing number of journals, and that he could represent this phenomenon as a geometric series. Thus we have as one statement of Bradford's Law, the following:
>
> $$N_k = \text{the number of journals in zone k} = N_{k-1}b = N_1 b^{k-1}, \qquad (9.2)$$
>
> where $b > 1$ is a parameter known as the scattering factor or Bradford multiplier, remains approximately constant for each distribution. (Kraft and Boyce, 1991, p. 115)

Bradford originally suggested three zones in his formulation without specifying any reason for doing so. Clearly more zones might be possible. The number of papers in each zone must be greater than one half of the single-paper journals (to be found at the bottom of the distribution), since otherwise the last zone would contain fewer journals than the preceding zone and thus $b < 1$, violating the assumptions of the law. We can specify the zones in a variety of ways, but we must maintain a structure such that for every zone k, $N_k > 0.5SP$, where SP is the number of journals contributing but one paper (Leimkuhler, 1967; Brookes, 1968).

Wilkinson notes the differences in two formulations of Bradford's distribution, one developed by Leimkuhler (1967) and the other by Brookes (1968). Wilkinson (1972) demonstrates that mathematical interpretations can vary based on Bradford's verbal formulation versus his graphical representations.

Thus conformity to the law may be measured by grouping the sources into the maximum number of zones and testing the status as a constant of both the multiplier and the number of papers in each zone. We might also measure conformity by plotting $R(n)$, the cumulative number of papers produced by n journals, on the y axis against log n on the x axis. This plot of the number of journals against the cumulative sum of their yield on semilog paper, for a bibliography conforming to the law, will produce what is sometimes known as the *Bradford bibliograph,* which is characterized by a short relatively concave curve, a linear rise, and finally a droop. This is the s-shaped logistic curve already mentioned in relation to our discussion of growth (Section 9.2).

The droop in the journals of low productivity is called the *Groos' droop,* shown in Figure 9.2. It has been suggested as a measure of the incompleteness of the bibliography under examination (Groos, 1967; Brookes, 1968). However, O'Neill (1970) has presented some considerable evidence that this is not the case.

9.6.2 Lotka's Law

Lotka's law describes the regularity inherent in the productivity of authors in terms of the papers they produce in a learned discipline. In other words, our source is now considered to be the author, rather than the journal, but the item remains the number of papers produced on the topic under consideration. The law states that:

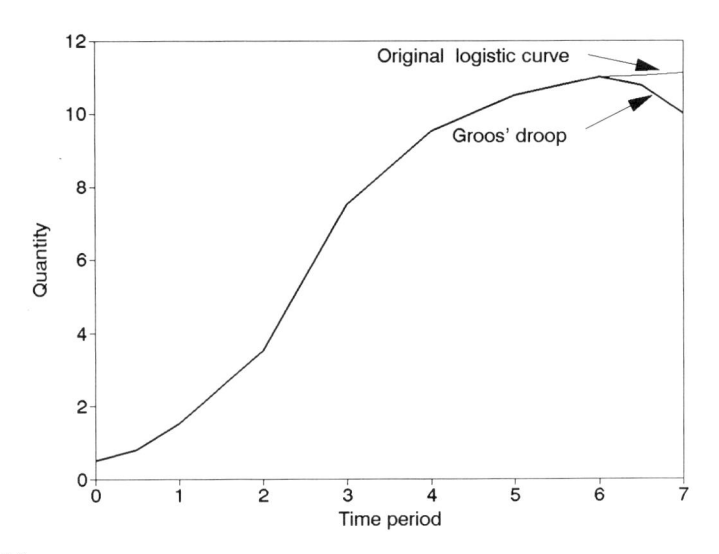

$$x^n \cdot y = K \tag{9.3}$$

Figure 9.2
Groos' droop. This is a logistics curve, applied to the publication of articles in journals. The y axis is the cumulative number of articles on a given subject; the x axis is the log of the number of journals considered. The number of journals may be large but is finite, hence the number of articles produced cannot increase without limit. The deviation of the actual curve from a projection of the linear central portion is called Groos' droop.

where x is the number of papers, y is the number of authors producing x papers, and n and K are constants. Since Lotka originally estimated n as 2, the law has also been called the inverse square law. In fact, $n = 2$ is a specific case and the constants must be determined from the data tested. A detailed procedure for carrying out the test may be found in Pao (1985).

There are, in fact, nearly a dozen such distributions relating sources to items. Egghe and Rousseau (1990, pp. 291–384) demonstrate that they all may be considered special cases of Lotka's law.

9.7
Information Theory

Information theory is a term used for the work of Claude Shannon and for those who have attempted to develop and generalize his work. Information for Shannon was a function of the number of possible messages available to the source of a communication system for transmission.

> The significant aspect is that the actual message is one selected from a set of possible messages. The system must be designed to operate for each possible selection, not just the one which will actually be chosen since this is unknown at the time of design.
>
> If the number of messages in the set is finite then this number or any monotonic function of this number can be regarded as a measure of the information produced when one message is chosen from the set, all choices being equally likely. (Shannon and Weaver, 1949, pp. 31–32)

This requires some additional explanation, since Shannon's definition of information does not include many of the common connotations of that word. Shannon's model of an information system includes a source, whose function is to choose from an available set of messages one message for transmission; a transmitter, whose function is to represent the message in a manner which will permit it to be transmitted over the third component; a channel, a medium which permits movement of an encoded message from one point to another; and a receiver, which reconstructs the message into a form understandable by the final component, the destination. The destination is that component which is transformed to some degree by contact with the message.

This is a one-way communication model, presumably for the purpose of generality. There are both one-way and two-way communication systems, but by considering each destination to be a source with its own file of potential messages, and each source a potential destination, the model can be applied in the other direction to include two-way communication.

Let us assume that our definition of information is the extent of removal of uncertainty. From the point of view of the destination, if we assume that the source has only two messages from which to choose, then we are far less uncertain about what is being transmitted than if there were 256 possible messages. It is from this perspective that the information in a message is a function of the number of messages available to the source for choice. If we have two equally probable messages the probability of each is 0.5. If there are four such messages the probability of any particular one would be 0.25, if eight messages 0.125, and so forth.

The simplest representation device for a message is a binary one. Assume we have an electric light as a transmitter. If the light is off, we will assume the first of two messages is being transmitted. If it is on, we will assume the second is being transmitted. One binary device will thus encode two messages. We might express this by saying that the number of states of the base device to the power of the required number of devices is equal to the number of messages. If the number of states of the base device and the number of messages is 2, the required number of devices is 1. The number of two-state devices needed to represent n messages is the power of 2 that will yield that number of messages. Stated algebraically, the number of binary devices required for n messages is $\log_2 n$.

It now becomes possible to use *bits,* the required number of binary state devices, as an indirect measure of the number of messages. To say that two bits are required to code four messages follows from $\log_2 4 = 2$. If n messages are of equal probability then $1/n$ is the probability of each, and the number of bits to measure the likelihood or probability of such a message,

$$I = -\log_2(1/n) = \log_2 n. \tag{9.4}$$

where I is the number of bits of information in a message. The uncertainty at the destination increases with the number of messages. The receipt of any one eliminates more uncertainty than if there were fewer messages. Uncertainty eliminated is information. The less probable the message, the more uncertainty is dispelled. Generally, we may say that the information I in the message m is equal to the negative log of the probability of the message, p_m:

$$I_{(m)} = -\log_2 p_m \tag{9.5}$$

If we are concerned with the average information in a system of messages we may use a formulation similar to that of Boltzmann, who was modeling the dispersion of molecules in a vacuum (Shannon and Weaver, 1949, p. 51). His measure is known as *entropy* and is a based upon the number of possible states of molecules in a space and their tendency to become less predictable as the number increases. Entropy is a measure of uncertainty; Shannon's formulation is a negation of thermodynamic entropy and thus rises with the amount of information toward $\log n$ when all the system probabilities are equal. Nonetheless, the term entropy without any concern for the inversion of the traditional meaning is commonly used for Shannon's formulation. For a system with n messages where p_i = the probability of message i, the information content is:

H *Information;* the number of bits of information in a system of n messages of probability p_i each.

$$H = - \sum p_i \cdot \log p_i, \qquad 1 < = i < = n \qquad (9.6)$$

H is a measure of the information (in Shannon's sense) in a *system* of messages.

Brillouin (1956) suggests a similar, but somewhat more general measure that avoids the use of probabilities and is based upon the assumption that the possession of information reduces the number of possible answers to a question and thus is a function of the ratio of the number of answers before and after the receipt of a message. Thus if B represents the sensible choices before receipt and A represents the number of sensible choices after receipt, we may define information from message m as

$$I_m = K \cdot \log_e(B/A) \qquad (9.7)$$

There are several other approaches to the measurement of information. Some, like Shannon's, are based upon probabilities that are dependent on the source alone. Others, like Brillouin's, attempt to measure some change in the destination as a result of the receipt of the message. Bar-Hillel and Carnap (1953) have come to an analogous measure of the content of a statement based upon the number of other possible statements excluded by the assertion of the measured statement in a well-bounded universe of discourse. An excellent review of the various proposed measures of information is available in the first chapter of Losee (1990). None have attained the wide popularity of Shannon's measure.

9.8
Application to Information Systems

While the investigation of bibliographic patterns has a certain theoretical interest, the results can provide insight for practical decisions. Measures of bibliographic phenomena can be used in such applications as evaluating university faculty members or entire faculties, deciding what journals a library should buy, or identifying the frontier areas of research in a given field.

The use of word frequency distributions leads to the selection of content-repesentative terms from documents in an objective manner. The commonality of these terms, or of citations and references in pairs of documents, permits the calculation of measures of closeness among documents in a file. Such measures can be used to create a file structure where content-related documents are grouped together.

9.8.1 Journal Selection

If we are interested in deciding which journals to purchase in order to maximize our coverage of a particular subject discipline, the use of Bradford type analysis can provide insight. By finding a fairly comprehensive bibliography of the topic in question, perhaps by electronically searching several databases and eliminating duplicate records, we can easily rank journal titles by their number of contributions to the list. The obvious strategy, for maximization of coverage of the topic for a fixed cost, is to buy down the ranked list as far as resources allow. This analysis, using an average journal price for the list, also permits estimates of what any particular level of coverage would cost.

This is, of course, a strictly quantitative procedure. We get the most papers on a topic for the least money. It is not quite so clear that the highest-impact journals are those that provide the most papers (Boyce and Funk, 1978; Boyce and Pollens, 1982). Naturally, enough journals can be ranked by their impact as well. It may be wise to check impact factors on candidate journals suggested by a Bradford procedure and then factor impact into any selection process.

Kraft (1979) discusses measures of journal worth for selection of journal titles in a library collection. He divides worth into three factors which can then be combined into a weighted measure of the worth of any given journal. The first factor is *usage,* which can be measured by citation count, interlibrary loan request count, photocopy request count, estimates of use from other libraries, and estimates of future use if the journal title is new.

The second factor is *relevance,* which measures subjective intrinsic values (see Chapter 13). A very broad meaning of relevance is used here, encompassing both content and utility. Such considerations as quality of paper and ink, length of run of the title in the library in question, technical expert opinions of the quality of the content of the articles, where the journal is indexed, who else owns the title in question, the original requester, the library population, and the reputation of the editors and editorial board might all enter into the evaluation.

The third factor is *availability elsewhere.* This measures how easily patrons could gain access to the title if the library decides not to acquire it. This factor is often a major consideration in the deselection process, a mirror image of the selection decision.

Although such decisions are often made without the benefit of the decision models Kraft provides, the factors discussed often play a decisive, if unquantified, role in journal selection.

9.8.2 Personnel Evaluation

Counts of citations can be used as a measure of the impact of a paper or of its author. Thus we may count not only the authorships of a person of interest over databases in which that person's papers are presumed to be collected but also citations to those papers, giving both direct and indirect measures of the impact of these papers and their author. Such evaluative measures can be improved by adding factors for rate of citation of journals or self-citation by authors. Presumably, a journal that is more often cited in a field carries more prestige as a vehicle for a candidate's publications than one not often cited. Self-citation being an easy way for an author to raise his or her citation rate, this practice can be countered by not including self-citations in an evaluation score. There is no fully accepted measure of this sort.

Within a particular subject literature, if we can collect a representative bibliography, we may look at the contributions of a particular author over time. Since Lotka's law establishes concentration of productivity among a few authors, such counts can be used to rate scholars as well. Although impact and productivity may not equate with quality, it seems likely that some degree of relationship exists. The same methods may be used to compare whole research groups or faculties.

9.8.3 Collection Maintenance

The concentration of use of materials in collections makes it possible to organize files so that high-use materials are easily accessible and lower-use materials stored in lower-cost, less accessible locations. Use may also be associated with value or quality. Thus high-use materials can be acquired and retained, low-use ones ignored and discarded. The use in question can be measured by circulation, by citation, or by recording each access to materials. It should be pointed out that the retention of high-use materials has a more firm basis than the acquisition only of materials similar to those currently in high use. That which has not been made available for use cannot be used. Thus low use of a class of materials that is seriously underrepresented in a collection may not indicate a true lack of demand.

9.9
Data Collection Issues

It seems useful to discuss some of the problems inherent in collecting the data for the measures discussed here. If we are concerned with analyzing the literature of a subject which we presume will follow the regularities named for Bradford and Lotka, we must have a bibliography which is representative of the subject. Ideally, such a bibliography should be complete. Unfortunately, completeness in a bibliography is a theoretical construct. We have no real way to determine if we have achieved it, and even if we had such a method, we should have to admit that the literature in question might well continue to grow after the point where we began our analysis. The decision as to whether or not some paper belongs within a topical bibliography is a fuzzy one. We will get a great deal of agreement that some papers belong in the literature of measurement, but we will find many papers whose inclusion or exclusion will generate a great deal of disagreement. The selection of the bounds of any bibliography for bibliometric analysis will involve many arbitrary decisions.

The study of an actual collection does not share the problem of theoretical boundaries. A physical collection actually exists at a location and its catalog is normally representative of it at a time somewhat prior to the current moment. Unfortunately, conclusions drawn from the study of a collection cannot necessarily be generalized beyond that collection. Bibliometric studies of a collection therefore normally concern the use of that collection. Here problems arise not in identifying the items to be considered, but rather in defining what is meant by use in a manner that is both countable and meaningful.

We can count the number of times an item circulates outside an information service, but this does not reflect in-house use, nor does it reflect the potential utility of other items that are not in the collection. Comparisons with the circulation of other similar collections will provide some information on materials not acquired, as will citation studies of these materials if such data exist. If users are not permitted to refile the materials they have consulted, counts of in-house use by those who do the filing are possible. This is labor intensive but is likely to prevent some misfiling as well as provide counts of uses. Since a great many items will not be consulted at all in a study period, some form of wrapper which will be destroyed by a consultation can be applied to all items. This will allow identification of unused items which may be candidates for less accessible storage or removal.

9.10
Summary

We see that regularities exist in the distribution and use of sources of information. These have considerable theoretical interest, but also some real practical applications in the design of systems for the collection, organization, and dissemination of information. It is possible to measure the productivity of information sources and to make use of these measurements to evaluate the usefulness of the sources. Relationships inherent in the sources may allow us to classify, rank, and organize them so that the most utility can be achieved from limited resources.

References

Bar-Hillel, Y., and R. Carnap. (1953). Semantic information. *The British Journal for the Philosophy of Science*, 4(13), 147–157.
Booth, A. D. (1969). On the geometry of libraries. *Journal of Documentation*, 25(1), 28–42.
Boyce, Bert R. and Mark Funk. (1978). Bradford's law and the selection of high quality papers. *Library Resources and Technical Services*, 22(4), 390–401.
Boyce, Bert and Janet Sue Pollens. (1982). Citation based impact measures and the Bradfordian selection criteria. *Collection Management*, 4(3), 29–36.
Bradford, S. C. (1934). Sources of information on specific subjects. *Engineering*, (37), 85. Reprinted in *Collection Management*, 1(3/4) Fall/Winter 1976–77, 95.
Brillouin, L. (1956). *Science and Information Theory*. New York: Academic Press.
Broadus, R. N. (1977). The application of citation analysis to library collection building. *Advances in Librarianship*, 7, 299–335.
———. (1987). Early approaches to bibliometrics. *Journal of the American Society for Information Science*, 38(2), 127–129.
Brookes, B. C. (1968). The derivation and application of the Bradford–Zipf distribution. *Journal of Documentation*, 24(4), 247–265.
Budd, J. M. (1992a). Bibliometrics: a method for the study of the literature of higher education. In *Higher Education: Handbook of Theory and Research*, Vol. VIII. Bronx, NY: Agathon Press, 345–378.
———. (1992b). *The Library and Its Users: the Communication Process*. New York: Greenwood Press, 50.
Cole, F. J. and W. B. Earles. (1917). The history of comparative anatomy. Part I. A statistical analysis of the literature. *Scientific Progress*, 11, 578–596.
Egghe, L. and R. Rousseau. (1990). *Introduction to Informetrics: Quantitative Methods in Library, Documentation and Information Science*. Amsterdam: Elsevier.
Garfield, Eugene. (1979). *Citation Indexing: Its Theory and Application in Science, Technology and Humanities*. New York: John Wiley & Sons, 24.
Goffman, W. and K. S. Warren. (1980). *Scientific Information Systems and the Principle of Selectivity*. New York: Praeger.
Groos, O. V. (1967). Bradford's law and the Keenan Atherton data. *American Documentation*, 18(1), 46.
Gross, P. L. K., and E. M. Gross. (1927). College libraries and chemical education. *Science*, 66, 385–389.
Hulme, E. W. (1923). Statistical bibliography, etc. *Library Association Record*, 1(4), 262–263.
Kessler, M. M. (1963). Bibliographic coupling between scientific papers. *American Documentation*, 14(1), 10–25.
Knuth, D. E. (1973). *The Art of Computer Programming. Volume 3, Sorting and Searching*. Reading, MA: Addison-Wesley Publishing Company.
Kraft, D. H. (1979). Journal selection models: past and present. *Collection Management*, 3(2), 163–185.
Kraft, D. H. and Bert R. Boyce. (1991). *Operations Research for Libraries and Information Agencies*. San Diego: Academic Press.
Leimkuhler, F. F. (1967). The Bradford distribution. *Journal of Documentation*, 23, 197–207.

Line, M. B. and A. Sandison. (1974). 'Obsolescence' and changes in the use of literature with time. *Journal of Documentation*, 30(3), 283–350.

Losee, R. M. (1990). *The Science of Information: Measurement and Applications.* San Diego: Academic Press.

Molyneux. Robert E., comp. (1989). *ACRL University Library Statistics, 1987–1988.* Chicago: Association of Research Libraries.

O'Neill, E. T. (1970). *Journal Usage Patterns and Their Implications in the Planning of Library Systems.* Ph.D. Dissertation, Purdue University (unpublished).

Pao, M. L. (1985). Lotka's law: A testing procedure. *Information Processing and Management*, 21(4), 305–320.

———. (1989). *Concepts of Information Retrieval.* Englewood, CO: Libraries Unlimited, Inc.

Price, D. J. de Solla. (1976). A general theory of bibliometric and other cumulative processes. *Journal of the American Society for Information Science*, 27(5/6), 292–306.

Seglen, Per O. (1992). The skewness of science. *Journal of the American Society of Information Science*, 43(9), 628–638.

Shannon, C. E. and W. Weaver. (1949). *The Mathematical Theory of Communication.* Urbana: University of Illinois Press.

Simon, H. A. (1955). On a class of skew distribution functions. *Biometrika*, 42(2), 425–440.

Small, H. G. and B. C. Griffith. (1974). The structure of scientific literature, I: Identifying and graphing specialities. *Science Studies*, 4(1), 17–40.

Trueswell, R. W. (1975). Growing libraries: who needs them? A statistical basis for the no-growth collection. In D. Gore, ed. *Farewell to Alexandria.* Westport, CT: Greenwell Press.

Virgo, J. A. (1977). A statistical procedure for evaluating the importance of scientific papers. *Library Quarterly*, 47(4), 415–430.

Wilkinson, E. A. (1972). The ambiguity of Bradford's law." *Journal of Documentation*, 28, 122–130.

Four

Measures of Databases and Information Retrieval

10

Introduction to Measurement in Information Retrieval

10.1
Models of Information Retrieval Systems

Our purpose in the chapter is to introduce the basic elements of information retrieval systems (IRSYS) and the basic measurements that are made of them, setting a framework for more deailed discussions in Chapters 11–14.

A *model* is an abstraction of an *entity,* which can be almost anything definable: a structure, system, process, person, organization, or even a philosophical concept. One type of model of an airplane, for example, is intended to sit on a table and *look* like an airplane. Its linear dimensions are uniformly scaled down from the original and it is decorated like the original. Another model type is used in wind tunnels for aerodynamic testing. It looks similar to the original in silhouette, but the dimensions are more precise and the scaling is more complex than a constant fraction of the original. No one bothers to paint airline markings on such a model. A mathematical model of the same aircraft, used for testing stresses on the wings, is a set of differential equations that do not, in any way, look like an airplane but are capable of accurately portraying certain of its characteristics.

The point is that if a model is to be used for testing or evaluation, then it is necessary to specify precisely what aspects of the real entity are to be represented in the model. This is true even when the system to be measured is the complete, real system but only selected aspects are to be examined. Since the measurements to be made may be precisely defined, it is something of a paradox that the system being measured may be quite ill-defined. Indeed, it has not been standard practice in information science for a journal paper reporting on a system evaluation in information retrieval to include a precise statement of exactly what is included in, and excluded from, the evaluation.

One way to define or describe an information system model is by *structure,* that is, by specifying what components are included and how they relate to one another. Another way to define a system model is by its *logic*—what it does, or how. The logic has great bearing on what kind of measurements are needed or useful. Hence, the first step in any measurement project must be to define carefully what aspects of the system are to be represented and measured.

10.1.1 Structural Definitions

Let us define an IRSYS as the set of computer programs that interpret queries, search for information in a file, and return information to the person who requested it. It will include some form of *retrieval status value* or *matching* or *membership function,* similar to that used in fuzzy sets (see Section 7.4), that either flags those records to be retrieved or provides a strength of association from which the user can determine which ones to retrieve. An *information retrieval service* (IRSVCE) may be defined as a larger system that includes an IRSYS and one or more databases and possibly an intermediary who (or which—it may be a program) converts a user's information need statement into a *query,* the formal sequence of retrieval commands to the IRSYS.

Sometimes a published evaluation of an IRSVCE is described as if it were only an evaluation of the IRSYS, thus excluding consideration of the role of the intermediary and of the database in satisfying user needs.

The components of a service and its users, some subset of which may become the object of a measurement effort, are the database, the language with which attribute values are represented, the information retrieval system, the intermediary, and the language with which users communicate with the IRSYS. The questions put to a retrieval system are not actually part of the system but do affect its performance, hence we may also be interested in measuring them. Just as, in Section 5.2, we stressed the importance of precise definition of a sample space if the sample data are to be meaningful, a system to be evaluated must be precisely defined in terms of configuration if its evaluation is to be meaningful.

10.1.1.1 The Database

A *database* is created in response to a policy of the producer that specified:

The *entities of interest,* such as all journal articles in chemistry, or all items in a newspaper except advertising, sports scores, and obituaries;

The *attributes* which are to be used to describe the entities, such as names, dates, titles, classification codes; and

The actual *selection of entities* for inclusion, such as which stories a newspaper editor selects for inclusion in a given issue of the paper.

Clearly, a retrieval service cannot be seen to perform well on behalf of a searcher if the database is not adequate to that searcher's needs and these are the basic elements of needs satisfaction.

10.1.1.2 Attribute Representation Languages

Given an entity about which information is to be stored and a set of attributes that are to be evaluated, the database design must also include, for each attribute, a language to be used for recording the values. If the attribute is *number of children,* the value language is simple enough—the set of integers from 0 to *n*. Although there is no legal limit on number of children a person may have, a database designer may set an upper limit, assuming that a value such as 1000 children for any one parent is probably an error.

If the entity is a book or a journal article and the attribute is *subject,* then there are quite complex languages for describing this information. The process of doing so includes such activities as *classifying* or *indexing.* For each entity a record may be created which includes attributes descriptive of *title, author,* and *subject.* One example of a language for describing subject is the Dewey Decimal Classification (see Sections 4.2 and 4.3). Another might be a set of individual words or desciptors that can be assigned to the document, collectively indicating its subject matter. The universe from which such a set is drawn is called a *controlled vocabulary.* If *any* word could be used, then a searcher would be hard pressed to guess which words had been selected by the indexer, the person who assigned the values. A controlled vocabulary enables users to look up the appropriate words in an *authority list,* or dictionary or thesaurus. It offers less freedom to choose the exactly right word but potentially reduces error.

A user who is not familiar with the vocabulary used with a given attribute will not be able to write query statements as well as one who is familiar with it. This is true with both natural and artificial languages. Familiarity with the language is not the same as familiarity with the subject matter. Many professionals do not know the controlled vocabularies used with bibliographic material in their profession, and many intermediaries know the vocabulary well but are not true experts in the subject matter.

Not all records consist of attributes for which special languages are in use. Increasingly, databases concerned with textual material will include the entire text, with little or no subject indexing. In these cases, there may be no controlled vocabulary or controls may exist only at the level of a style guide for a publication.

10.1.1.3 The Information Retrieval System

The information retrieval system (IRSYS) is the mechanical heart of the service. In many present-day commercial systems the IRSYS performs no real interpretive function; i.e., the user gives only commands containing precise, binary, Boolean expressions which leave no need for judgment to be exercised by the IRSYS in order to execute, hence provide little basis for evaluation. Other IRSYS accept broad or imprecise expressions and convert them into commands, by various means, and often improve them. Hence there is a need for evaluation of their performance. Very recently, we see commercial interest in interpretive systems that rank output for users.

10.1.1.4 The Intermediary

Traditionally, the intermediary is a person, typically a librarian, who receives the user's statement of information need, which may be quite informal or vague, and converts it into a query, the formal expression that is to be interpreted and executed by the IRSYS. This interpretive function is not limited to computer-based retrieval. It could as well be a matter of manually determining which subject headings to use for a card catalogue or online catalogue search, Dewey Decimal Classification codes for a search of the bookshelves of a library, or a recommendation of what reference work might hold the desired information. The skill of the intermediary in performing the translation of a user's stated need into search terms and in helping the user articulate his or her needs is critical to the success of the retrieval operation. This and other activities of an intermediary are described in Soergel (1985, pp. 371–372) and Auster (1990).

In recent years a number of computer programs that perform the intermediary function have been developed (Croft and Thompson, 1987; Marcus and Reintjes, 1981a,b; Meadow, 1990; Vickery and Brooks, 1987a,b; Waters, 1986; Weyer, 1989; Williams, 1985). These programs may be incorporated as part of an IRSYS or kept separate and even run in a separate computer from that of the IRSYS. But the functions undertaken are the same as when the human performs the job, even for a noncomputer search.

10.1.1.5 The User Language

A query language or IRSYS command language is a computer programming language in every respect, albeit a highly specialized one. Languages used may range from natural almost to assembly language level. Some are or can be highly expressive, some simply do not permit certain types of relationships among record attributes to be expressed. For example, we know of no IRSYS command language that enables the user to express, in a single command, the requirement "I want all news articles that mention new product releases by the XYZ Company, in the week preceding any

10.1 Models of Information Retrieval Systems

rise in XYZ's share value of more than 10%." This might be what a securities analyst really wants—to see how product announcements affect share prices. To a significant extent, the language determines how effective the human user, hence the retrieval service, can be. In linguistics the Whorf hypothesis (Whorf, 1956, p. vi) states essentially that the language we speak shapes our perceptions of the world. Similarly, a command language may shape a user's perception of what an IRSYS can do. Subject headings or classification codes in libraries are forms of query language used in manual systems. Knowledge of these languages, or lack of it, affects how we ask questions in libraries, whether or not through the medium of a computer.

In some cases, by means of a graphical user interface (GUI) or a menu interface, users indicate actions desired by placing values in specified positions or by selecting an action from a list of possible actions. In such interfaces the means of expressing commands is different from one in which the user types the name of a command, but the functions available for execution do not differ. They are still command-driven interfaces.

Another variation is to describe desired output, rather than provide the commands necessary to produce the output. Such languages are called *nonprocedural* and may be easier for novices to learn, but may lack the degree of precision and control desired by professional users.

10.1.1.6 The Question or Query

Saracevic and others proposed that there are the following "aspects of information seeking and retrieving" in a major study (1988, p. 162): (1) user, (2) question, (3) searcher, (4) search, and (5) items retrieved. We have tended to consider the question (our term is *query*) as a form of text or document, hence subject to the same measurements as other texts. But, as we shall discuss in Chapter 11, the Saracevic study did propose some measures of questions that cannot reasonably be applied to all texts in a database.

10.1.2 Logical Definitions

A number of authors have defined models of information retrieval in terms of the manner in which the queries are expressed by a user and interpreted by the IRSYS. Principal among them is the *Boolean model*, both the oldest and most frequently used commercially. Others include the *probabilistic model* and the *fuzzy set model*.

10.1.2.1 The Boolean Model

In the Boolean model a query consists of two kinds of statements: (1) *equivalence* or *conditional statements,* each of which defines a set of records of the database in terms of values of attributes, such as $SALARY > 40000$

or SUBJECT = CHEMISTRY, and (2) Boolean *algebraic statements*, which specify operations to be performed on the sets defined by the equivalence statements, such as SALARY > 40000 AND DATE-OF-BIRTH > 1970. This last statement creates a new set which is the intersection of the two defined by the individual equivalence statements.

An equivalence relation in Boolean algebra (see Section 4.1.2) is *binary;* it admits of the values TRUE or FALSE only. Hence, each record in a database is either in or not in the set for which the equivalence statement is true. While primitive, this is a matching or set membership function.

This sort of logic is very convenient for computer programmers as well as for theorists looking for a concise method of measuring outcome. For a nontext file, such as one showing inventory status, it is easy for users to visualize what it means to ask for the current stock level of white or beige refrigerators or freezers (COLOR = WHITE OR COLOR = BEIGE) AND (TYPE = REFRIGERATOR OR TYPE = FREEZER). But there is something disquieting about the thought that a document must be treated as either matching or not matching a query, with no in-between values or degrees of match. For example, does the color IVORY match the query just stated? Should it?

10.1.2.2 The Probabilistic Model

In the case of the probabilistic model, the objective is to discover the probability of a match between a query and a stored document, hence doing away with the strictly binary nature of the matching function (see Section 7.5.1 and Bookstein, 1983). Proponents suggest that this is a more meaningful way to respond to a user than to say "These match. These do not." Inherent in such a model is the concept that the query should contain more information than is usually given in a Boolean query, and probably with less formally restrictive requirements than are used with Boolean expressions.

The additional information in the query is usually a weight assigned to the terms and this weight allows us to assign some sort of match function or retrieval status value, *rsv,* to each record. This, in turn, permits sets of records to be ranked on the basis of their presumed value as responses to the query. If these weights are based on the probability of a term being present when a record is relevant to a query, then we are using a probabilistic model. Using Bayes' theorem, the probability that a term will appear in a record judged to be relevant can be generated from the probability that a relevant record has been assigned or contains the term. The second value can theoretically be attained by storing the frequency of a term's appearance in a relevant record retrieved by the system. We are unaware of any operational systems of this sort, but considerable theoretical discussion has ensued since the original suggestion by Maron and Kuhns (1960).

A probabilistic IRSYS may use a form of economic consideration when evaluating records, such as the value of retrieving a record or the cost of not retrieving it. These estimates would be based on word frequencies in the text, the query, or both.

10.1.2.3 The Fuzzy Set Model

This is a generalization of the Boolean model (see Section 7.5 and Bookstein, 1985). Here, we define a measure of the strength of association of each document with a query. This measure can be the probability that the document is in the set of matching documents, or the degree to which it is in the set. There is no single function for measuring strength of association of query with text. Any function that measures the similarity of texts (see Section 7.2.3) may be used. No new set is created until after the computation of the functional values, when the user may set a threshold for values to be included. Since the creation of a retrieval set is a second-stage operation, after the query has been used to assess the database records, a different kind of measure of retrieval effectiveness is needed than for the Boolean model.

If the term weights are viewed as fuzzy membership functions, then a 0 for a term occurring in a record indicates no set membership, a 1 indicates certainty of membership, and a weight in the interval (0,1) indicates partial membership. Retrieval status values can be constructed using the redefined Boolean operations of fuzzy logic. Suppose we wish to search for records containing terms a and b. Suppose further that A and B are membership functions for a and b, respectively, for any given record. This means that these functions describe the strength of association of the term with the record. Such a function can be the binary 0 or 1, indicating whether or not the term appears in a record, or a value based on frequency of occurrence, as a term weight. Then, we may compose a query A AND B which calls for retrieval of those records for which the membership values are as stated. And, we may define another function that measures each record's degree of association with the query. One such function is MIN(A,B), which assigns to the record the minimum of the individual term membership functions. If we were using the traditional term occurrence values, 0 or 1, indicating that the term is present or not, then MIN(A,B) for a record is 0 unless both terms are present—the usual situation for the Boolean searches, given a query of a AND b. If we have a multivalued weighting function, in the range [0,1], and for some record $A = 0.5$ and $B = 0.3$, then MIN(0.5, 0.3) = 0.3. Similarly, the function for A OR B can be calculated as MAX(A,B) and for NOT A as $1 - A$ (Buell and Kraft, 1981).

10.1.2.4 The Vector Space Model

As described in Section 7.2.3.3, one way to represent a text is to assume an n-dimensional Euclidean space where n is the number of potential word types in use. For each word there is a vector of length 0 if the word is not present in the document, 1 if it is. In this way, each document is represented by a point in n-space, the resultant vector of all the individual

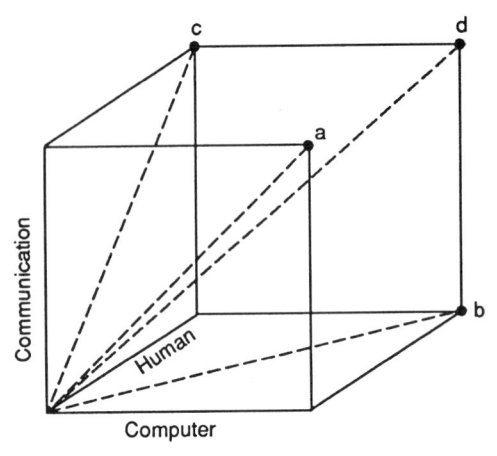

Figure 10.1
Vector space. This is a three-dimensional vector space for a vocabulary consisting only of the words *communication, computer,* and *human.* A text containing the words *computer* and *communication* would be represented by a point at *a;* one containing *human* and *computer* by a point at *b;* and one containing *human communication* by *c.* These points are equidistant from the origin and from each other. The point at *d* represents a text with all three words. We cannot, of course, illustrate a space of several hundred dimensions in this manner.

ones. See Figure 10.1. Two documents with similar subject matter will probably use a similar set of words and, if so, their resultant vectors will be close to each other. This method is more useful with a controlled vocabulary than an uncontrolled one because of the large number of dimensions of the latter and the number of different words having similar or identical meaning. The terms may have assigned weights other than 0 or 1 based on their frequency of occurrence in the record or the file or both.

A query can be similarly represented as the resultant vector of all the words used in the query. Hence, one way to match a query with a stored document is to find the resultant vector for each and compute the difference between them. We shall consider this method in more detail in Chapter 11.

10.2
Types and Goals of Measures

What is it we want to measure in an information retrieval system or service? What measures would be useful, and to whom? van Rijsbergen (1981, p. 32) says that we want an IRSYS to have "the ability . . . to retrieve relevant documents while at the same time suppressing the retrieval of non-relevant documents." Hence one measure is the extent to which this

10.2 Types and Goals of Measures

is done. B. C. Vickery (1961, p. 140) quoted Cyril Cleverdon, one of the pioneers of information retrieval measurement, as saying that economic efficiency is the ultimate measure, because what we really want to know is how much it will cost to solve a problem. Cleverdon was probably assuming, not unreasonably, that most systems would ultimately retrieve the same materials, hence that the question of cost is the ultimate one. Cooper (1973, p. 99) says that "a retrieval system must ultimately be judged on the basis of a comparison of some kind involving costs and benefits." Cooper also says (1973, p. 87) that "the search for a *single* measure of effectiveness is misguided—. . . there is not . . . one 'correct' way of measuring retrieval success." The elapsed time since this was written has not diminished its truth.

The van Rijsbergen approach is to evaluate the extent to which the system meets user needs. The Cleverdon approach is to determine how cost-effectively it meets needs, i.e., at what cost in various resources, such as money, time, or tying up of resources. This approach is useful in comparing systems all of which are likely to produce essentially the same result when in the hands of a skilled user, or when evaluating the skill of the user.

Lancaster (1981, pp. 106–109) points out that information services, which include retrieval systems, can be evaluated at these levels:

Cost, the price of the time and effort required to find information;

Effectiveness, the extent to which user needs are satisfied and often the only the factor considered in an evaluation;

Benefit, the frequently subjective, perceived value of a system or its use;

Cost-effectiveness, a comparison of achieved effectiveness per unit of cost;

Cost–benefit, a comparison of benefits, as defined above, per unit cost;

Cost–performance–benefit, a comparison of costs with both measured effectiveness and perceived benefits.

In any case, we can agree that it is possible to evaluate a retrieval service overall, or in terms of individual components or combinations of them. The kinds of measurements applied to the major components are briefly introduced here and enlarged upon in subsequent chapters. The measurement of relevance is covered in more detail in Chapter 13.

10.2.1 Database Measures

The aspects of a database that can be measured, to varying degrees of success, fall in the following categories:

Coverage, or the intended scope of the domain of entities included, such as all articles on physics published anywhere in the scientific literature, or all articles published in any of a list of physics journals. Also, the attributes represented, the actual selection of entities for inclusion, and the number of entities (database magnitude) represented.

Relationships, including the extent to which the entities represented in one database are also found in another (overlap) and the relationships among attribute values.

Timeliness, or the delay between occurrence of an event and its recording in the database. An event can be the withdrawal of an item from inventory or the publication of a book. It is a report of the event which is then represented in a database.

Cost of buying or leasing a copy of the database, searching it remotely, or printing a record from it.

Reliability, or accuracy of the information. This is undoubtedly the most difficult aspect to measure.

10.2.2 User Measures

We may be interested in measuring the performance of the person who interacts directly with the IRSYS for several reasons: to assess the performance of employees, to assess the effectiveness of training, or to be sure that, in an assessment of the mechanical system or overall service, the human participants in the service are of uniform or comparable levels of skill. As with most measures of human performance, those related to information retrieval are not well defined and some are subject to considerable subjective judgement (Meadow et al., 1994; Chignell et al., 1990). Those that are used include:

Experience, always a convenient measure, never a perfect one. This may be experience as an intermediary or merely as a user in knowing how to ask questions. Experience is becoming recognized as a multifacted characteristic—experience at what?

Skill in use of the command language.

Skill in using the data representation languages or databases.

Skill in expressing the user's own information needs.

Skill in the subject matter of the search, i.e. in recognizing the relevance or value of retrieved records, or the lack thereof, and of what makes a record relevant. This, too, is rarely, if ever, measured, although the ability to recognize a target as such, when seen, is a consideration in formal search theory (Janes, 1989).

Skill in using the data representation languages and in evaluating output is the major benefit of *subject domain knowledge,* i.e., knowledge of the subject matter of the database. The other major aspect of skill is in the use of the

10.2 Types and Goals of Measures   **141**

IRSYS or IRSVCE. High degrees of these two do not often reside in the same person. A different kind of user characteristic is that of the user's perception or understanding of the system, called the *user's mental model*. These measures are discussed in greater detail in Chapter 14.

10.2.3 Query Language Measures

The language is intimately tied to the IRSYS software but is not the same as the software. Furthermore, it is possible to introduce a language other than that intended for use with an IRSYS and to use an intermediary program for translation. Hence, the language in actual use should be evaluated separately from the software that executes the commands. Aspects of language subject to measurement are:

Ease of learning by users;
Logical power of the language, i.e., the kinds of statements that can be made and the precision of defining information needed.

10.2.4 The IRSYS Software

It is sometimes difficult to separate aspects of user skill or of logic of the command language from the software that executes language commands. Measures that exist are largely concerned with resource use, including:

Interpretation of queries, if done by the IRSYS. How successfully or how accurately is this translation done?
Cost of use of the system, in monetary terms (software can be bought, licensed for long-term use, or rented by the minute).
Nonmonetary resources consumed. Although resources such as memory can be measured in money terms, memory demands and the like may be constrained for a using organization independent of purely financial cost. For example, there may be procurement freezes in an organization that do not take value received into consideration, but only dollars expended.
Time to execute various kinds of commands, which is also a resource not entirely measurable in money terms.

10.2.5 Operation of the Service

Here, we consider the entire service, viewed as a single entity. Measures of such broad scope may be composites based on combinations of other measures listed herein or simply on users' overall evaluations of the outcome. End users are often unable to perceive the role of various system components and, for example, to rate the language separately from query interpretation. When, as is often the case, it is impossible or too expensive to make all the detailed measures that may combine to indicate overall level of performance, the single-question user evaluation may be the best approach.

10.3
Issues in Information Retrieval Measurement

We shall go deeper into the measures introduced above in the chapters to follow. But first let us consider some of the problems of performing measurement in this field. The first and most important is defining the system or service and the measures. When a prospective buyer is evaluating an automobile and knows as little as most of us about the automobile as a machine, there are certain standard measures that can be used, of which the following are only a sample:

Acceleration; the time required to go from standing to 60 mph. This always seems of interest in advertising, even though few of us have occasion to push the car to its maximum acceleration.

Fuel consumption; of general interest, but must be phrased carefully as consumption is different in highway travel, when the vehicle will be operated at a high but fairly constant rate of speed, and in city travel, when the car will usually be operated at low speed, with frequent stops and starts. Always, there is a footnote to the effect that the mileage depends on the individual driver's habits.

Reliability; the likelihood of need for repairs or mean time to failure of a component or the entire vehicle.

Cost; always difficult to determine in the automotive world and virtually never quoted as inclusive of repairs and maintenance, insurance, licensing, etc.

Resale potential; the probable market value after n years of use.

Similarly, in deciding on the purchase of an IRSYS, measures are usually incomplete and as heavily dependent on users as the automotive measures are on the driver and conditions of use. To extract meaning from them, the user of these measures must take the trouble to inquire into their definitions and the manner of collecting the data.

The measures or attributes which can be expected to vary during the course of an experiment or field study include:

User's *mental model;* or the perceptions by the user about what the

10.3 Issues in Information Retrieval Measurement

system consists of, how it is structured, and how it actually operates. These can vary to a great extent, and when a user thinks the system performs differently than it actually does, he or she will probably use it differently than intended. Measurement, or even full and accurate recording, of the mental model in use by a user has been an elusive factor. Even defining it has no standard, but psychologists (Carroll and Olson, 1988) are convinced that the model that is perceived affects user performance.

User *changes during a search,* particularly their perceptions of which records are related to, or of value to, their information needs vary as they proceed through a search, as different sets are defined and examined. (Boyce, 1980; Eisenberg, 1988) Hence, the first judgment about a record may not hold up as the search progresses. Similarly, the searcher may grow more or less impatient and may find information not explicitly sought, which may change the overall attitude toward the activity of searching.

Nature of the relationship between query and records, which can be evaluated in absolute terms or relative to the query's relationship to other records. Some experimenters have operated on the assumption that the relationship of a query to a record is virtually fixed, hence a person other than the requester or end user can evaluate the output in terms of its relationship to an assumed information need. Others believe that relationship varies with the immediate needs of the user. While either approach may be valid, care must be taken that all attribute evaluations for one system or service are based on the same assumptions.

Experimental procedures; there being a number of procedural factors that can affect the quality of data collected in a laboratory or field test setting, such as:

Selection of subjects. The number of subjects used and the extent to which the sample truly represents the population under study.

Selection of measures. As pointed out above, the measures to be used must be consistent and well defined.

Selection of scales. Defining a scale is not the same as ensuring that subjects asked to use it in an evaluation understand it. For example, a decile scale has been used in evaluating personnel; i.e., a rating of 6 means the person is superior in performance to 60% of others in the same job category. But only 40% of people can achieve a rating this high. What if, in spite of instructions, 80% of persons are rated as 6 or higher? What this suggests is that the users of the scale are ignoring the definition and in fact using an equal-interval scale with 10 intervals.

Treatment of subjects. The tasks assigned to users under study must be difficult enough to bring out differences in subject capability, but not so difficult that almost none can perform well.

Laboratory procedures. Even simple procedures such as what a laboratory assistant says to a subject who may not understand what to do can introduce bias and affect performance.

10.4
Summary

In this chapter we have concentrated on defining the major elements of information retrieval and information service systems in preparation for investigations of their measurement. We have distinguished among (1) various models of an IRSYS, a mechanical system for storing information, interpreting queries, and searching for and retrieving information; (2) the database which the IRSYS searches; (3) languages used to represent information in a database; (4) query or command languages for instructing an IRSYS what to retrieve; (5) the information retrieval service which offers an IRSYS and database plus often some help in needs translation and query formulation; and (6) users, the people who operate and make use of the output of an IRSYS.

In Chapter 11 we concentrate on databases and various measures that can be made of them. Chapter 12 is concerned with the operational performance of an IRSYS in the sense of what a system does, how fast, and at what cost. It also deals with users and their speed, errors, and so on. Chapter 13 deals with outcome, the question raised earlier in this chapter of what a retrieval system is supposed to accomplish and how effectively it produces the information desired. Chapter 14 deals with other measures of user performance that were raised in Chapters 12 and 13.

References

Auster, Ethel. (1990). *The Online Searcher.* New York: Neal Schuman Publishers.
Bookstein, Abraham. (1983). Outline of a general probabilistic retrieval model. *Journal of Documentation,* 39(2), 63–72.
———. (1985). Probability and fuzzy-set applications to information retrieval. In Martha E. Williams, ed., *Annual Review of Information Science and Technology,* Vol. 20. New York: Knowledge Industry Publications, Inc., 117–151.
Boyce, B. (1980). Beyond topicality. A two-stage view of relevance and the retrieval process. *Information Processing and Management,* 18(3), 105–189.
Buell, D. A. and D. H. Kraft. (1981). A model for a weighted retrieval system. *Journal of the American Society for Information Science,* 32(3), 211–216.
Carroll, John M. and J. R. Olson. (1988). Mental models in human–computer interaction. In M. Helander, ed. *Handbook of Human-Computer Interaction.* Amsterdam: Elsevier Science Publishers, 45–65.
Chignell, Mark H., Lee Jaffee, Philip J. Smith, Deborah Krawczak and Stephen J. Shute. (1990). Knowledge-based search intermediaries for online information retrieval. In Rao Aluri and Donald E. Riggs, eds. *Expert Systems in Libraries.* Norwood, NJ: Ablex Publishing Corp., 170–191.
Cooper, W. S. (1973). On selecting a measure of effectiveness. *Journal of the American Society for Information Science,* 24(2), 97–100.

References

Croft, W. B. and R. H. Thompson, (1987). I³R: a new approach to the design of document retrieval systems. *Journal of the American Society for Information Science*, 38(6), 389–404.

Eisenberg, M. B. (1988). Measuring relevance judgement. *Information Processing and Management*, 24(4), 373–389.

Janes, Joseph W. (1989). The application of search theory to information science. *Proceedings of the 52nd Annual Meeting, American Society for Information Science*. Medford NJ: Learned Information, 9–12.

Lancaster, F. W. (1981). Evaluation within the environment of an operating information service. In Sparck Jones, Karen, *Information Retrieval Experiment*. London: Butterworths, 105–127.

Marcus, Richard S. and J. F. Reintjes. (1981a). A translating computer interface for end-user operation of heterogeneous retrieval systems. I. Design. *Journal of the American Society for Information Science*, 32(4), 287–303.

——————————————. (1981b). A translating computer interface for end-user operation of heterogeneous retrieval systems. II. Evaluations. *Journal of the American Society for Information Science*, 32(4), 304–317.

Maron, M. E. and J. Kuhns. (1960). On relevance, probabilistic indexing and information retrieval. *American Documentation*, 7(3), 216–244.

Meadow, Charles T. (1990). The making of an information retrieval interface. *The 5th Jerusalem Conference on Information Technology*. Los Alamitos, CA: IEEE Computer Society Press, 787–795.

Meadow, Charles T., Gary Marchionini and Joan Cherry. (1994). Speculations on the measurement and use of user characteristics in information retrieval experimentation. *Unpublished manuscript*.

Saracevic, Tefko, Paul Kantor, Alice Y. Chamis, and Donna Trivision. (1988). A study of information seeking and retrieving. I. Background and methodology. *Journal of the American Society for Information Science*, 39(3), 161–176.

Soergel, Dagobert. (1985). *Organizing Information: Principles of Data Base and Retrieval Systems*. Orlando: Academic Press.

van Rijsbergen, C. J. (1981). Retrieval effectiveness. In Sparck Jones, K., ed. *Information Retrieval Experiment*. London: Butterworths, 32–43.

Vickery, A. and H. M. Brooks. (1987a). Plexus: the expert system for referral. *Information Processing and Management*, 23(2), 99–118.

Vickery, Alina and Helen Brooks (1987b). Expert systems and their applications in LIS. *Online Review*, 11(3), 149–165.

Vickery, B. C. (1961). *On Retrieval System Theory*. London: Butterworths.

Waters, Samuel T. (1986). Answerman, the expert information specialist: an expert system for retrieval of information from library reference books. *Information Technology and Libraries*, 5(3), 204–212.

Weyer, Stephen. (1989). Questing for the 'Dao': DowQuest and intelligent text retrieval. *Online*, 13(5), 39–48.

Whorf, Benjamin J. (1956). *Language, Thought, and Reality: Selected Writings*. J.B. Carroll, ed. Cambridge: MIT Press.

Williams, Philip W. (1985). The design of an expert system for access to information. *Proc. of the 9th International Online Meeting*. Abingdon, UK: Learned Information Ltd., 139–149.

11
Measurement of Databases

11.1
Introduction

Although the term *database* is relatively new, we have had databases for as long as we have had symbolic recording of information. Indeed, many of civilization's earliest records concerned what we now call commercial accounts (Innis, 1991; Ascher and Ascher, 1991). But in all the time since, we have developed remarkably few measures of these databases, or even of precisely defined attributes for describing them. Sheer magnitude seems, informally, to matter a great deal. Libraries are often described in terms of their number of holdings and the larger ones seem to do little to discourage this form of evaluation. We rarely hear of a library or an academic accrediting agency emphasizing the extent to which user needs are filled, rather than collection size. The Sunday *New York Times* is a prodigious work, impressing any reader with its size—almost independent of its content, and possibly leading readers to rate its content based on its size.

In the spirit of scientific inquiry and sound management, we must look for other attributes that may be used to convey useful information about databases for use in decision making. Such decisions might concern which database to buy or use, how reliable one is, or how well its producers' objectives are being met. We can identify a number of database attributes, most of which are not quantitative. These are briefly introduced in Section 11.2 and then the more quantitative ones are covered in more detail in sections to follow. Prior work in measurement (see, for example, Struminger, 1984; Tenopir, 1982) has mostly concentrated on computing the number or percent of records in common to two databases, the coverage of a database (set of entities included), and on methods for detecting duplicate records in two databases, where slight differences may occur in the representation of the same entities.

11.2
Database Characteristics

Fidel (1987, pp. 197–216) proposes the following attributes or characteristics (which term we shall use to avoid confusion with *attribute* as a component of a database) of databases. These are not quantitative, but perhaps someday our art will develop to the point where they can be. They may refer to entities, relationships among entities or attributes, or to the attributes themselves.

Intrinsicality is the extent to which each element of a database relates to the function of the database, or the extent to which all components serve the purpose of the database.

Reliability is the extent to which information is available to provide the necessary data element values. See a related definition in Section 11.3.

Representability, the extent to which a desired data element can be represented. Color and shape, for example, are difficult to represent in words.

Continuance is the stability of the *definition* of a data element or the likelihood the definition may change. A person's name may change but the definition of the attribute *name* is unlikely to. On the other hand, an attribute called *eligibility*, applied to almost anything from membership in a club to admissibility to a nation, may change often.

Resolution is the extent to which any component can be distinguished from others. (See also *resolution* in Section 3.1.1.)

Consistency is the extent to which definitions of elements are consistent among themselves and could, for example, refer to consistent use of *Système Internationale* measurement units throughout a database.

Flexibility is the degree to which data elements can be added, deleted, or changed, if necessary (cf. *continuance*).

Clarity is the desirable quality in any undertaking that component definitions be clear and unambiguous.

Efficiency, a term with multiple meanings which Fidel uses to mean economy of use of data elements—no more than necessary. (See also Section 16.1.)

Semantic integrity is the ability of a database to support meaningful inferences. This is almost impossible to define with great precision, but consider the company that goes bankrupt without warning to management that this condition was imminent. What can we say of the semantic integrity of its accounting system? Almost this exact situation in regard to the production of a commercial airliner was reported in *Fortune* magazine (Smith, 1962).

Completeness is the degree to which all elements needed to accomplish the purpose of the database are, in fact, included in it. In the example of the previous paragraph, if the company has not created the data elements by which to compare forecasted expenditures with actual costs or forecasted sales, it may be doomed.

Specificity is the ability of a database to provide answers to questions at various levels of detail. (See also Section 11.5.6.1.)

Domain specificity is the range or fineness of definition of attribute values, for example, the extent to which data elements can distinguish between two similar entities.

Domain expressiveness is the ability of the attribute values to adequately describe an entity—the right set of attributes. See also Sections 11.5.2 and 1.5.3.

Saracevic et al. (1988, pp, 166–167) use some similar categories to decribe a *question,* by which they mean the central concept of what we have called the information need statement or the query. Still, the question is a text and it can be operated upon or measured in the same manner as other texts. A *subject* is defined as the main concept of a question. They use the word *query* to mean the particular aspect of the subject being searched for. Thus, to them, a query is a narrowing of a subject. Values of the metrics are taken from judges, hence they are subjective. *Subjective* simply means determined by a subject or participant in an experiment or study. It has no pejorative implication. Their categories are:

Domain, the subject class of the question. A nominal scale measure.

Clarity, how well understood the question is to judges, measured separately in terms of *semantic clarity* (meaning of terms) and *syntactic clarity* (relation of terms to each other). Measured on a Likert scale of 1 to 5, 5 meaning *clear.*

Specificity measures the judge's feeling of the relative broadness of definition of terms. Separate values are recorded for terms from the subject and query part of a question. Again, a scale of 1 to 5 is used, 5 here meaning *narrow.*

Complexity, essentially a measure of the judge's opinion of the effect of the number of terms in a question. It is evaluated separately for each subject concept, on a 1 to 5 scale, 5 meaning *high complexity.*

Presupposition, a measure of the extent to which a question contains implied concepts. For example, a question asking "Where is . . ." implies that its subject exists, but verifying existence is not stated as part of the question. Again, a 1 to 5 scale is used, 5 meaning *many suppositions.*

11.3
Survey of Database Measures

We shall briefly review nine measures. The first two, *scope* and *attributes represented*, are applied to a database as a whole, on the basis of intent or design. The next six, *selection of entities, magnitude, timeliness, selectivity, reliability*, and *cost*, are measures usually applied to the database as a whole and as actually realized, not to its intent. The final one, *overlap* or *comparability with other databases*, deals with comparisons and relationships between databases.

> *scope* Scope; the intended population of entities about which records are acquired or maintained. A database producer may declare its intent to provide bibliographic coverage for all published works in computer science, or all securities transactions on a particular stock exchange. There is a tendency to overuse the word all; it is frequently impossible to include all records that are produced outside the control of the database producer, or to measure the extent to which it has been done. Scope is unlikely to be more than a nominal measure, i.e., a description rather than a numeric measure.
>
> *attr* Attributes; the set of descriptors, fields, or data elements which describe an entity. The entities needed to describe a stock market transaction may be few, perhaps stock symbol (abbreviation of company name), number of shares sold, price, and time of transaction. When it comes to what attributes should be included in the description of a human being for use by police intelligence, a hospital, an employer, or a dating service, the list is not so obvious. The attribute list also constitutes a nominal measure.

A prime purpose for the existence of a database is to enable certain records to be selected or separated from the others. The basis for selection is a set of values of attributes used in a query. The set of attributes available in the data record and the nature of their values, along with user skill, determine the ability of any retrieval system to select those records wanted and to ignore those not wanted.

> *selectent* Selection of entities; the measure of the reality of the selection process compared with the intent. While scope is the set of entities intended to be included in the database, their selection does not necessarily coincide with the intent. We may have intended to include a record for every published work on physics, but has that goal been realized? If not, to what extent has it been realized? This is probably not a quantitative measure in most cases.

> *m* Magnitude; defined in Section 4.1.2.
> *timels* Timeliness; the elapsed time between the occurrence of an event and its recording in a database.

This can be used to describe when information arrives relative to its need ("Timely information was provided by the poison control center"), but in database measurement it will refer to attribute values in a database, not to user perceptions. In a daily newspaper, we expect most news items to have occurred no earlier than yesterday; in a stock market ticker display serious traders are intolerant of more than a few minutes delay.

Timeliness can be quantitative in some cases. The sale of a block of shares in a stock market is an almost instantaneous event for which time is recorded. But an election campaign is an event spread over a considerable time range.

> *selectvy* Selectivity, or *discriminating ability*, is the ability of an information system to make distinctions between records or entities.

The degree of selectivity depends on the attributes represented as well as the values assigned. There is no overall measure of selectivity. A database in which *publication date* is represented as *day, month,* and *year* can be more selective than one using only *year*. Similarly, if one database can have ten subject descriptors per item it can be more selective than one having only a single descriptor. Of course, it depends on what attributes and values the searcher wanted. See Fidel's definitions of specificity and expressiveness in Section 11.2.

> *reliab* Reliability; a term without a precise definition in terms of database content.

It seems clear that we cannot directly measure truth. We *can* measure comparability. Hence, if we are inclined to trust one database, similarity of a second to it may provide a measure of the reliability of the second. But an objective measure of the reliability of the standard is unlikely in most cases. There is no established form such a measure should take. Military intelligence analysts try to rate the reliability of their sources by carefully maintaining histories of previous reports, but it is not clear exactly what average readers mean when they declare a newspaper reliable or unreliable.

> *cost* Cost; the price a user pays for a service.

Cost measures the market value of the database, but the concept can be extended to cover other than the monetary direct price. Cost normally is determined by a number of components, rather than directly as a total.

> *overlap* Overlap; or comparability of one database or set with another, measuring the extent to which two databases share entities in common.

This measure has been used in practical studies comparing databases. The complete meaning of comparability should, ideally, cover not just mutual inclusion of entities but mutual inclusion of attributes of these entities, timeliness in their reporting, and attribute values assigned. Overlap measures can be applied to subsets as well as to complete databases.

11.4 Definitions and Terminology

A file or database consists of a set of records, each descriptive of an *entity*. The *record* is the set of attribute *values* descriptive of the entity. A record *structure* is a specification of the attributes intended to be present to describe an entity. In practice, some may be missing. An attribute value may be made up of more than one individual word. A word is an essentially atomic symbol, one that can be treated partially (e.g., by truncation or removal of a suffix) but which might not contain semantically meaningful subordinate words. Although there are compound words, such as *database*, in general a word in English is not made up of other complete words. An attribute such as *name*, however, may consist of subordinate attributes denoting *title* or *honorific, family name, given name, initials,* and *affix*, such as III or Jr. A book may have an attribute *title* which might have the value MEASUREMENT IN INFORMATION SCIENCE. That string of words constitutes a *term*, or attribute value. Not only can an attribute value consist of more than one term, but there can be more than one value for an attribute in a record. If an attribute of a book is *author*, then there must be provision for multiple authors, hence more than one value of the attributes of an author, such as *name*.

The definition of *record* just given does not exactly agree with the modern terminology of data management, a branch of computer science, because the information elements descriptive of an entity can be grouped and combined in many ways, not necessarily all kept together as a single contiguous whole. But we are primarily concerned with the conceptual record, the set of information about an entity, not with how it is physically stored in memory.

The terms *database* and *file* are sometimes used interchangeably, but sometimes a database is defined as a set of interrelated files. A file is a set of records. A database may be viewed as a set of information about a set of entities and may consist of more than one subordinate file. For our immediate purposes, the two terms are synonymous.

We designate a file by a name, such as A. We might want to emphasize that it is a collection of records by a usage such as $\{A_k\}$, meaning the set of records comprising file A, where k is a record index number. The count, or total number of records contained, or the *magnitude* of A, is signified by | A | or, if the context is obvious, simply by *m*.

11.4.1 Measures of Occurrence of Values

We are usually interested in the frequency of occurrence of an attribute value, sometimes the probability of its occurrence, and sometimes merely the fact that it occurred, regardless of frequency. The fact of occurrence can be viewed as a binary representation of frequency: 1 if the value occurred at all, 0 if not. Following linguistic terminology (see Section 8.2.2), a *type* is a generic symbol; a *token* is an occurrence of a type. In the preceding sentence, the symbol 'a' occurs four times. It can be treated as a single type, distinct from other types such as 'of' or 'an.' There are four 'a' tokens. Most of the symbols and measures defined in the following represent individual occurrences or sums. In practice, it will often be parameters of frequency distributions of these variables—means, ranges, standard deviations, etc.—that are used. The symbols we shall use for denoting values and frequency and probability of value occurrence were defined in Section 7.2.3. Here, we define some additional measures related to term occurrences in a database:

$bf(k)_{i,j}$ Binary term frequency of term $t_{i,j}$ in record k; taking the value, for type i of attribute j of record k, of:
1 if $t_{i,j}$ occurs in record k,
0 if $t_{i,j}$ does *not* occur in record k.

$brf(t_{i,j})$ Binary record occurrence frequency; the number of records in the range $k = 1$ to m in which $t_{i,j}$ occurs. *In information retrieval terms, this is the size of a retrieval set for the term $t_{i,j}$.*

$$brf(t_{i,j}) = \sum_{k=1}^{m} bf(k)_{i,j}$$

$ntyrec_{j,k}$ Number of term types in a record; the total number of term types occurring in attribute j, in a single record k.
$ntyset_j$ Number of term types in a set or vocabulary size of attribute j; the the total number of types in attribute j over a range of records.

$$ntyset_j = \sum_{k=1}^{m} ntyrec_{j,k}$$

This might, for example, denote the number of different author names found in a database, or of words in a set of text records, but each type is counted one per record. If a term has subordinate terms then it must be established which level is indicated.

11.4 Definitions and Terminology

$ntkrec_{j,k}$ *Number of term tokens in a record;* the number of tokens occurring in attribute j of record k. (Recurrences of the same type are counted each time.)

$ntkset_j$ *Number of term tokens in a set;* the number of tokens occurring in attribute j over the range of k.

$$ntkset_j = \sum_{k=1}^{s} ntk_{j,k}$$

where s is the magnitude of a subset of the database. If the set is the entire database, then $s = m$.

$p(t_{i,j,k})$ *Probability of occurrence of a type;* relative frequency of type i in attribute j, in record k.

$$p(t_{i,j,k}) = f_{i,j,k} / ntkrec_{j,k}$$

$pcum(t_{i,j})$ *Cumulative probability of term type;* or cumulative probability of occurrence of $t_{i,j,k}$ over the range of records, or the probability that the type occurs somewhere in the range.

$$pcum(t_{i,j}) = \sum_{k=1}^{s} p(t_{i,j,k}) = \sum_{k=1}^{s} f_{i,j,k} / ntkrec_{j,k}$$

$\bar{f}(t_{i,j})$ *Mean frequency of type $t_{i,j}$;* or average number of occurrences of the type $t_{i,j,k}$ over the full record range.

$$\bar{f}(t_{i,j}) = \sum_{k=1}^{m} f_{i,j,k} / ntkset_j$$

11.4.2 Additional Measures of Value Co-occurrence

Measures concerned with co-occurrence of values, beyond those defined in Section 7.2.3.3, are:

$bcof(t_{i,j} o t_{l,j,k})$ *Binary co-occurrence frequency in record k;* the frequency of co-occurrence of two terms, t_i and t_l, taking the value:
1 if $t_{i,j,k}$ and $t_{l,j,k}$ both occur in record k,
0 if $t_{i,j,k}$ and $t_{l,j,k}$ do *not* both occur in the record.

As with bf, this metric is independent of the actual frequency of occurrence of either term. It simply notes whether or not they have co-occurred at least once.

$rbcof(t_{i,j} \cap t_{l,j})$ *Binary co-occurrence record frequency;* the number of records in which $t_{i,j}$ and $t_{l,j}$ both occur. In information retrieval terms, it is *the size of a retrieval set* for the intersection of the sets containing $t_{i,j}$ and $t_{l,j}$.

$$rbcof(t_{i,j} \cap t_{l,j}) = \sum_{k=1}^{m} bcof(t_{i,j} o t_{l,j})$$

Note that *rbcof* could denote co-occurence withn a text, a paragraph within that text, or a sentence within a paragraph, depending on how the database defines fields and subfields.

$pco(t_{i,j,k} O t_{l,j,k})$ Probability of co-occurrence of two types; $t_{i,j,k}$ and $t_{l,j,k}$.

$$pco(t_{i,j,k} O t_{l,j,k}) = rcof(t_{i,j} O t_{l,j})/m$$

11.5
Database Measures

Here, we undertake more complete discussions of the measures introduced in Sections 7.2 and 11.3.

11.5.1 Scope

It is far more common than not for a database producer to state complete coverage of some defined domain as a goal. We are certainly not used to hearing scope stated as "most publications in . . . ," "most news about . . . ," or " records of some of our employees . . . ." The difficulty may lie in the definition (of *publications* or *employees* in these examples) rather than in the quantitative statement. Is a privately circulated research paper a publication for bibliographic purposes? Is an employee who took 30 days' sick leave 90 days ago and has not yet returned still an employee?

Where the database producer has control over the events, the goal of complete recording is more likely to be met. No one organization can control all publications in any discipline. But a company is expected to have complete control over who is added to its payroll and how and when this is done. It is inconceivable that any news organization can cover all aspects of any major world event. However, secondary publishers can conceivably record all that has been published on that event, or at least can come closer to it than can the primary publisher to covering all aspects of the event.

We must generally accept that scope is not a quantitative measure and frequently is not even a precisely defined nominal one because so often no one really knows exactly what it means. It deals with design or intent rather than the database as it currently exists. Still, the expression of scope is useful in order to understand intent. This is especially true if it makes clear what is *not* intended to be covered: that a newspaper does not cover sports news, or that a library does not collect children's material or non–English language material.

11.5.2 Attributes Represented

In a computer database, information on the attributes represented and the manner of representing them (8-digit character field, real number, . . .) is required if programs are to be executed correctly. A semantic description of the meaning of an attribute is not necessary for the computer programs and is not always provided. Hence, users may not understand what an attribute means, even if well defined in computer terms. A computer programmer can confidently assert that the biosystematic code requires n digits without understanding how the code works or what it represents.

If a person is searching a library for all red books set in Garamond type, the search will surely fail because these attributes (*color* and *font*) will rarely if ever be found in a bibliographic database. If a searcher wanted all books with FORESTRY in the title, written by an author named EDWARD OLSON, in 1981, then most retrieval systems using bibliographic databases could extract exactly these records.

In a noncomputer file, there is no absolute requirement for complete definition. Hence, whole generations of schoolchildren may mature without understanding the meaning of all the items on a library catalog card. News reporters may be told to answer the five W questions about an event—who, what, where, when, and why—but few stories are actually written to provide only this information and often some of the information is not available. That does not prevent the story from being written or published. Rarely does the text make explicit which W's are covered.

Attributes represented is an entirely nominal measure, being but a list of attributes, and applies both to the design and to the current state of the database. The complete specification of an attribute should include a definition, the relationship of the attribute to the entity it describes, and the manner of representing values, including any restrictions on values. For example, does *color* as a descriptor of a person refer to acutal skin pigmentation or to the person's race? (And if the latter, exactly what does *that* mean?) Skin coloring can change with seasonal exposure to sunshine and to state of health. Before classifying a person as DARK COMPLECTED it must, or should, be recorded or determined relative to whom. When Jamaicans call a person light complected, they do not necessarily mean Caucasian, because most Jamaicans are descended from non-Caucasian ancestors; when some British people speak of dark complected, they may have in mind a French Caucasian.

Relationships among attributes can be stated explicitly using various forms of *data declaration languages* or the more modern *entity relation maps* (Korth and Silberschatz, 1986). Brief examples of each are given in Figures 11.1 and 11.2.

```
TYPE
    NAME = RECORD
        FAMILY: STRING[20];
        GIVEN: STRING[30];
        END;
    ADDR = RECORD
        STREET: STRING[25];
        CITY: STRING[20];
        STATE: STRING[10];
        POST: STRING[12];
        COUNTRY: STRING[15];
        END;
    COURSEID = RECORD
        COURSENO: STRING[10];
        COURSENAME: STRING[20];
        CREDITS: INTEGER;
        END;
    EMPLOYID = INTEGER:

VAR

STUDENT
    STUNO: INTEGER;
    STUNAME: NAME;
    STUADDR: ADDR;
    COURSELIST: ARRAY[1..10] OF TYPE COURSEID;
    END;

COURSE
    IDENT: COURSEID;
    COURSEPLACE: STRING[25];
    COURSEINSTR ARRAY[1..20] OF TYPE EMPLOYID;
    END;

INSTRUCTOR
    INSTNAME: TYPE NAME
    INSTRID: EMPLOYID;
    INSTRADDR: ADDR;
    END;
```

Figure 11.1
An example of the structure of a database as defined using a data declaration language.

11.5.3 Selection of Entities

As noted in Section 11.3.1, there may be significant differences between the scope, or intended range, of entities and the actual content of a database. The typical cinematic portrayal of a newspaper city editor making snap decisions while in telephone contact with reporters, or being told by the evil bosses to suppress some story, exemplifies one concept of a *gatekeeper*, who decides what comes in and what stays out: what stories are

11.5 Database Measures

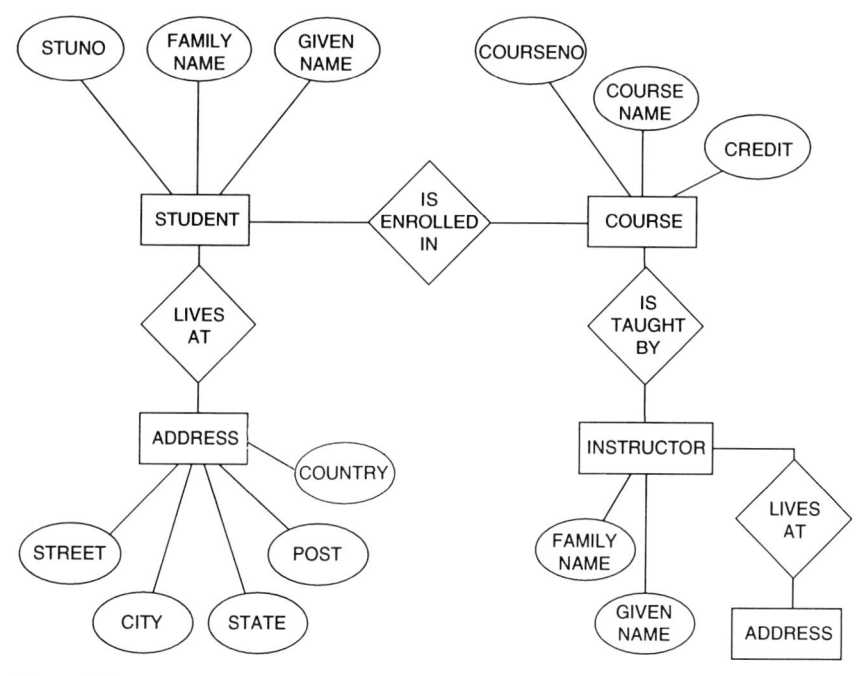

Figure 11.2
This shows how the same database design illustrated in Figure 11.1 might be presented using an entity-relation map.

printed, what books are purchased, what kind of people are hired. Another meaning of gatekeeper is a person to whom others turn to find information, whether this is a formally appointed intermediary or someone who works on an informal, voluntary basis (Allen, 1978, pp. 141–181), but this is an advisory role and does not normally control acquisition or distribution of records.

Selection of entities is a nominal measure applied to the current state of the database. Since there is usually a scope statement associated with a database, the measure of selection should be the difference between intent and reality. In most cases the only way to perform such a measurement is by comparison with another database, although Brookes (see 9.6.1) does propose a method for predicting the size of a bibliography. In many cases, we cannot make a direct comparison with the goal, because there is no quantitative measure of such concepts as *all the news about* . . . or *everything published about* . . . . We return to the most basic concept of measurement. There must be a standard in order to have measurement and there rarely is one for expressing scope statements.

11.5.4 Magnitude

Hearing that a library has 5 million volumes in its collection or that a newspaper edition consists of 200 pages, we are likely to make certain assumptions. It is reasonable to assume (but only that) that the respective contents are broad, deep, and carefully selected to meet some objective for breadth, depth, and timeliness of coverage and for quality or reliability of the records (books or articles) contained. Would any organization go to the trouble and expense of compiling such a collection *without* regard to these attributes? Would a newspaper, presumably a commercial enterprise, risk the considerable capital required to produce such an edition without making it attractive to a wide and discerning audience? ("Attractive," of course, has different meanings, hence the difference in coverage and content of the *National Enquirer* and *New York Times*.)

While the reasonable answer to these questions is *no*, that is not proof. We must accept that a measure of magnitude is just that, a count of records. Implications to quality, reliability, or other attributes must be separately ascertained. Magnitude is, normally, a ratio measure and is applied to the current database. It is or can be quite precise, although there can always be minor uncertainties: What constitutes an article in a newspaper? Does it include obituaries, advertisements, or baseball box scores? Most such questions can be resolved by careful definition before counting.

11.5.5 Timeliness

Probably the records of most files anywhere do not include the date of the record's creation or last modification. But in a growing number of cases, some or all of the individual attribute values may be dated or timed: date of a deposit to a bank account, time of a patient's blood pressure reading in a hospital, date of a grade received by a student in a university course. When such times or dates are available it is possible to compute the average age of data by comparing the recorded time with current time (in both cases, including date). *The true measure of timeliness is the elapsed time between event occurrence and the appearance of a record of it in the database.* In air traffic control, for example, it is important to know the time since the last radar contact with an aircraft. Newspapers can be evaluated, in one sense, by average age of the events reported. Unfortunately, it is more common that date of entry will be present than date of origin. The difference between date of entry and current date is not necessarily a useful measure. Something has to be known about how often new information is generated in order to know whether the date of an attribute value is a useful measure of timeliness. If dates or times of origin of information and their entry into

11.5 Database Measures

the database are available, then timeliness can be a ratio measure, but if data are lacking, it may be only ordinal.

In secondary publications and databases, such as bibliographic files, and in libraries, the only date might be the publication date of the item reported on, but not the date of the report. This, too, gives a means of measuring the timeliness of the databases—by computing the average age of records added since the last evaluation. Or, some systems do include in a record the date on which it was added to the database (which is *not* necessarily the date on which the record was created).

11.5.6 Selectivity

Attribute values may be perfectly accurate or truthful, but the attributes so badly designed or selected as to convey no meaningful information to users or searchers. So, we must consider how *completely* a set of attributes potentially describes an entity separately from how *accurately* the values of these attributes are recorded. The selection of attributes, combined with the precision and accuracy of their values, determines the discriminating ability of the database. Again, we have here a situation in which there can be no objective standard for completeness, i.e., for how well the attribute set describes the entity. Again, it is possible to compare one database with another or to compare attributes represented in one database with the considered opinion of "experts."

11.5.6.1 Specificity

If a comparable database exists, then a comparison can be made attribute by attribute: Is attribute a included in the records of database T (the one to be tested), S (the standard), both, or neither? Or, if L(AVC) is a list of *a*ttribute *v*alues (for attribute j) to be used as the basis of a comparison, then the measure is the number of items in L that are also in T, S, and T·S. Then we can define:

$L_j(T)$ List of the Values of attribute j represented in T.
$|L_j(T)|$ Number of Values of attribute j in $L_j(T)$; or the magnitude of $L_j(T)$.
$|L_j(T·S)|$ Number of Values of attribute j in common to T and S.
$relspec_j(T,S)$ Relative specificity; the number of attributes in common divided by the mean number of attributes in the two databases.

$$relspec_j(T,S) = \frac{2 \cdot |L_j(T·S)|}{|L_j(T)| + |L_j(S)|}$$

One reason for doing this kind of measurement is to be able to do some prediction on how well a retrieval system can discriminate or separate one class of records from another. If a library catalog card contains only *title, author,* and a few *subject headings* to aid the searcher, then the catalog cannot perform the task of discriminating among books whose texts mention some particular word from those that do not. Modern, online database search systems contain many more attributes than the traditional catalog card, hence they provide this discriminating ability or provide it to a much greater extent. The number of keywords in a modern catalog record enables subject discrimination of great specificity. Whether the system can perform to the satisfaction of a given user depends on that person's selection of attributes and values for use in a query.

If there is no other database or list of attribute values to compare with, then some approximation is possible by relying on users. In this case, it might be best to conduct a formal poll of users, collecting information on their background, rate of use, and opinion on whether the database provides enough specificity to allow isolation of the records wanted.

11.5.6.2 Distribution of Attribute Values

If it were possible to compile a list or frequency distribution of values of each attribute, then it would be possible to make some approximation to the size of various intersecting subsets and hence to the selectivity of the database. Such approximations depend on knowing or approximating the functional relationships among attribute values as well as the distribution of values of each attribute, e.g., the probability that a U.S. telephone area code of 201 coincides with a state code of NJ is 1. The probability that a graduate of Rutgers University (in New Jersey) has a 201 area code is high, but is not 1. Such relationships are not always known, perhaps even rarely so.

Databases can be characterized by the distribution of attribute values, as can any population. This can be done in such ways as:

1. Determining the frequency of occurrence of values of scalar attributes or of attributes that have multiple values in a record.

2. Determining the frequency of occurrence of words or strings occurring *within* an attribute value, such as words in a text field.

3. Computing values of functions of attributes, symbolized by $F(t_{i,j,k})$, where F can be any function (this is not f, the frequency) and t is the attribute value.

Examples of the use of such measures are:

1. A frequency distribution of individual values of a single attribute across the database, for example, a list of journal names and their frequencies of occurrence, extracted from a bibliographic file. Such a list would show which journals are dominant in a field and also the range from which the database producers do their selection. The same can be done for authors or

11.5 Database Measures

subject headings or for institutions reporting research, companies being assigned patents in various fields, etc.

2. Frequency distributions of individual values occurring in any of several attributes. Perhaps the most common use of value frequencies, at least in information retrieval, is in matching a natural language query (which is a text) with the text of a stored document. The usual approach is to compare the relative frequencies of terms in each text and compute some function of the two frequency distributions such as the sum of squares of the corresponding frequency differences. This is covered in more detail in Chapter 13. The words may come from the text of the stored document or its title, abstract, or subject descriptors.

3. Functions of values or their frequencies. The preceding example uses a function of frequencies in order to compare two distributions. We may also be searching for the record of any company showing a gross sales increase of more than 10% over the past two years.

Information such as that just illustrated can be used to predict search outcome and to assess the value of an attribute as a means of discriminating records from other records. The word *the* will have high frequency in almost every record. Therefore, it does not play much of a discriminating role. If every automobile in inventory is black, then *color* is a useless attribute upon which to discriminate records of cars. The inverse document frequency weight, $W_{i,k}$, was defined in Section 8.2.2 as a measure of relative frequency of a term in one document compared with its frequency in a set of documents.

In addition to the frequency of occurrence, it may be useful to assign a rank to each value, based on frequency, e.g., rank 1 to the highest frequency value. Many statistical procedures and relationships are based on rank. Rank is usually symbolized by r_i, the rank of the ith frequency in order of rank. In a frequency distribution of $f_1 = 12$, $f_2 = 6$, and $f_3 = 117$, the f_3 value has rank 1, f_1 has rank 2 and f_2 rank 3.

This kind of measure begins with simple counting, hence it can be a ratio measure. It applies to the current state of the database. Individual frequencies may refer only to selected sets of attributes or even to individual records or entities.

11.5.7 Reliability

When dealing with *reliability* we venture into the morass of grappling with the question of what is truth, or at least what is true, or what is true enough. Taking a highly pragmatic approach, we can measure truth or accuracy of attribute values by comparison of one source of information with another. Accuracy has been defined earlier (see Section 3.1.3) as meaning, in effect, how close to truth a value is. The standard by which truth is judged can only be another version of the same datum, one in which the user or measurer has some reason to have confidence.

11.5.7.1 Finding Errors

Attribute values can be compared between databases on a systematic basis or even by a panel of experts, people with a strong knowledge of the database content and the subject domain of the information contained. If the values are ratio measures, then precise deviations can be computed and statistics, such as mean and standard deviation, computed on the population of differences. If measures are nominal, then it is only possible to count instances of agreement or disagreement, not the extent of disagreement. The color of this author's eyes have been variously described as being blue, gray, hazel, and green. There is no established ordering among these values, no way to determine by how much any value is in error. These all represent different mixes of wavelengths of light, but where in the spectrum does hazel fall? In comparing two texts, say two news stories covering the same event, it is virtually impossible to tell which is true or false or even the degree to which they are either, without ascribing to one of them, or a third version, the status of a standard. But it is possible to compare the sets of names, places, objects, or concepts mentioned in the articles. Basically, this might be done by creating a third database, a list of words and phrases [the L(AVC)], identified by type (personal name, place name, event, etc.). We could then count the instances of members of L(AVC) in the two databases being compared.

The title of a best-selling novel of the 1950's was Robert P. Smith's *Where Did You Go? Out—What Did You Do? Nothing*. Most parents are familiar with such a "conversation" and most former children have probably contributed their share in such an exchange. The two questions call for values of the attributes *destination* and *activity*. The parent asking the questions is presumably looking for answers such as "I went to the park and played baseball" or "I went to Sam's house and we worked on our science project." The child may be implying "You don't really need the information you are asking for." That the answer given is not entirely factual does not mean it is a lie or wrong. It can mean as little as that two people disagreed on what kind of value would be appropriate for a given attribute.

Reporting of errors found by users is a practical source of error detection. While it is not systematic, it does represent what may be the best opinion available and costs little to acquire. It requires only that database producers and distributors make known to their users that reports of errors will be appreciated and that corrective actions will be taken as a result.

11.5.7.2 Measurement of Error

Unless there is a standard by which the contents of one database can be tested for reliability, then as a practical matter, error measurement will have to be indirect or incomplete. We can easily count content errors *reported* and we can easily count missing values. But counting values that are out of date or no longer valid or that are incorrect but unreported is not possible, in general. The measure, then, is on a ratio scale and applies to the current state of the database. It could be applied to a subset of the database, defined almost any way. A measure could appear in the form of an opinion, as in a book review, in which case it would be a nominal one.

11.5.8 Cost

Databases are sold or licensed for use in many different ways. The most obvious is that a copy of the database, whether a magnetic or optical disk or a printed book, is transferred for a fixed, predetermined price. But there may be a combination of fixed price plus royalty payments that depends on volume of sales. There may be restrictions on ownership, such as copyright protection prohibiting copying and retransfer of the information, or various forms of disclosure control that prohibit even showing the information to someone else, typified by military security classifications. These may affect value as perceived by a user. Nonetheless, the price is known, even if there may be limitations on what may be done with the product purchased or rented.

The cost of database *access* is different from that of database purchase or lease. Access implies use of telecommunication facilities, computer software and hardware, and supporting services such as training, documentation, and consultation. The method of computing cost of access varies considerably from service to service. Some charge only for *connect time,* the amount of time that a user's computer is connected to the database search computer. Some charge for connect time and then make a separate charge for each record retrieved and possibly also for each term used in a search because number of terms looked up is a measure of the work performed on behalf of the user.

That database cost is not a simple scalar number should not be surprising. Neither is the cost of a computer, house, or automobile: each involves purchase, maintenance, and add-on costs which make the actual total an obscure concept. Cost may be a ratio measure, but may only be, or partially consist of, a nominal measure where such factors as redistribution restrictions come into consideration. The measure generally would apply to the current database as a whole; prices tend not to vary from record to record.

11.5.9 Comparability with Other Databases

We cannot generally measure the entity selectivity of a database against the standard of its own scope, i.e., how well the scope, as a target, is met. We *can* measure selectivity against another, existing database.

So long as there is a means of recognizing an entity as represented in different databases, then it is possible to compute or compile for any two databases the sets A∪B, A∩B, A − B, B − A, and conceivably X − (A∪B). The last of these is the set of entities that are possible to exist but are not represented in either database and forming it requires knowing what entities are possible. A simple measure of overlap, using only numbers of records in the two databases or sets of records and their intersection, not the term counts is

overlap$_j$ Overlap; the number of records or entities in common divided by the average number of records in the two databases being compared.

$$overlap_j = \frac{2 \, |A \cap B|}{|A| + |B|}$$

This is restatement of the formula for Dice's coefficient, introduced in Section 7.2.3.4 as a measure of text similarity. Any of the similarity measures for comparing texts can be used, with minor modification, as measures of overlap, or similarity, of databases. Marczewski and Steinhaus (1958) and later Shaw (1986) used the 1's complement of *overlap* to express how different two sets are:

setdist   Set distance; the complement of *overlap* expresses how different two sets are, in terms of the entities included.

$$setdist = 1 - overlap = 1 - \frac{2 \, |A \cap B|}{|A| + |B|}$$

Tenopir (1982) gave some examples of the use of a list of attribute values to compute a measure of overlap. Clearly, such a measure of overlap has to specify by what criterion overlap is recognized, which will usually mean naming the attribute whose content determines membership in the sets or subsets being compared. It may be a combination, such as *title, author, journal,* and *date*. Even though the number of records in common may be relatively large, $|B - A|$ or $|A - B|$ may still be greater than zero, implying that both databases may be needed for full coverage. The range of both *overlap* and *setdist* is [0,1].

In addition to counting records in common or exclusively held, we can examine the actual entities exclusively held or omitted and determine their characteristics. It might be that B has a greater number of records of European origin than A, but that A has more Asian records. It might be

11.5 Database Measures

that A has everything B has and more, and costs more, but that the set A − B contains relatively low-grade information for the purposes of a given evaluator, hence is not worth the extra price. At least, this kind of computation enables that sort of analysis and decision making to be made.

Comparability or overlap will normally be a ratio measure and applies to the current state of the databases being compared. It would be possible to perform a similar comparison only on a selected subset, such as only electrical equipment manufacturers, out of a database of all public companies. Once again, comparisons must be based on an attribute set, because even identifying which entities are represented in common requires designating the attributes that identify the entities.

The creation and enumeration of these sets can be time-consuming and expensive. For example, the price of an online search to test each record of one database against another database could well exceed any value of the analysis. However, random sampling can be used and since the information sought is quite precise, standard statistical sampling procedures can be used. These enable us to make significant decisions based on a small percent of the total number of records in a pair of large databases.

> $attr_d$ *Attributes contained;* a nominal measure of the attributes of database d, really a listing of them.
> $|\,attr_d\,|$ *Number of attributes;* the magnitude of the attribute list, or number of attributes of the database.

Comparing two attribute lists may require more than counting overlap; it may also involve determining which attributes are important to the comparision. That one bibliographic database may give the page size of a journal and another not is of little importance to most users.

Comparing content is a far more complex problem. First, it is necessary to be able to compare the sets of attributes represented in each database's records. This is not necessarily trivial because quite similar attributes can be differently named in different databases. Worse is that the representation of values can vary greatly. The date of publication of a book, to be entered into a bibliographic database, might be called *date, publication date, date of publication, publication year,* etc. As is well known, the date can be represented in a variety of formats. Authors' names can be represented in a wide variety of fashions, such as: WINSTON S. CHURCHILL; CHURCHILL, WINSTON S.; CHURCHILL, W.S.; and CHURCHILL WS. Income can be represented as an integer expression (47500), as an element expressing a range (1 = 0–10000, 2 = 10001–30000, etc.), or in unconverted pounds sterling, whose relation to the dollar is uncertain unless a date or current conversion rate is given.

In bibliographic work, because there can be so much variation even in what should be such straightforward attributes as *title* and *author,* complex algorithms have been devised to compare bibliographic records and decide whether or not a match has indeed occurred. An example is the method of Hickey and Rypka (1979), designed for use with a database of over five million bibliographic records. Various attributes are encoded or truncated and the resultant values used in matching. Matches on any attribute may be exact or partial. Examples of the encoding or transformation procedures used are: For names, use a three-part code consisting of abbreviation for the attribute, length of surname, and a string consisting of first two letters of surname and first initial of given name (DONALD H. KRAFT becomes KRD and the attribute value becomes AU5KRD). For a title, use a string consisting of letters of the title numbered by the Fibonacci sequence 1,2,3,5,8, ... MEASUREMENT IN INFORMATION SCIENCE becomes MEAUMNT. All these transformations do is convert values into other values that are physically shorter and more abstract: minor variations could be carried into the transformed values. The matching, not strictly binary, nonetheless gives an approximation to the computation of the number of co-occurrences of term values from record to record.

The next level of difficulty is that of comparing content for other than identification purposes. How do we compare what one database's text attribute says about an entity with what another says? There is no generic answer to this question. There is a whole discipline of content analysis (Holsti, 1969) but there is no simple measure of the difference. If the data are numeric and well defined, then simple mathematical operations might suffice, say comparing estimates of population or of predicted high temperatures in a geographic region.

11.6
Summary

The measurement of databases, as contrasted with measurement of what is retrieved from them, has had little research attention. Magnitude, m, the number of records, is an easy and obvious metric but it carries with it the temptation to use m as a measure of quality or comprehensiveness of coverage of an intended scope. In comparing databases, A and B, the magnitude of the intersection (number of records in common), or this number normalized by dividing by the magnitude of one of the databases being compared or their mean, provides a measure of how alike they are. More information can be gained, for comparison purposes, by considering the magnitude and content of $A - B$ and $B - A$.

A number of other measures were introduced, in full recognition that they are not in common use. There is no *right* measure. Experimentation may tell which is best for a particular application. But the measures of closeness described here are entirely statistical.

References

Allen, Thomas J. (1978). *Managing the Flow of Technology: Technology Transfer and the Dissemination of Technological Information within the R&D Organization.* Cambridge: MIT Press.

Ascher, Marcia and Robert Ascher. (1981). Civilization without writing—the Incas and the quipu. In D. Crowley and P. Heyer, eds. *Communication in History. Technology, Culture, Society.* New York: Longman, 36–43.

Fidel, Raya. (1987). *Database Design for Information Retrieval.* New York: John Wiley & Sons.

Hickey, Thomas B. and David J. Rypka. (1979). Automatic detection of duplicate monographic records. *J. Library Automation*, 12(2), 125–142.

Holsti, Ole R. (1969). *Content Analysis for the Social Sciences and Humanities.* Reading, MA: Addison-Wesley.

Innis, Harold. (1991). Media in ancient empires. In D. Crowley and P. Heyer, eds. *Communication in History. Technology, Culture, Society.* New York: Longman, 39–36.

Korth, Henry F. and Abraham Silberschatz. (1986). *Database System Concepts.* New York: McGraw-Hill, 21–44.

Marczewski, E. and H. Steinhaus. (1958). On a certain distance of sets and the corresponding distance of functions. *Colloquium Mathematicum*, 6, 319–327.

Saracevic, Tefko, Paul Kantor, Alice Y. Chamis, and Donna Trivision. (1988). A study of information seeking and retrieving. I. Background and methodology. *Journal of the American Society for Information Science*, 39(3), 161–176.

Shaw, W. M., Jr. (1986). On the foundation of evaluation. *Journal of the American Society for Information Science*, 37(5), 346–348.

Smith, Richard Austin. (1962). How a great corporation got out of control; the story of General Dynamics. *Fortune*, Part 1 65(Jan 1962), 64–69, 138–184. Part 2 65 (Feb 1963), 120–122, 178–188.

Struminger, Leny. (1984). *Methodology for Evaluating Related Databases and a Computerized Algorithm for Merging Their Output.* Ph.D. dissertation. New Brunswick, NJ: Rutgers University, The State University of New Jersey.

Tenopir, Carol. (1982). Evaluation of database coverage: a comparison of two methodologies. *Online Review*, 6(5), 423–439.

12

Measures of the Retrieval Process

12.1
Introduction

The process of information retrieval is the sequence of events that, together, constitute a database search. The term is usually applied to those searches involving natural language text or its surrogates. Traditionally, measurement has been applied to preparation of a database (especially indexing, abstracting, and cataloguing), to the internals of retrieval system (IRSYS) operation, or to human–computer interface, but less so to the interaction of a user with a human intermediary who may help to prepare for a search. As we shall bring out here, this can lead to misunderstandings about what has been measured or what the measures mean.

Process measures do not deal with outcome. They do not deal with any of the various aspects of the user's satisfaction with results of a search. Process is largely concerned with mechanical actions. A rough analogy may be drawn to operation of a taxi. One set of measures of the process of operating a taxi might include fuel consumption per mile, number of accidents and their repair costs, number of traffic citations and their cost, hours of actual availability out of hours of potential availability, and gross and net revenue. But outcome might be measured by customer satisfaction or tips. Knowledge of the city, or its complement, geographic and traffic pattern mistakes, might be construed to be in either category: it can be measured by examination, it contributes to selection of a most time- or fuel-efficient route, and it contributes to customer satisfaction.

Most of the actions taken by a user, once the query has been decided upon, are manifested as commands issued to the IRSYS. If the IRSYS operates by use of menus or filling in blanks, we treat choosing a menu

12.1 Introduction

option or entering a value in a form as essentially equivalent to issuing a command. We divide process measures into two broad categories: (1) those concerned with *direct monetary cost* and *use of resources* and (2) those concerned with *time* and *numbers of commands* issued. There are two related categories of importance: (3) *errors* made and (4) *patterns of use* of the command language. The elapsed time of use of an online service can be the major factor in monetary cost. But the time of the persons involved may be an even greater cost, although rarely considered in determinations of system cost, partly because human costs vary so much from organization to organization. We shall consider patterns of language use to be primarily measures of the user, rather than of the system, hence this topic is dealt with in Chapter 14. Errors are ambiguous. From one viewpoint they reflect ease of use (or its opposite) of the IRSYS, hence may be considered measures of process; from another they represent user, not system, characteristics. We shall deal with them both here and in Chapter 14.

In general, the metrics we shall discuss, possibly excepting resources used, actually measure the process of a user using a system, not the system alone. Similarly, the database being searched plays a role in performance, albeit passive. Process measures that are completely independent of the person using the system would be specific to hardware and software, e.g., computer speed or the efficiency of a search algorithm. Possibly the only way to measure a *system* is to make a large number of measures of uses by different people with different data, where the selection of users and data are statistically controlled and their effects can therefore be minimized or eliminated.

Lancaster (1981), as noted in Chapter 11, says that an information service (IRSVCE) can be evaluated at any of six levels: cost, effectiveness, benefit, cost-effectiveness, cost-benefit, and cost-performance-benefit. He defines *effectivness* as the extent to which user needs are satisfied and *benefit* as "perceived value" of a service, recognizing that these are not always easy to keep separate. The hyphenated terms represent comparisons, e.g., of benefits obtainable for a given cost. Barraclough (1981, p. 128) suggests a reason why detailed performance studies have not been in great demand. She says that IRSVCEs or "system providers rely on the provision of extensive databases accessible to the user to sell their system. From the commercial point of view they are very successful. Users do tend to opt for the system with the most data available." This coincides with Cleverdon's view (Vickery, 1961, p. 140) that cost is the ultimate measure, seemingly because most operational services provide about the same service in terms of process. Thus, data availability, rather than IRSYS performance, is likely to have the most effect on users' attitudes toward, or procurement decisions affecting, retrieval services.

12.2
Cost and Resources Used

The price a user pays (direct monetary cost to the user) for an IRSYS varies with the mode of use, principally whether the user or using organization buys or leases a complete database for use on a local computer, or uses a remote computer operated by an IRSVCE. There is typically a high one-time price for the complete database, but few restrictions once it is procured. If a search is performed through an IRSVCE then, again typically, the user pays only for one search at a time and the cost consists of a set of charges for different aspects of the search. Both these modes have many variations on how an actual price is determined. What we are discussing here is price charged or cost to the user. This is not necessarily the same as cost to the provider of a service. A vendor's charge to customers may range from a charge below actual cost to attract customers, to cost recovery and no more, to cost recovery plus an overhead or profit charge, to "all the traffic will bear," independent of cost.

Cost is an essential variable in decision making. We need to know what we have spent in order to pay invoices and to plan the use of funds remaining. We need to predict cost in order to plan for most effective or efficient use of resources.

Components of cost generally are:

$costdb_d$ *Database cost;* the charge for a complete database, d, with few restrictions on use.

$costct_d$ *Connect time cost;* a charge for a unit of time during which a user's computer is connected via telecommunications with that of an IRSVCE.

Connect time cost is usually a uniform charge, i.e., not based on the actual computer components being used. It may be reduced by a discount based on total usage over a period of time.

$costtc_n$ *Telecommunications cost;* charge for long-distance telecommunications, using network service n, from user's location to the IRSVCE's computer; typically a fixed rate within a country, independent of actual distance.

$costrc_d$ *Record charge;* charge for viewing or retrieving a record of database d, or a portion thereof. This may be a variable depending on the format or portion of the record viewed or downloaded.

$costtrm_d$ *Search term charge;* a charge sometimes applied on each term used in a query.

$costfl_d$ *File size charge;* a charge sometimes applied to a query, based on the number of records in the database being searched.

12.2 Cost and Resources Used

Price, as defined above, is a direct cost to the user. From the point of view of the IRSVCE, or even of a user organization that buys databases and offers search service to its employees, costs beyond that of acquiring the database may be largely a matter of what computer resources are consumed by the information retrieval system in use. Of concern are the base cost of a computer, the base cost of information retrieval software (the IRSYS), and the amount of various computer resources used by the IRSYS (random access memory, hard disk memory, communication ports, etc.) There are too many cost components and the manner of allocating them is too variable to be able to list all the individual possibilities. When using any service, its price formulas should be known to the user.

Any individual's manner of use, or any organizational policies affecting use, may affect the actual cost. For example, obviously a slow user of a remote, online system will incur more costs than a faster user performing the same functions. Some institutions place a dollar limit on the cost of any one search and this may have an effect on the searcher's behavior.

As an example of a decision-making use of cost information, Boyce and Gillen (1982) proposed the following measure of the cost of printing when performing an online database search:

costpr Printing charge; a composite measure used to help decide whether to ask for retrieved records to be transmitted online to the user or printed at the IRSVCE and mailed to the user.

$$costpr = (R/S) \cdot (costct_d + costtc_n)/3600 + onpr$$

where R is the length of a record, in bytes, S is the speed of communication in bytes per second, *costct* and *costtc* are charges per hour converted to per-second charges by the 3600 factor, and *onpr* is a one-time extra charge for off-line printing that may be applied.

Then, the cost of printing a retrieved record set is the sum of this value over all records in the set. Since this measure was proposed, pricing practices as well as technology have changed somewhat. The cost of transmission may depend on the speed. What was once offline printing transmitted by post may now be that or transmission via express mail or electronic mail, making *onpr* a variable, not a constant, for any one IRSVCE.

It is useful to have the value of the total cost of a search.

costtot$_j$ Total cost of search j; the sum of all costs associated with a given search.

Unfortunately, there is no precise formula for computing *costtot$_j$* since the components of the cost vary so much from service to service and database to database.

12.3
Time and Command Rate

There are two time variables of importance: total time to complete a search and average time per command, or rate of issuance of commands. We use the term *command* to refer to actual commands in a procedural language [e.g., FIND HAZARDOUS (W) WASTE or DISPLAY S1/TI/1-3], or to choices selected from a menu, or to attribute names or values entered into a graphic user interface. All are for the purpose of directing the operation of an IRSYS. The specific measures are:

> *timelaps$_i$*   Elapsed search time; for search i. If only one search is being discussed, the subscript may be omitted.
> *timecmd$_{i,j}$*   Command time; the time required to select, enter, and execute command j of search i.

Total time devoted to a single command consists of at least three components, starting at the instant an IRSYS response to a previous command or prompt for a new one is displayed. The user needs time to read the display, which might involve a lengthy text, and then consider what action to take. The time for taking the action may range from the duration of a single keystroke to the typing of a lengthy text. Finally, the IRSYS must act upon this input, which, again, can range from a near-instantaneous action to one requiring several minutes.

Hardly any IRSYS, and few telecommunications interface programs, will provide all the detail on timing of these three steps, so that while the data are conceptually simple they may be difficult to acquire. In any case, we can define the following three time-related measures and we would probably be more interested in their mean values than their raw values:

> *timeplan$_{i,j}$*   Time to plan; to consider or think about the action to be taken as step, or command, j of search i.
> *timeent$_{i,j}$*   Time to enter the command; or to enter the selection or message for step j of search i.
> *timeproc$_{i,j}$*   Time to process; the time for the IRSYS to process the command or message entered at step j of search i.

Having the three measures available enables us to pinpoint the cause of most major delays in system operation. The exact boundaries between any two of these elements may be difficult to define. For example, slowness in entering data may be due to slow manipulation but also to pausing between keystrokes to consider the remainder of the input message. Delays imposed by the telecommunications network may not be separable from system or user delays. But these tend to be minor, over a large number of cases. If, in spite of definitional difficulties, all three measures are available, then of course:

$$timecmd_{i,j} = timeplan_{i,j} + timeent_{i,j} + timeproc_{i,j} \qquad (12.1)$$

It has been our experience (Meadow, 1983) that the number of commands used during a search is so highly correlated with the elapsed time of a search as to make the use of both measures largely redundant. One use of time data, other than as a general average, is to identify those commands or sequences that seem to give the user the most trouble. These are likely to be the ones consuming the most time.

Time data can be used for more or less raw assessments of system or user speeds, but also to identify which commands or situations consume the most time and, by implication, cause the most trouble for users or require extra attention in training. Time data are not always available, but in their place we can often use:

$nocmds_i$ *Number of commands used;* in search i.
$ratecmds_i$ *Rate of command entry;* in search i.

$$ratecmds_i = nocmds_i / timelaps_i$$

12.4 Errors

The most difficult aspect of using error occurrence as a measure is defining an error. Here, since this chapter is devoted to measurement of the system or service, not the user, we will define an error as a command or user input which is rejected by the system. Such rejections add to user cost without increasing value received. There are times when syntactically valid commands may be treated as errors, for example, when a search command generates a null set, but that is an action more indicative of how the system is used than how the system performs and is left for Chapter 14. The rate of occurrence of errors, in general, may be indicative of how well the system was designed for its user group.

Retrieval systems do not always provide a diversity of error messages, those used by the system to respond to invalid commands, nor are they always comprehensible to users (e.g., the infamous "Syntax error"). We can compile the frequency of occurrence of each type of error message sent by the IRSYS. Hence,

$errcnt_{i,j}$ *Number of occurrences of an error message;* for message type j in search i.

$errrate_{i,j}$ *Rate of occurrence of an error message;* for message type j in search i.

$$errrate_{i,j} = errcnt_{i,j}/nocmds_i$$

$totalerr_i$ *Total number of errors;* the combined number of occurrences of all error types in search i.

$$totalerr_i = \sum_{j=1}^{J} errcnt_{i,j}$$

where J is the number of possible error types for the IRSYS under study.

Just as the commands taking the most of a user's time may be indicators of difficulty in using the language, the error count by type of commands can help designers find system problems or trainers discover weaknesses in training programs (Shi, 1990). Furthermore, such factors as the time between an error message and the next user input may be an indirect measure of its comprehensibility to the user, but it may also measure the difficulty of rectifying the error.

12.5
Summary

With the measures defined in this chapter, we can compute the cost of use of an IRSYS and measure in several ways the rate at which persons use the system's commands or equivalent and make errors. These measures must all be used with caution because all, to some extent, measure how a user uses the system, not the system as an entity unto itself. Furthermore, we have indications, although not proofs, that user decisions that might be expected to depend upon performance skill may depend upon data retrieved from a given system. Thus, to measure the *system*, not the *users*, would require careful statistical control of the selection of users for study, the data involved, and types of uses or applications.

References

Barraclough, Elizabeth D. (1981). Opportunities for testing with online systems. In Sparck Jones, Karen, *Information Retrieval Experiment*. London: Butterworths, 128–135.

Boyce, Bert R. and Edward J. Gillen. (1982). Is it more cost-effective to print on- or off-line? In: Danuta A. Nitecki, Online Services, *RQ*, 21(2), 117–120.

Lancaster, F. W. (1981). Evaluation within the environment of an operating information service. In Sparck Jones, Karen, *Information Retrieval Experiment*. London: Butterworths, 105–127.

Meadow, Charles T. (1983). *A Study of User Adaptation to an Interactive Information Retrieval System*. Research Report OCLC//OPR/RR-83/6. Dublin, OH: OCLC Online Computer Library Center, Inc., 28.

Shi, Xirong. (1990). *Usage of the Online Catalogue at the University of Toronto: An Analysis of Computer Monitoring Data*. Research report. Toronto: Faculty of Library and Information Science, University of Toronto.

Vickery, B. C. (1961). *On Retrieval System Theory*. London: Butterworths.

13

Measurement of Retrieval Outcome

13.1
Introduction

In Chapter 10 we quoted van Rijsbergen's view of information retrieval effectiveness as "the ability of the system to retrieve relevant documents while at the same time suppressing the retrieval of non-relevant documents" (1981, p. 32). If we accept this view then the basic measure of how well a system performs in terms of achieving the desired outcome is the extent to which it retrieves records that are wanted by the user and does not retrieve records unwanted by the user. However, the situation is not quite that simple. We must consider who is making the judgments and on what basis. For example, a user might be content with a few useful items, even if embedded in a larger number of nonuseful ones, or a few very good ones may be better than many somewhat good ones. Or, the user may insist on retrieving *all* records that meet the specifications of the query and *none* that do not. Since *all* is the goal of relatively few searchers, we are justified in assuming that users want a retrieval set that satisfies their information need without undue cost in reading extraneous or redundant texts. This, in effect, is the point Cleverdon made about economics being the dominant consideration.

There is also the question of whether the extent to which a record meets a user's needs is a constant. Can the extent of the "goodness" vary over time and by comparison with different records, thus increasing or decreasing as other records are viewed? A truly useful measure should reflect variations in what the user wants and should recognize that records meet users' needs to a variable degree, not on a binary basis, and that this degree can change with time.

13.1 Introduction

13.1.1 Concepts of Relevance and Utility

The principal measure in common use for assessing outcome is *relevance*, a term having many definitions (Saracevic, 1975; Cooper, 1971; Bookstein, 1979; Wilson, 1973) which tend to cluster around two meanings: relevance as *relatedness* or *aboutness* and as *utility* or *value*. Two records (or a record and a query) are related in the first sense if they are *about* the same thing. This can happen because they have the same or a similar entity or because they have attribute values in common. Thus, if one record is about George Bush and another about Bill Clinton then they are related because the two entities (Bush and Clinton) have held the same high office. A record about Bill Clinton may be related to one about William Clinton because these may be the same person. But, there is no assurance in either case, at least until the records are read. Two records concerned with different entities may be related if, in a text attribute, many words occur in both records, but not in all records. For example, *the* will occur in virtually any English language text, but *osteoporosis* will not; hence its co-occurrence in two records carries a greater implication of a subject relationship between them.

Utility refers to the value or usefulness of a record to its reader. Value can have many meanings (see Section 1.5.4.), such as useful for background reading or containing the exact solution to a problem. *Relatedness* is a measure with a possibly high degree of intersubjective agreement, at least among judges with backgrounds in the same subject domain. However, the *value* of a record to one person cannot easily be judged by another, hence we would expect far less intersubjective agreement on this variable.

Generally, a record must be subject related to the information need statement (INS) of its requester to be considered subject relevant, which is virtually a truism. But relatedness does not necessarily imply value. Nor does value imply relatedness. People find valuable information on subject B when searching for subject A, a phenomenon often called *serendipity*. The very act of browsing allows a user to recognize information of value in other contexts than that in mind when the search was started (Bates, 1989). On the other hand, a record may be closely related to a query or other record, in the subject sense, but the user may already have seen the record, or may not trust or understand it, or may find it too simplistic. Conversely, a user may be ecstatically happy with a single record out of a large number retrieved, if it completely solves a pressing problem, resulting in complete satisfaction but possibly a low average rating of retrieved records.

When we refer to two records being related, this can mean two records in a database or a query and a record of the database. The various methods and procedures for determining relatedness are the same for any two texts.

Relevance, per se, is not really an outcome measure. It measures the relationship between a question and an answer. But it serves as the basis for most measures of outcome which tend to deal with the likelihood of retrieving relevant records or the ratio of relevant to nonrelevant records. We shall discuss relevance more fully in the following. For now, let us consider the question of *to what* a record is relevant. In Chapter 10 we described the progression from a user or a user community sensing the absence of some information, to a person approaching an information system or service and expressing an information need, to a formal query being addressed to an information retrieval system. The recognition of absence of information has been called an *anomalous state of knowledge,* or ASK, by Belkin (1980) and a *gap* by Dervin (1977). The statement a user makes to a retrieval system or service is what we call the *information need statement,* or INS. The statement made to a retrieval system is the *query*. If the purpose of the IRSYS is to separate relevant from nonrelevant materials, we must consider to what they are relevant, which is equivalent to determining who is judging relevance and with what version of ASK, INS, or query the retrieved records are compared. All three of these representations of need are subject to change, possibly as a result of the search process.

Many databases contain only references to or descriptions of documents which are not, themselves, in the database. These are sometimes called *surrogate records*. Library catalog cards or their modern electronic equivalents are examples. Beghtol (1989, p. 19) points out that relevance judgments on such records are measuring "perceived *potential* worth of the document to which the reference points." The "ultimate usefulness" can be assessed only by examining the actual document.

When a query is presented to an IRSYS, in a formal, symbolic language, using such expresssions as FIND AUTHOR = SMITH? AND ACID RAIN, most retrieval systems will assume that AUTHOR denotes an attribute of a record, because it appears to the left of the = sign. They will assume a default attribute for the undesignated second value (ACID RAIN) and will then look for exact matches of records with this query. An exact match means that the first five characters of the author's name are SMITH (the ? indicating any string of zero or more characters) and that the character string ACID RAIN occurs somewhere in the default attribute, such that the string is preceded and followed by a blank, punctuation mark, or the start or end of the attribute value. That is, ACID RAIN is accepted but ACID RAINS will not be, as the query was written. Barring a programming error or an error in the composition of the record (e.g., the author's name should properly have been spelled SMYTH) *all retrieved records are relevant to the query* based on the *rsv* or matching function. Relevance in this sense means that subject attribute values are found in both records. With only the information given, it is not possible for a computer to determine the *value* of a record retrieved in response to this query. Indeed, the concept of a computer judging the value of a record to a query has little meaning.

If the person with the question, the user, has expressed it to an intermediary, then that expression is what we called an INS. The intermediary translates the INS into the query. This translation, like most, will be imperfect. Therefore, when records are retrieved in response to the query, they are not necessarily subject-relevant to the information need. It may well happen, perhaps even is likely to happen, that if the intermediary is asked to judge the outcome, he or she would rate records according to subject relatedness, whereas the user would be concerned only with value relatedness. In other words, the user asks what good the record is to himself or herself, rather than whether or not the record should have been retrieved by a well-formulated query to meet the stated information need, which is all the intermediary has to work with. The INS might become a record. One form of dialogue between user and intermediary may involve the intermediary writing down his or her understanding. This can then be used for formal comparison with database records. Some IRSYS allow a natural language query to be presented directly to the IRSYS, which would then translate it into whatever form is necessary to control retrieval operations. In this case, judgment of outcome will be based on the INS because the query into which it was translated by the IRSYS may never have been seen by users or other judges.

To compare retrieved records with the ASK is difficult because it may never have been articulated. Although both relatedness and value judgments can be made with respect to it, it may well be that no two people share the same sense of what the ASK is, hence of the relevance of records to it, under either meaning of relevance.

13.1.2 Uncertainties in Relevance Measurement

The various uncertainties in understanding what information is needed or in how to express the need are part of the reason why relevance measurement is so problematic. Other reasons are that relevance judgments tend to be relative, there is no established standard for comparison; that a user may judge a record highly relevant until a more relevant one is seen and then change his or her mind about the first one; or that the user is asked to judge on the basis of a surrogate, not the actual document.

We have five questions to contend with when measuring relevance: (1) What goal, objective, or standard is to be used? (2) What measurement scale should be used? (3) Which meaning of relevance is to be used by a judge? (4) Relative to what is relevance being measured? and (5) Is the judgment to be treated as constant, or is the relationship between an INS and a record constant? Before trying to answer these, let us consider some derivative measures which are the ones commonly used.

13.2
Measures Derived from Relevance

In one of the earliest studies of measurement of information retrieval systems, Vickery (1965) proposed the following model of retrieval outcome. All records are assumed classified as either relevant or not, for a given query using a binary *rsv*. Then, records are either retrieved or not in response to the query. Newer systems may retrieve a set, compute an *rsv*, and inform the user of how many were retrieved and what the measurement of relatedness to the query was, but older systems simply retrieved records or did not. Then, a two-by-two matrix or *contigency table* is formed, as in Figure 13.1, where rows represent the number of records retrieved or not retrieved and columns represent the number relevant or not. The letters *a–d* represent the number of records with the indicated attributes; e.g., *a* is the number that were both relevant and retrieved.

Based on this, we can define the following quantities, first proposed in slightly different form by Kent et al. (1955):

P *Precision;* the ratio of the number of relevant records retrieved to the total number retrieved.

$$P = \frac{a}{a + b}$$

In case $a + b = 0$, i.e., no records are retrieved, a value of 1 could be assigned to P (See 13.5.4.) P can be measured by having the searcher rate

	Relevant	Not Relevant
Retrieved	a	b
Not Retrieved	c	d

Figure 13.1
The contigency table showing possible retrieval outcomes based on binary relevance measures.

13.2 Measures Derived from Relevance

each retrieved record, on a binary scale, the number of relevant records retrieved being a and the number of irrelevant ones retrieved being b.

R *Recall;* the ratio of the number of relevant records retrieved to the number of relevant records existing in the database.

$$R = \frac{a}{a + c}$$

R poses a more difficult measurement problem than does P. If some relevant records have never been retrieved, how do we know they exist or how numerous they are? The value c can be measured indirectly by doing a search, then broadening the query and seeing if any more relevant records are retrieved. This process can be repeated until no more, or only an insignificant additional number, are retrieved. Then, count the number now retrieved but missed by the initial query. This is not a perfect method of measuring for several reasons. There may be more than one way to broaden a query, and the end user may not agree that additional records are relevant. Another, somewhat similar approach, has been to use a small experimental database, small enough that some group of judges can be familiar with its contents and can *know* what records were missed. This has the disadvantage of limiting the database to a possibly unrealistic size and assumes the judges have the same basis for judgment as the end user.

N *Noise* or *false drop rate;* the ratio of nonrelevant records retrieved to total retrieved; the complement of precision $(1 - P)$.

$$N = \frac{b}{a + b}$$

Whatever procedure is used to measure P can also measure N.

F *Fallout;* the ratio of nonrelevant records retrieved to total nonrelevant records, or the proportion of the unwanted records that were nonetheless retrieved.

$$F = \frac{b}{b + d}$$

O *Omission factor;* the portion of relevant records not retrieved; the complement of R. Like recall, O requires measurement of the number of relevant records not retrieved.

$$O = \frac{c}{a + c}$$

S *Specificity;* the proportion of nonrelevant records not retrieved, or rejected. This measures the ability of a system to reject what we want to reject.

$$S = \frac{d}{b + d}$$

The most commonly used of these measures are precision and recall (Baker and Lancaster, 1991), and it seems to be implicitly assumed by most of those who use it that searchers have the goal of maximizing both P and R, retrieving all relevant records and only relevant records. The importance of goals in measuring relevance is discussed in Section 13.4.

This assumption that the goal is always to maximize P or R is not necessarily correct. Relatively few users of a library, for example, really want *everything* on a subject. For most users, most of the time, only a few records are really wanted and an indication that a large number, say hundreds or thousands, of records have been retrieved is likely to lead to a quick redefinition of need. Similarly, a retrieval set consisting of one or two extremely valuable records, among a total of 10 or 20, may mean a low value of P but by no means an unhappy searcher.

A searcher can always improve P by making another iteration of a search, if necessary by asking only for the relevant records by exact title or accession number. Thus, P measures only the precision achieved up to a point. It does not measure the potential of the query or the information need statement. Another way to consider precision is that it, or its complement, N, measures the amount of work necessary to achieve a pure result of only relevant records. If the retrieval system fails to produce only relevant records, it is left to the searcher to do the work necessary to reach this goal. In case $a + b = 0$, or no records are retrieved at all, we might artificially assign the value 1 to P, hence 0 to N. Although the search has failed to find useful records, no work is necessary to separate relevant from nonrelevant ones. (See Section 13.5.4.)

A related measure, defined by Blair (1980), is the *futility point,* i.e., the point in a search at which a user decides it is no longer worth trying to improve results. While the reaching of this point can be readily observed—it is quickly followed by a log-off or similar command—its value lies in seeing what situation has brought the user to it. How many cycles, or how large a retrieval set, or what average relevance or utility has made the user feel that further work is not worth the effort? Cooper (1970) and Kraft and Lee (1979) propose attention to the more general concept of measuring how long a search is or when a termination point is reached, not necessarily just a futility point. We shall discuss these in Chapter 14 as measures of user performance.

The definitions of precision and recall can be modified for use of multivalued or nonbinary scales for relevance. If relevance is not binary then we cannot use the contingency table of Figure 13.1 because we cannot divide the database into mutually exclusive relevant and nonrelevant sets. What we can do is use the relevance measures to decide which records to retrieve. This assumes the IRSYS is making at least the first relevance judgment. The user then retrieves all records above a certain threshold, presumably applies his or her own relevance judgment (reflected by changing the threshold, revising the query, or changing term weights), and repeating the process.

We can then use a measure such as

$|R|$ *Quantity or amount of relevance;* to provide an indication of how much relevant material has been retrieved.

$$|R| = \sum_{k=1}^{a} r_k$$

as an approximation to the measure of the quantity of relevance retrieved. Here, r_k is the relevance assigned by user or system to record k and a is the number of records retrieved. This may also be expressed as

$$|R| = \Sigma \, r_k \\ r_k \geq RT$$

where RT is the relevance threshold for retrieval. This is the essence of probabilistic retrieval (see Section 10.1.2.2). When Tiamiyu and Ajiferuke (1988) proposed retrieving a quantity of relevance, this implied use of system-assigned relevance values.

13.3
Measuring Relevance

We shall now discuss the five questions raised in Section 13.1.2 as a guide, not a prescription, to an experimenter or observer collecting relevance data.

13.3.1 Goals, Objectives, and Standards

We have no accepted standard by which to measure relevance or its derivatives, that is, no value such that we can say that the average relevance of a retrieved set of records should be x. Instead, we can use the user's goal or objective in conducting a search if it has been stated. There is no point measuring against an arbitrarily assumed standard of, say, *precision* = 0.8 if the user feels, in advance, that a level of 0.6 is satisfactory. Users, unfortunately, rarely express a goal in terms of relevance. We can, however, identify a reasonable set of possible goals, any of which might be used in an experiment, which are not all-inclusive and which are not mutually exclusive:

Maximum recall. The user's goal is retrieval of all relevant items. Ideally, $R = 1.0$.

Maximum precision. The user's goal is retrieval of relevant items only. Ideally, $P = 1.0$.

Maximum separation of relevant from nonrelevant. This goal is one of minimizing retrieval error, i.e., of retrieving nonrelevant items or failing to retrieve relevant items. Ideally, $N = 0$ and $O = 0$.

Maximizing the amount of relevance. Insofar as relevance weights can be assigned to all records of a database, this goal is to retrieve the maximum sum of weights. It is not the same as maximum recall, because maximum recall may result in retrieval of low-relevance items.

Satisficing. In our opinion, this is probably most people's goal most of the time. Satisficing is the quest for a *good* outcome, at a reasonable cost; it does not demand optimality of any variable.

Minimizing cost for a minimum level of outcome. This is a common goal for institutions offering service to a wide range of people without cost recovery. It aims to provide a decent result, but limits the cost of each effort, sometimes in money terms, sometimes time.

13.3.2 Measurement Scale

Historically, relevance has been measured on a binary scale—a record is treated as either relevant or not relevant to a query or INS—and this scale is still often recommended by researchers. Eisenberg and Hu, for example, say that "the dichotomous relevance judgement is . . . a fundamental element in information science research and system evaluation" (1987, p. 66). They are not necessarily advocating dichotomous measures, but indicating their widespread use. But it almost challenges intuition. Given three texts retrieved in response to a query, are we to say there can be no ordering among them, that although all may be relevant, no one can be more relevant than the others?

How, then, should relevance be measured? The next most commonly used scale is an ordinal one, such as: OF NO RELEVANCE, OF MINIMAL RELEVANCE, MODERATELY RELEVANT, VERY RELEVANT, EXTREMELY RELEVANT, which can be encoded numerically as 0, 1, 2, 3, 4. Note that there is no meaning to negative relevance, hence the middle value is not a neutral one; all values range from zero relevance up. The difficulty with the scale is that people tend to use the upper end of such a range. We see the same phenomenon in school grades, where grade escalation leads to mean scores in a range that once indicated above-average performance. Thus, the equal-interval scale suffers mostly from the manner of its use, plus its inability to measure the difference between "extremely relevant" and "the complete solution to my problem, worth millions to my company."

An alternative to the equal-interval scale is an n-ile scale (see Section 5.3.4). This kind of scale does allow for recognizing extreme differences in value. But, again, peoples' actual usage has been known to ignore definitions and use the rating as an ordinal scale with equal intervals. Thus, if used for employee ratings, it could well be (and in this author's experience has been) that most employees are rated as better than 70% of all others, reminiscent of Garrison Keillor's fictional Lake Wobegon, where all the children are above average. Use of n-ile scales requires skill and experience on the part of users.

Yet another possibility is to use an unequal-interval scale, but not defined as an n-ile scale. For example, we might assume a range of 0–1000 for relevance scores, but ask users to specify one of the subranges 0–10, 10–100, 100–1000. Again, this meets the criterion of allowing for extreme differences but is not likely to be used properly due to lack of user experience.

Saracevic et al. (1988) measure utility as a composite of time spent on a search, monetary cost, an estimate of whether the time was worth the cost, the extent to which the outcome contributed to the resolution of the problem leading to the search, and the user's satisfaction with results. Although these are not all cleanly separable, they do bring into consideration the many factors that contribute to *value*.

13.3.3 The Meaning of Relevance Being Used

We have discussed two primary meanings of relevance. There can be others. It is not the function of the science of measurement to specify which should be used; this is a decision of the person doing the measurement and depends on the precise objective of the experiment or study being designed. But the traditions of measurement science do dictate the importance of being sure that all concerned share and understand the definition being used. Conventionally, research reports seem not to state explicitly (a) which definition was used or (b) that those asked to make relevance judgments were informed of and understood which definition was to be used.

It is *not* necessary to choose between the major meanings; it is necessary only to differentiate between them. While relatedness and utility have some similarity of meaning, they are also different. Both can be measured in an experiment or field study, but this would demand even greater care in assuring that respondents understood the measures. Indeed, Saracevic et al. (1988) report that they did just this.

13.3.4 Relevance as a Relative and a Variable Measure

Not only is relevance multivalued (not binary), but experimental evidence (Eisenberg and Hu, 1987; Boyce, 1980) and intuition both indicate that the value of relevance, for records retrieved by a given information need, may vary during the course of a search. Given a set of n records that users have been shown for evaluation, the values assigned may differ depending on the order in which they are viewed. This appears to mean that the relevance of a record is influenced by the relevance of others. Seeing one of higher relevance may lower a previously assigned value. Then, different users may make different judgments, further indicating that relevance is not a constant.

What a user expects may also enter into the variability. Expecting little, the user may be impressed by the first few records seen, but become progressively less so as it becomes apparent that there are many midrange relevant records, causing a reassessment after this fact becomes known. Becoming familiar with the content of a database also may affect the user's judgment, reflecting such possibilities as overall disappointment with content or results that are better than expected.

Some research projects have used the evaluation of retrieved records by a panel of subject experts to decide what records should have been retrieved in fulfillment of an information need (Sparck Jones, 1981; Salton and McGill, 1983, p. 164). This assumes that the combined opinions of the experts define "truth," that is, define the true set of records relevant to a stated subject or a reasonable outcome of a search. Then, users can be evaluated in terms of their ability to write queries that achieve the "true" or reasonable set of records or the system can be evaluated in terms of its ability to produce the true results. *System* in this context can mean the system of database production, which includes the creation of record content, or the system of query interpretation and retrieval. This approach suggests that the relevance of a record to a query is constant or nearly so. But that assumption implies that, for a given statement of information need, all users would, or should, interpret the relatedness or value of records the same way. This means that two users, even with the same sense of relatedness and value, but having a different history of previously reading texts they have now retrieved, might still rate the values equally.

Harter (1992) described the concept of *psychological relevance,* which essentially is the idea that relevance judgments by users are personal or individual, contrary to the older theory that experts would tend to agree on what is relevant to a query. Of course, this also implies that users are judging utility or value, rather than topicality or pertinence, where the latter is more likely to be constant across different judges.

Tiamiyu and Ajiferuke (1988) suggest that records are related to each other and these relationships affect relevance measures. The relationship can be one of *substitutability* if there is significant duplication of informational content. The relationship is one of *complementarity* if two texts discuss different aspects of a subject and the two together provide more relevance than the two considered separately. These relationships help explain why relevance judgments are not constant, why a newly retrieved text that is on the very subject of a previously retrieved one may be perceived as of little value, or why a complementary one may receive a very high rating if tied to a previous text.

Barry (1994) suggests that we can identify factors in any relevance judgment that are beyond topical appropriateness. Twenty-three categories of relevance criteria were identified by interviewing end users as to how their decisions on particular documents were made. These, she suggests, can be grouped into seven classes. Criteria pertaining to content (but not topic, e.g., clarity), criteria pertaining to experience and background, criteria pertaining to beliefs and preferences, criteria pertaining to other information sources, criteria pertaining to sources of documents, criteria pertaining to the document as an entity (e.g., its cost), and criteria pertaining to the user's situation (e.g., relationship with the author).

In summary, there are at least two meanings of relevance in fairly common use: subject relatedness or topicality and value or utility to the user. There are three variations on the basis for making relevance judgments: relatedness to the formal query, to the INS, or to the ASK. When a user may encounter and judge a given record more than once during the course of a search, there is the question of which relevance judgments to accept, for either definition or basis for comparison. Assessments can vary as a function of time elapsed, cost, content of other records seen, etc. Finally, there is the question of whether the assessment of relevance can legitimately vary from individual to individual, i.e., whether relevance is a personal, subjective matter or objective truth.

13.4
System-Computed Relevance, Ranking, and Feedback

Ranking records means to put them in order based upon their probable relevance to a user. To perform such ordering requires that we have a measure capable of representing the user's opinion of relevance. We do not expect a perfect representation, but hope to improve on random ordering or ordering by an attribute such as *date*. It is not surprising that measures proposed lean toward the *relatedness* meaning of relevance. Predicting value to a user remains an unsolved problem. Being able to rank on the basis of relevance means the IRSYS does not simply make a retrieve or no-retrieve decision. It rates *all* records, then retrieves the number the user wants to see. This moves us away from binary relevance judgments.

13.4.1 Ranking

There are many possible ways to rank the members of a retrieval set. We could, for example, take the attribute values used in a query and count the number of times each occurs in a record, then rank the records according to the total number of query term occurrences. Or, use the number of query terms represented in the record, regardless of their individual frequency of occurrence. The principal drawback of these is that terms that occur very frequently in a database will receive high rankings. Their use does not provide a good discriminating technique.

The inverse document frequency weight, $W_{i,k}$, can be used to add extra weight or importance to terms that occur often in some records, but are not generally of high frequency across the database. Words like EDUCATION in an educational database or COMPANY in a directory file of corporations are likely to have high frequency. But words like CHEMISTRY in the former database or DISTILLING in the latter are probably of low frequency in general, but if they are of high frequency in any one record a user may assign extra weight to show that they are important in separating these documents from others. If each term is assigned a weight based on this measure, the record weight can be the sum of the Ws for each term. Then, the user is presented with an initial set of records and their weights and may browse as much as desired.

Losee (1991) suggests a method of using system-determined relevance to affect the retrieval decision for each record considered. He defines the costs of retrieving and of not retrieving each record. These measures can then be used to set a threshold for deciding which to retrieve. Cost of retrieval is defined in more detail as

> *costret* Cost of retrieval; the cost of retrieving a record, whether or not relevant.

$$costret = P(\text{Rel} \mid a) \cdot C_{\text{Ret,Rel}} + P(\text{NonRel} \mid a) \cdot C_{\text{Ret,NonRel}}$$

> where a is a set of attributes of the record to be used for decision making, $P(\text{Rel} \mid a)$ is the probability that a record with attribute set a is relevant, and $C_{\text{Ret,Rel}}$ is the cost of retrieving a relevant record.

13.4 System-Computed Relevance, Ranking, and Feedback

The cost of retrieving a relevant record is, presumably, the mechanical cost or the IRSVCE charge for a record. The cost of retrieving a nonrelevant record is compounded by the added burden to the user of retrieving unwanted material—an extremely difficult value to compute.

costnonret   *Cost of nonretrieval;* the cost of not retrieving a record, whether or not it is relevant.

The cost of nonretrieval of a nonrelevant record is, presumably, zero or close to it. (Possibly, the cost of searching must be factored into this.) But the cost of not retrieving a relevant record brings up computational difficulties similar to those of retrieval of an irrelevant record.

$$costnonret = P(\text{Rel} \mid a) \cdot C_{\text{NonRet,Rel}} + P(\text{Nonrel} \mid a) \cdot C_{\text{NonRet,NonRel}}$$

An IRSYS with access to this information would decide to retrieve if *costret* < *costnonret*; i.e., the cost of retrieving is less than the cost of not retrieving. System-determined relevance is not the same as user-determined relevance. If the system estimates relevance, this is only a step in the retrieval operation. The user must still make the ultimate decision.

Bookstein's *retrieval status value (rsv)* (1983) can be used to weight each record in terms of its closeness to a query. The *rsv* can then be used to rank records according to their likelihood of relevance to the user. One form of *rsv* is *expected cost*, which considers both the probable relevance and the cost of retrieval in arriving at a ranking of records. This is defined as:

Expcost or *ec(a)*   *Expected cost of retrieval of a record.*

$$ec(a) = \Sigma \; f(r,a,h) \cdot costret(r)$$

where a is as defined above, r is the computed relevance, h is the history of retrieval and evaluation of the record in question, f is the particular function in use, and *costret(r)* is the cost of retrieval of a record with relevance r. At one time, a would have been a set of index terms or descriptors, but in fact it can be any set of attributes. None of these variables can be determined easily and objectively. But it is possible to use approximations, especially since the alternative is usually no system help in ranking retrieved records.

13.4.2 Computing the Quantity of Relevance Retrieved

Tiamiyu and Ajiferuke (1988) introduce the concept of a *total relevance function*. They point out that records retrieved in response to a query may interact with each other in three ways: no relationship, substitutability, or complementarity. Substitutability means that one record provides essentially the same information as another, or adds no new relevant information. Complementarity means that one record provides information that enhances the value of another.

Unfortunately, no proven method of measuring the total relevance function is given, but one might be calculated by asking a user for each record the degree to which it is relevant to the INS and then whether it is substitutable (adds no new total relevance) or is complementary (increases the provious total). The authors present the function as bounded in maximum value; it is not really clear that adding new, complementary records to a collection does not continue to increase the relevance or value of the set.

Hence, a simple total of relevance ratings, where complementarity adds relevance to the total but substitutability does not, might provide a basis for comparison between iterations of a search. It is not likely to provide a meaningful absolute value.

13.4.3 Relevance Feedback

The concept of relevance feedback is simple. (Salton and Buckley, 1990). A user rates retrieved records and these ratings are used to revalue terms which can then be used to revalue records in a subsequent retrieval. One such method (Salton and McGill, 1983, pp. 142-143) assumes that an original query is a set of weighted terms:

$$Q_0 = (q_1, q_2, q_3, \ldots q_n)$$

where the q_i are weights of individual terms. A revised query adds to or subtracts from these weights on the basis of weights assigned to retrieved records. Thus:

$$Q_1 = Q_0 + 1/R \sum_{\text{rel}} D_i - 1/N \sum_{\text{nonrel}} D_i$$

where R is the number of records deemed relevant after the first query, N is the number deemed not relevant, and D_i and D_j are the sets of term weights for relevant and nonrelevant records, respectively. Summation is over the set of relevant or nonrelevant records.

This and similar methods are based upon the notion that records are relevant or nonrelevant and that it is the terms used that make them so. Clearly, this implies the relatedness meaning of relevance.

13.5
Measuring the Question

Saracevic et al. (1988) use the following categories of decription of a question, by which they mean the central concept of what we have called the information need statement or the query. They use the word *query* to mean the aspect of the subject being searched for, whereas we have used this term to mean the interpreted INS as presented to an IRSYS. The following measures are more of the semantics than the statistics of the question text. Values are taken from judges; i.e., they are subjective. *Subjective*, here, simply means determined by a subject or participant in an experiment or study. It has no pejorative implication.

Domain, the subject class of the question. A nominal scale measure.

Clarity, how well understood the question is to judges, measured separately in terms of *semantic clarity* (meaning of terms) and *syntactic clarity* (relation of terms to each other). Measured on a Likert scale of 1 to 5, 5 meaning *clear*.

Specificity measures the judge's feeling of the relative broadness of definition of terms. Separate values are recorded for terms from the subject and query part of a question. Again, a scale of 1 to 5 is used, 5 here meaning *narrow*.

Complexity, essentially a measure of the judge's opinion of the effect of the number of terms in a question. It is evaluated separately for each subject concept, on a 1 to 5 scale, 5 meaning *high complexity*.

Presupposition, a measure of the extent to which a question contains implied concepts. For example, a question asking "Where is . . ." implies that its subject exists, but verifying existence is not stated as part of the question. Again, a 1 to 5 scale is used, 5 meaning *many suppositions*.

These authors used an overlap measure to compare questions or queries posed by two different searchers. We have, again, changed the symbols for internal consistency.

$asymovrlp_{1,2}$ or $S_{1,2}$ *Asymmetric overlap;* the ratio of the number of terms in common in two texts or sets to the number of terms in one of the texts.

$$asymovrlp_{1,2} = \frac{|S_1 \cap S_2|}{|S_1|}$$

where S_1 and S_2 are sets. Note that $asymovrlp_{1,2}$ is not is not the same as $asymovrlp_{2,1}$. The measure is not symmetric. The relationship of text 1 to text 2 is not the same as that of text 2 to text 1. Dice's coefficient (see

Sections 7.2.3.3 and 11.5.9) is essentially the same measure, but uses the mean of the magnitudes of S_1 and S_2 as denominator, thus giving a symmetric measure.

Although this attempt to measure questions and the differences in how various people interpret them is welcome, there is too little comparative information to know how successful it is.

13.6
General Measures of Outcome

The concept of a general measure of outcome is that there be a single scalar measure descriptive of the outcome of use of an IRSYS, that is, a measure of the extent to which an IRSYS or IRSVCE satisfies a user's information needs. If such a measure can be found for a single instance of use, then the statistical parameters of a frequency distribution of such measures, over a wide range of users, can measure the system's or service's overall capability. Several such measures have been proposed, all based on relevance. Before considering them in detail, let us consider whether such a single metric is desirable and what it is capable of measuring.

13.6.1 Definition of the System to Be Measured

When a set of records has been retrieved and a judgment made on the quality, suitability, relevance, or utility of the records, the following events will have occurred: a user has expressed an information need or presented an information need statement (INS); this has been rendered into a query, the statement actually presented to the retrieval system; the IRSYS searches a database and retrieves some records; judgment is passed by someone on these records. The judgment expresses the relationship between a record and the query or INS. If this judgment is to be used for any other purpose, such as to evaluate the IRSYS, then great care must be taken to delineate exactly what is being evaluated and what controls may be necessary on other factors or variables.

For example, it is very tempting to test a new IRSYS by inviting a set of experimental subjects to conduct searches where the topic or INS is given to them. The subject then converts the INS to a query which the IRSYS executes and the output records are judged. Retrieved records are evaluated and the question arises whether the set of judgments constitutes a measure of performance of the IRSYS. There is no clean answer to this

13.6.2 The Relationship between Precision and Recall

Precision and recall are sometimes shown as related by approximately

$$P = K/R \qquad (13.1)$$

or
$$PR = K$$

where K is a constant. This is presented graphically in Figure 13.2.

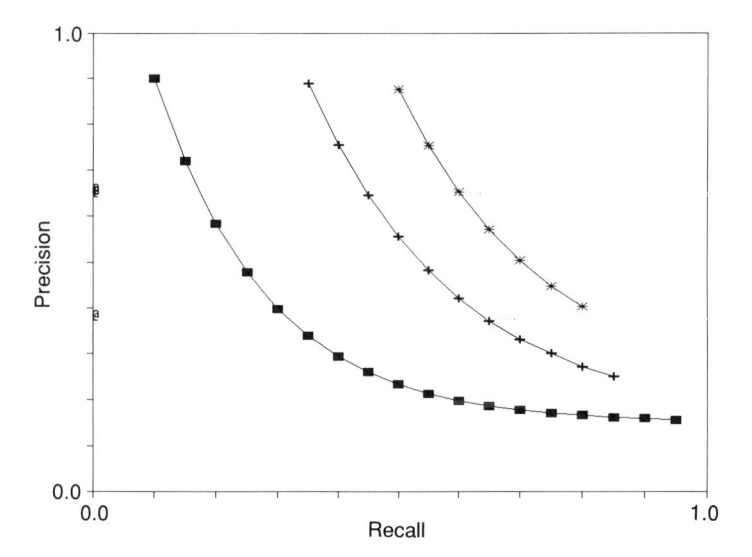

Figure 13.2
The generally assumed approximate relationship between precision and recall. There is no precise mathematical formulation; the curves will vary by user and circumstances of use.

That there is approximately an inverse relationship seems obvious. If the result of a query shows high precision, it is likely to have been achieved by not retrieving borderline records, which omission tends to lower recall. That is, when the selecting person or mechanism is in doubt, the doubted record is omitted on the assumption that the end user might see it as nonrelevant. In order to eliminate all extraneous or nonrelevant material from the retrieval set, it is probably necessary to be severely restrictive on what is retrieved and this tends to mean that some definitely relevant material will probably not be retrieved. Similarly, to ensure high recall, meaning that no, or very few, relevant records are missed, some irrelevant ones will probably be in the retrieval set, and this will lower precision. These are related to Type I and II errors in statistics, a false acceptance or rejection of a hypothesis. High recall tends to imply false acceptence of some records; high precision tends to imply false rejection of some. For a given query, the searcher can modify it to produce either higher precision or higher recall than characterized the original retrieval set. As these variations are made, the successive recall and precision values are precisely related as in Eq. (13.1). The second form of the equation eliminates the appearance, in the first form, that P is a dependent variable, R an independent one. They are mutually interdependent.

That the P-R relationship is an inverse one is still debated (Harter, 1986, p. 201). In fact, all we can be reasonably sure of is that as one variable decreases, the other tends to increase.

Salton and McGill (1983, p. 168) and Gordon and Kochen (1989) have pointed out that the actual curve is more like that of Figure 13.3, which shows that, as a value of 1.0 is approached for either P or R, the other goes to or nearly to zero. A recall value of 1.0 can always be achieved, by retrieving the entire database, but possibly at the cost of driving precision to near zero. A precision value of 1.0 can be approached by retrieval of only a very small number of records, with consequent very low recall. As we have noted previously, a value of $P = 1.0$ can be guaranteed by performing one extra query iteration, calling only for the specific relevant records of the previous iteration. The real question seems to be how close we can come to high values of either, without excessively low values of the other. See Section 13.6.4 for a discussion of zero retrieval.

Gordon and Kochen proposed the following variation on Eq. (13.1) (their original symbols have been changed to correspond with other usage in this book)

$$P = R \cdot p(rel)/p(retr) \qquad (13.2)$$

where $p(rel)$ is the probability that a randomly chosen record is relevant and $p(retr)$ is the probability of a randomly chosen record being retrieved.

13.6 General Measures of Outcome

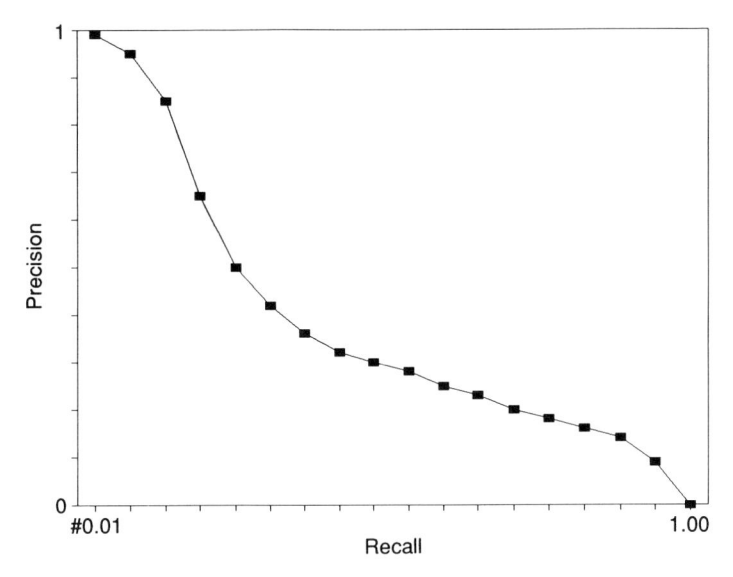

Figure 13.3
The precision–recall relation according to Gordon and Kochen, demonstrating that an extreme value of either P or R sends the other toward zero.

Then,

$$p(rel) = \frac{a + b}{m} \qquad (13.3)$$

and

$$p(retr) = \frac{a + c}{m} \qquad (13.4)$$

where a, b, and c are the Swets values and m is the magnitude of the database searched ($m = a + b + c + d$). Then

$$P = R \cdot \frac{a + b}{a + c} \qquad (13.5)$$

or

$$P = R \cdot \frac{\text{number retrieved}}{\text{number relevant}} \qquad (13.6)$$

Equations (13.2)–(13.6) use the two probability variables: $p(relevance)$ and $p(retrieval)$. If these are interpreted as providing information about the database as a whole, as it relates to a single query, then the fraction by which R is multiplied in (13.6) is a constant, hence the R-P relationship is a straight line. Since most surmise and experimental data suggest it is not a line, the retrieval and relevance probabilities cannot be fixed for the query–database combination as a whole and we are back to having no readily computable relationship. Missing from any version of these equations is a measure of the user: how skillful is the user at separating relevant from irrelevant records? If the user is not skillful, then does a measure based on that person's query and evaluation of outcome measure performance of the system or the user?

13.6.3 Overall Measures

To have a single measure of overall effectiveness of a retrieval system would be convenient and desirable. Several have been proposed to date which tend toward some form of averaging of P and R. Cooper (1973), van Rijsbergen (1981), Robertson and Hancock-Beaulieu (1992), and Salton (1992) provide reviews of work that has been done. Since users do not tend to try a series of variations of their queries in order to test the limits of recall and precision (unless engaged in a formal experiment), we can never be completely sure what the distribution of values would be.

Here are several measures of overall outcome or effectiveness that have been proposed, originally using different names and symbols:

Meadow (1973) proposes

effect1 or *EM*   Effectiveness (Meadow).

$$EM = 1 - \frac{\sqrt{((1-P)^2 + (1-R)^2)}}{\sqrt{2}}$$

which assumes average values of P and R and measures the average distance from the supposed ideal of 1.0 for both, i.e., complete retrieval of all relevant records and only relevant records.

B. C. Vickery (in Cleverdon et al., 1966) suggests

effect2 or *EVi*   Effectiveness (Vickery).

$$EVi = 1 - \frac{1}{2/P + 2/R - 3}$$

where, again, P and R are average values over a series of retrieval operations. As either P or R approaches zero, the denominator of the fraction approaches a very large number, the fraction a small number,

13.6 General Measures of Outcome

and *effect2* approaches 1.0. If both P and R approach zero, indicating a very poor search, *effect2* again approaches 1.0, not the value we would intuitively assign to a search with zero value of P and R.

Heine (1973) offers

effect3 or *EH* Effectiveness (Heine).

$$EH = 1 - \frac{1}{1/P_i + 1/R_i - 1}$$

where the subscript i indicates that the measure applies to an individual measure of P and R.

For a measure of a complete search or set of searches, the *effect3* values would be aggregated. Actually, the other two measures could be treated similarly, i.e., the base measures taken from individual variations of a query and the mean value used for the overall measure. *effect3* gives results very similar to those of *effect2* and has the same difficulty with extreme values.

van Rijsbergen (1979, pp. 173–176) proposes a more general expression of which he shows the Vickery and Heine measures are special cases. van Rijsbergen's measure is:

effect4 or *EVa* Effectiveness (van Rijsbergen)

$$EVa = 1 - \frac{1}{\alpha(1/P) + (1 - \alpha)\cdot(1/R)} \qquad (13.7)$$

where α is the relative importance or weight assigned by the user to *precision*, on a scale of [0,1]. Implicit is the assumption that the importance of *recall* is the complement $(1 - \alpha)$ of that of *precision*.

In this function, if $\alpha = 1$, i.e., the user places the full weight of importance on *precision* and none on recall, then *effect4* $= 1 - P$. Conversely, if full weight is placed on *recall*, then *effect4* $= 1 - R$. Again, we should have preferred that a value of 1 indicate perfect performance and 0 total failure, but these values can be achieved by eliminating the "1−" portion of the function.

Unfortunately, there is no evidence to show that users have a fixed importance rating for P or R. In fact, users may ignore P if they have reached the futility point, or they may treat retrieved sets as serving only to help find appropriate terms to define a subsequent set. They may also set and then change P and R goals during the search.

Shaw (1986) shows that these measures derive from a basic measure of the amount by which one set of retrieved records differs from another set relevant to a particular query. The meaning of *query* tends to vary from author to author. Shaw's measure is similar to that of Marczewski and

Steinhaus (1958). Again, slightly changing the symbols for consistency, Shaw's measure is

effect5 or *ES*   *Effectiveness* (Shaw).

$$ES = 1 - \frac{1}{1/2P + 1/2R}$$

which is very close to Vickery's measure. Shaw also shows that this metric can be derived from van Rijsbergen's if α has the constant value 1/2, in the latter's meaning implying equal emphasis on recall and precision.

A difficulty with all these measures is that they do not recognize that what is measured is someone's *opinion* of the relevance of records retrieved. They do not directly measure the performance of the retrieval system or service. The most we can use them for is to be able to say that, for a given set of users, the system was able to perform at this level. An untrained user with a good system can give the same outcome as a poorly designed system in the hands of a trained user.

Goffman and Newill (1966) propose a measure of effectiveness by analogy with medical screening tests. In medicine, *sensitivity* is the probability that a test will classify as positive a subject who, in fact, has the condition being tested for. The meaning of *specificity* (See also 13.2) is the probability that a subject will be declared negative who does *not* have the condition. An ideal test has the value 1 for both measures, i.e., always identifies positives, always rejects negatives. Real life is rarely so ideal. These authors define the following measure, using the Swets model (but our symbols):

effect6 or *EGN*   *Effectiveness* (Goffman & Newill).

$$EGN = \frac{a}{a + c} + \frac{d}{b + d} - 1$$

The first term, here, is *recall* and the second *specificity* as defined in Section 13.2. Since these measures both have a range of [0,1], their sum would be in the range [0,2]. Goffman and Newill subtracted 1 to give a range of [−1,1]. This measure requires knowing the relevance of nonretrieved items, which may be approximated but usually not accurately observed.

13.6.4 The Case of No Retrieved Relevance

Almost all the foregoing measures assume that some records are retrieved, i.e., that | Retrieved set | > 0 or $a + b > 0$ (something is retrieved) and $a > 0$ (something relevant is retrieved). In practice, this does not always happen. Since a and b cannot, by definition, be negative, the critical condition is whether or not anything relevant is retrieved. If nothing is retrieved, then, of course, nothing relevant is retrieved.

What are the values of such measures as P and R when $a = b = 0$? Technically, if a search results in a null set, i.e., $a + b = 0$, the computation of P is indeterminate, $0/0$. If $a = 0$ but $b > 0$, then $P = 0$. Indeterminate values can be set by definition or by examining what happens as the zero value is approached. If a and b are both very small, say between 1 and 3 records, then the ratio of a to $a + b$ is around 1.0. Since these numbers are integers and we are assuming they are both small, their ratio cannot be very large, as could be the case if either were a fraction or if either were a very large integer. We are inclined, then, to assign a value of 1 to P when $a = b = 0$.

A justification for this decision is that the complement of precision $(1 - P)$ measures the amount of work needed to separate relevant from nonrelevant records. If there are no records, no work is needed. Hence, $1 - P = 0$, or $P = 1$. This definition may prove useful to experimenters whose programs abort when computing P for the case of no relevant retrieval.

13.7
Summary

Measures of outcome have traditionally been measures of the relationship between queries or information need statements and retrieved records. *Relevance* is the most frequently used basic measure and, from it, the composites *recall* and *precision* are computed. A good bit of controversy surrounds the use of these measures because they involve human judgment, which has been demonstrated not to be constant over time or over different sequences of viewing records, and because relevance is a *relative* judgment. If a database has relatively little to offer on the subject of a query, evaluations of some records may be high because they are the best there are, but they would be lower if viewed in the context of a better-suited database. Furthermore, there is the issue of what component or set of components of a retrieval system or service is evaluated if the relevance judgments are applied to the "system." Is it the computer software, the database, or the skill of an intermediary?

These sometimes disquieting questions do not invalidate the use of relevance or its derivatives. They place more demands on the users of the measures for careful definitions and controls.

References

Baker, Sharon L. and F. Wilfrid Lancaster. (1991). *The Measurement and Evaluation of Library Services.* Arlington VA: Information Resources Press, 284–287.

Barry, Carol L. (1994). User-defined relevance criteria: An exploratory study. *Journal of the American Society of Information Science* 45(3):149–159.

Bates, Marcia J. (1989). The design of berrypicking techniques for the online search interface. *Online Review,* 13(5), 407–424.

Beghtol, Clare. (1989). Retrieval effectiveness: theory for an experimental methodology measuring user-perceived value of search outcome. *Libri,* 39(1), 18–35.

Belkin, N. J. (1980). Anomalous states of knowledge as a basis for information retrieval. *Canadian Journal of Information Science,* 5, 133–143.

Blair, Daid C. (1980). Searching biases in large interactive document retrieval systems. *Journal of the American Society for Information Science,* 31(4), 271–277.

Bookstein, Abraham. (1979). Relevance. *Journal of the American Society for Information Science,* 30(5), 269–273.

Bookstein, Abraham (1983). Outline of a general probabilistic retrieval model. *Journal of Documentation,* 39(2), 63–72.

Boyce, B. (1980). Beyond topicality. A two-stage view of relevance and the retrieval process. *Information Processing and Management,* 18(3), 105–189.

Cleverdon, Cyril W. and M. Keen. (1966). *Factors Determining the Performance of Indexing Systems.* Vol. 2. Bedford, U.K. Cleverdon, 49.

Cooper, W. S. (1970). On deriving design equations for information retrieval systems. *Journal of the American Society for Information Science,* 21(6), 385–395.

Cooper, W. S. (1971). A definition of relevance for information retrieval. *Information Storage and Retrieval,* 7, 19–37.

Cooper, W. S. (1973). On selecting a measure of retrieval effectiveness. *Journal of the American Society for Information Science,* 24(2), 87–100.

Dervin, B. (1977). Useful theory for librarianship: communication, not information. *Drexel Library Quarterly,* 13(3), 16–32.

Eisenberg, M. and X. Hu. (1987). Dichotomous relevance judgements and the evaluation of information systems. *Proceedings of the ASIS 50th Annual Meeting.* Medford NJ: Learned Information Inc., 66–70.

Goffman, William and Vaun A. Newill. (1966). A methodology for test and evaluation of information retrieval systems. *Information Storage and Retrieval,* 3(1), 19–25.

Gordon, Michael and Manfred Kochen. (1989). Recall–precision trade-off: a derivation. *Journal of the American Society for Information Science,* 40(3), 145–151.

Harter, Stephen P. (1986). *Online Information Retrieval. Concepts, Principles, and Techniques.* San Diego: Academic Press.

Harter, Stephen P. (1992). Psychological relevance and information science. *Journal of the American Society for Information Science,* 43(9), 602–615.

Heine, M. H. (1973). Distance between sets as an objective measure of retrieval effectiveness. *Information Storage and Retrieval,* 9, 181–198.

Keillor, Garrison. From the the radio series *A Prairie Home Companion,* National Public Radio System.

Kent, Allen, M. M. Berry, F. U. Leuhrs, and J. W. Perry. (1955). Machine literature searching VIII. Operational criteria for designing information retrieval systems. *American Documentation,* 6(2), 93–101.

Kraft, Donald H. and T. Lee. (1979). Stopping rules and their effect on expected search length. *Information Processing and Management,* 15(1), 47–58.

References

Losee, Robert M. (1991). An analytic measure predicting information retrieval system performance. *Information Processing and Management*, 22(1), 1–13.

Marczewski, E. and H. Steinhaus. (1958). On a certain distance of sets and the corresponding distance of functions. *Colloquium Mathematicum*, 6, 319–327.

Meadow, Charles T. (1973). *The Analysis of Information Systems*, 2nd ed. Los Angeles: Melville Publishing Co.

Robertson, S. E., and M. N. Hancock-Beaulieu (1992). On the evaluation of IR systems. *Information Processing and Management*, 28(4), 457–466.

Salton, Gerard and Chris Buckley. (1990). Improving retrieval performance by relevance feedback. *Journal of the American Society for Information Science*, 41(4), 288–297.

Salton, Gerard and Michael J. McGill. (1983). *Introduction to Modern Information Retrieval*. New York: McGraw-Hill.

Salton, Gerard (1992). The state of retrieval system evaluation. *Information Processing and Management*, 28(4), 441–449.

Saracevic, Tefko. (1975). A review of and a framework for the thinking on the notion in information science. *Journal of the American Society for Information Science*, 26(4), 321–343.

Saracevic, Tefko, Paul Kantor, Alice Y. Chamis, and Donna Trivison. (1988). A study of information seeking and retrieving. I. Background and methodology. *Journal of the American Society for Information Science*, 39(3), 161–176.

Shaw, W. M., Jr. (1986). On the foundation of evaluation. *Journal of the American Society for Information Science*, 37(5), 346–348.

Sparck Jones, Karen. (1981). The Cranfield tests. In K. Sparck Jones, ed. *Information Retrieval Experimentation*. London: Butterworths, 256–284.

Swets, J. A. (1969). Effectiveness of information retrieval methods. *American Documentation*, 20(1), 72–89.

Tiamiyu, Mutawakilu A. and Isola Y. Ajiferuke. (1988). A total relevance and document interaction effects model for the evaluation of information retrieval processes. *Information Processing and Management*, 24(4), 391–404.

van Rijsbergen, C. J. (1981). Retrieval effectiveness. In Sparck Jones, K., ed. *Information Retrieval Experiment*. London: Butterworths, 32–43.

———. (1979). *Information Retrieval*, second edition. London: Butterworths.

Wilson, Patrick. (1973). Situational relevance. *Information Storage and Retrieval*, 9, 457–471.

Vickery, B. C. (1965). *On Retrieval System Theory*. London: Butterworths, 165.

14

Measurement of Users

14.1
Introduction

We mentioned in Chapters 12 and 13 that for all but the most basic measures of system performance or outcome it is difficult to separate measures of the system from measures of people using the system. We have the complementary problem if we wish to study users, alone. Normally, we can observe behavior related to database searching only while users are engaged in searching, and this means engaged in using a particular system, with a particular database.

In this chapter we first introduce some measures of users in the sense of who they are, not what they do or how they do it. Then we go on to performance measures that are closely related to users and are fairly objective, not based on an observer's opinion. Some of these have already been discussed in previous chapters. Finally, we look at outcome measures which are concerned with achievement or assessment of achievement and which are highly subjective.

14.2
User Characteristics

The purpose of measuring user characteristics separately from the search process is to be able to use them to predict performance or to explain differences in performance. If, for example, people with characteristic a were seen to perform differently from those with characteristic b, then these characteristics could be used to predict how a user would act during a search or to determine how best to approach instruction, which presumably affects how that person will act. At one time, there was almost a fad to look for facile measures that might explain differences in search performance. These included age, gender, intelligence, and major subject studied in university.

Assumptions were made that younger people would be more adaptable to the new mode of searching (via computer vs. manually) than older ones, that men might be more "logical" than women, that more intelligent people would perform better, and that scientifically trained people would be better equipped to cope with artificial languages and symbolic logic than those with arts or humanities background. Intelligence might be the easiest of these to put to rest, since information retrieval is an activity that is generally performed by well-educated people, hence the intelligence spread is likely to be much smaller in the population of searchers than in the general population. (As database searching becomes more generally available, for example, through public libraries, we may see a greater spread of intelligence and may be able to find a way to use it in predicting performance or assisting users. Its measurement will probably always be controversial.) Age and gender did not work well as discriminators of good performance, and subject matter failed also as musicians and literature scholars began to become computer users.

Then came a period of interest in cognitive style, that is, in measuring a person's thought style. Intuitively, this seems the ideal measure with which to predict or explain performance but it has never worked out. The world still lacks a reliable, generally accepted method of measuring this extremely complex variable (Hockey, 1990; Huber, 1983). We can, however, make some other biological and psychological measures relatively easily. Their value in this context remains uncertain. Then, there are measures of experience, knowledge, or skill, factors that seem important and for which there is some statistical proof of value. There are also what may be called organizational factors, for example, an organization's rules as to how much money can be spent on any given online search. Finally, we are beginning to be able to record and measure users' mental models, their personalized images of the systems they are using.

We still lack generally agreed upon measures and we certainly lack a reliable set of data describing the characteristics of various types of users, a set which can be drawn upon by new researchers. Borgman (1989) and Bellardo (1985a,b) have published reviews of various measures of users.

14.2.1 Biological and Psychological Measures

Included in this group are *age, gender, intelligence,* and *cognitive style.* As noted, the first two have never been proved to be of significance in predicting performance. They can, of course, be easily collected, since most people will give the values readily.

Intelligence is usually measured by standardized tests (Wolman, 1985) even though the originator of such tests cautioned against treating intelligence as a single entity (Gould, 1981, p. 151). It does correlate fairly well with grade average and number of years of education, which it is often used to predict. But the correlation is not 1 and many people might resent the use of their grades to measure their intelligence. Also, as already noted, the people who use information retrieval services tend to be well educated (university graduates with a fairly high probability of an advanced degree) who may be assumed, by this fact, to be of high intelligence in the sense implied by the standardized tests. The relatively small differences among the high educational achievement segment of the population may not be enough to make use of intelligence a measure of significance.

Cognitive style, again, is a measure of how a person tends to think. If fully understood and measurable, it would surely be among the most valuable factors in predicting performance. But we have a double problem with it. First, there is no proven, accepted measure. Second, if there were, users would have to submit willingly to testing and be motivated to perform well. Taking such a test to provide a credential for admission to a university or award of a fellowship seems motive enough. If the purpose of an examination is simply to provide data for someone else's experiment, participants may not be highly motivated or serious about their effort.

14.2.2 Education and Aptitude

Borgman (1989) and others have shown high correlations of information retrieval performance with "scientific" training or aptitude, but until recently query languages were rather mathematics-like, requiring the use of symbolic logic. Hence, the ability of scientists to learn these languages is not unexpected.

14.2.3 Experience and Knowledge

There is an old aphorism that ten years of experience can be ten years of ever new experience and new learning or one year of new learning repeated ten times. *Experience* is an easy measure to collect and use, but it may lack precision. Ten years of experience do not always lead to the same or even to a similar outcome in terms of the performance of a person with this amount of experience. But its actual measurement is straightforward. It requires no tests or other elaborate measuring procedures. When a person volunteers his or her own length of experience, the value can be reasonably presumed to be accurate.

But as we try to use this variable as a basis for prediction of performance we may find it not serving as an accurate basis for prediction. Meadow

14.2 User Characteristics

et al. (1994) propose the following taxonomy, of experience that encompasses knowledge, skill, and purpose in using an information retrieval system. A similar taxonomy was proposed by Chignell et al. (1990).

1. *System Knowledge.* [K]nowledge of a system does not, in itself, make a person a skilled user, any more than a knowledge of ballistics makes a person a skilled hunter. Yet, a lack of systems knowledge will almost certainly inhibit acquisition of information-seeking skill. Aspects of system knowledge are:
    1.1 *Knowledge of the hardware and software components,* essentially the internals, typically best known by the computer programmers and system designers who design, implement, or maintain information retrieval software. This includes knowledge of formal database or file organization and physical structure.
    1.2 *Knowledge of the command language,* essentially the interface between user and system, the linguistic means by which a user conveys to the system what is wanted. We mean command language in the most general sense; it includes menu-based systems and graphical user interfaces (GUI). This involves knowledge *about* the language.
2. *Information-Seeking Knowledge and Skill.* Knowledge of how to search is a broad area of knowledge, bounded at the low end by the minimal "information literacy" necessary to function in today's world and unbounded at the upper end, and including the knowledge and skills possessed by experienced professional intermediaries. Components include:
    2.1 *Skill in identification, clarification, and elicitation of information needs.*
    2.2 *Knowledge of a variety of information sources and information-seeking strategies.*
    2.3 *Knowledge of* how to use *(the mechanics of using—in contrast to knowledge "about" the language) command languages* for query formulation and iteration.
    2.4 *Skill in use of techniques for examination, extraction, and evaluation of information.*
3. *Subject Domain Knowledge.* We apply the term *subject domain* to the subject matter of a search, including:
    3.1 *Knowledge of the subject field.* Knowledge entirely outside the context of information retrieval systems and databases. It is medical knowledge for the medical researcher, law for the lawyer, etc.
    3.2 *Database knowledge.* Knowledge of the databases actually or potentially in use. It includes knowledge of how attributes are

represented, such as how to represent an author's name in a bibliographic file, or how to use a controlled vocabulary such as a subject heading system. This could be considered a form of system knowledge, as well. There is considerable overlap with knowledge of formal structure, which includes such information as type of field (character, numeric, . . .), field length, or structure, such as the rule that a name is represented as <lastname>, ",", <firstname>, " ", <initials>. But one can know this kind of information well and yet not understand how to read a chemical ring structure or to use the biosystematic code.

4. *Searcher's Role.* The role is primarily a matter of whether the search is being done on behalf of the actual searcher or by a searcher on behalf of someone else. Persons searching for themselves are able to make value judgments that cannot be made by an intermediary on behalf of an absent end user.

   4.1 *End user searcher.* This searcher's primary role is to find information for his or her own use. The true meaning of end user is the person who will evaluate and use the information resulting from a search. If this person is also the searcher, then we have an end user searcher.

   4.2 *Intermediary searcher.* This searcher's primary role is to serve others. If the searcher is not the ultimate consumer of the information, then he or she may not be the person best suited to assess its value to the end user. What is important about the role of acting for another is whether or not the searcher can make content judgments on behalf of the other.

5. *Retrieval Goals.* An important aspect of searching is what the searcher is trying to accomplish. Of concern is the goal in terms of completeness (recall), precision, and magnitude of the retrieval set. This can be expressed in such terms as "a few good items," "everything pertinent," or "high precision." End users may have this goal fixed in their minds but they may not articulate it well, sometimes insisting on "everything," with no concept of what that may really mean. Intermediaries may be heavily influenced by institutional policy on expenditures in time or money per client.

6. *Searcher's Individual Characteristics.* Although our work did not specifically address individual searcher differences, these may be important to understanding search outcomes and are included as a category without extensive commentary. See work by Bellardo (1985a), Borgman (1989), Fidel (1987), and Saracevic and various others (1988, 1990) for discussions of user personality styles, abili-

ties, training, mental models, experience, and biases. While we recognize that it is only the rare experiment or field study in which all these attributes can be accurately measured, we also feel that lack of consideration or control of such specifics can contribute otherwise unexplained variation in data. (Meadow et al. 1994)

If we could measure all these attributes we could distinguish between a person with much search experience but little subject knowledge, a system designer who understands completely how an IRSYS functions but rarely uses it for a real (vs. a program test) search, and a subject domain expert whose knowledge of any aspect of the system is minimal.

Recording these measures is an uncertain undertaking. Knowledge can be measured by an examination or may reasonably (but not infallibly) be inferred from experience in specific kinds of activities. The use of an examination, which can provide finer distinctions on knowledge or skill than can experience alone, introduces some behavioral problems. Many people will readily volunteer to participate in an experiment or field study to investigate user behavior, but might balk at being asked to take a test of knowledge in their own professional field. Examinations that do not particularly affect persons' lives or challenge their professional qualifications might not be taken seriously (Carlisle, 1974).

14.2.4 Organizational Factors

Organizational factors are policies imposed on users that may affect their behavior as searchers. Examples are rules requiring charging of search services to end users or rules limiting the amount that can be spent on any one search. Such rules may have the effect of forcing a quicker search, without full use of feedback and iteration.

Fenichel (1981, pp. 26–27) found that those who worked with an imposed time or spending limit showed different behavior from those who did not, even if the rules were not in force during a test period. On the other hand, completely free searching may encourage more experimentation and browsing, activities not always characteristic of for-pay searches (Bates, 1989).

There are no established ways to characterize institutional restrictions. Within the context of any study, those restrictions that may come into play, either in the activities to be studied or in the habit-forming backgrounds of experimental subjects, should be ascertained for possible use as a variable partially determining user behavior.

14.2.5 Users' Mental Models

A mental model of an entity is a person's own internal image of that entity—what it is, how it is constructed, how it works. We often find that a person's mental model does not correspond to objective reality and that, indeed, *objective reality* may be nothing more than someone else's mental model.

Those of us who are teachers like to think that when we explain an entity, such as an IRSYS or an arithmetic procedure, students will correctly perceive it, will form a mental model consistent with the "reality" being taught (i.e., the teacher's view). But such is not always true. Students *do* sometimes perceive entities differently from how teachers or writers think of them and the subsequent student behavior can appear random, "wrong," or inexplicable to the teacher. Burton and Brown (1978) reported on such problems in the teaching of arithmetic to children. An example is a child who learns the "carry" operation in addition as meaning that any carry is brought to the leftmost position of the numbers being added. Thus, in adding 127 and 246, the "correct" action is to add the units column, 7 and 6, and carry 1 to the tens column. But some children learn to carry the 1 all the way to the leftmost (here, hundreds) column. Such behavior appears wrong to most teachers and, since the carry does not occur in all problems, may seem a random error. Thus, the error in the student's mental model might not be readily perceived. Arithmetic tests do not ask about models: they pose problems to be solved.

Borgman (1983) taught two sets of subjects how to do database searching, intending to impart to one group a particular model and not to impart it to the second group, in an attempt to see the behavioral differences caused by different models. Differences were not detectable, partly because it was not possible to compare the actual models held by the two groups, since only the model *intended* for the first group was known.

An important question for the designer of any artifact, hard or soft, is what the user's image or model of the artifact is or will be. To ask the question outright does not guarantee an answer, nor does receiving an answer guarantee that it actually represents the respondent's mental model. If a person does not understand the artifact or is inarticulate or inhibited, the verbal model may inaccurately portray the mental model.

It would be desirable to compare the models held by two persons or by two groups and even to measure by how much they differ. There is not, at the present time, any generally accepted, calibrated measure of the difference between two mental models. Indeed, there is no generally accepted method of recording a mental model.

One method that has shown some promise, as a means both of recording and of measuring differences between models, is the *repertory grid technique* (Kelly, 1970). Basically, this involves selecting a set of elements which are attributes or components of an entity. Then, a person is asked to select two elements on the basis of similarity and a third which is different from the other two, on the same basis. If the entity were a computer, elements might be: *random access memory, secondary memory, read only memory, video display, keyboard,* etc. Two elements that may be seen as similar are *random access memory* and *video display*. One that is different is *read only memory* (ROM). The basis for these relationships is permance or volatility: the first two are temporary forms of information storage and will be lost if power is lost. The third element, ROM, is permanent. Thus, a *construct,* or basis for comparision, is permanence and we may assign a scale ranging from highly volatile to permanent and then rate every element on this basis. The set of elements, constructs, and ratings then collectively constitute one form of representation of a mental model. Because the ratings are numeric, on an ordinal scale, it is possible to make numeric comparisons of average ratings, and thus of how different two people are or two groups of people. Latta and Swigger (1992) report some work toward this end, but more investigation and application is necessary.

14.3
User Performance Measures

We can adapt some of the same measures used for systems to the measure of users of the system. The reason is that most such measures describe a *user using the system.* Proper statistical controls and sampling procedures can enable the effects of system variations to be removed from a study of user variations. We have divided a recommended set of measures into two broad categories: those that are relatively mechanical and those that primarily describe the vocabulary and command language usage of the user. As with measures of the system, those considered first are measures of *process,* how the user goes about the task of searching. In Section 14.4 we consider the results, or outcome, obtained.

14.3.1 User Process Measures

The general model of a search proposed originally by Penniman (1975) was that a user performing a search progresses through a sequence of states. A state is the condition of having issued a particular command or type of command. A search is in the *display* state if the most recent command called for display of a record. Typically, the user begins a search by selecting a database (BEG), then looks up some terms or words in a dictionary or thesaurus (DIC), creates some sets defined by presence or absence of terms (SET), and displays the content of one or more records (DSP). There are other (OTH) types of commands, such as one for setting the margins on a printout or displaying a history of the search to this point. The order of their occurrence is not deemed significant in analyzing a searcher's performance, although the numbers of such commands used might be.

Penniman suggested that when a user issues a BEG command or issues any command that comes before the last-entered command in the sequence just shown, a new *cycle* is starting. For example, if after viewing a few records, the user thinks of a new term and wishes to look it up in a dictionary, this begins a new cycle. Similarly, if the user adds a new restriction, e.g., *date*, to a search, redefining the desired output, that too starts a new cycle. The number of cycles is then a measure of how the user performs a search.

Largely in parallel with system measures, we define the following user process measures where k designates a user, i a search, j a command entered during a search, and l a set formed during the search.

14.3.1.1 Measures Based on Time

Some of these measures were introduced in Section 12.3, where their purpose was to measure system performance. Here we have added a subscript identifying the user.

$timelaps_{k,i}$ Elapsed search time for user k to perform search i.

$timelaps_k$ Average elapsed time for user k to perform a search.

$$\overline{timelaps_k} = \sum timelaps_{k,i}/n$$

where n is the number of searches by user k for which we have data.

$ratecmds_{k,i}$ Rate of entry of commands by searcher k in search i.

$$ratecmds_{k,i} = 1/\overline{timelaps_k}$$

$timeplan_{k,i,j}$ Time for user k to plan command j of search i.
$timeent_{k,i,j}$ Time for user k to enter text of command j of search i.
$timeproc_{k,i,j}$ Time for the system to process command j of search i for user k.
$timeexe_{k,i,j}$ Time for user k to select, enter, and execute command j of search i.

$$timeexe_{k,i,j} = timeplan_{k,i,j} + timeent_{k,i,j} + timeproc_{k,i,j}.$$

14.3 User Performance Measures

14.3.1.2 Measures Based on Number of Commands Used

Again, we repeat some measures introduced in Section 12.3, adding a subscript for the specific user.

$nocmds_{k,i}$ Number of commands used by searcher k in search i.
$nocycles_{k,i}$ Number of cycles used by searcher k in search i.
$cmdcycle_{k,i}$ Average number of commands per cycle used by searcher k in search i.

$$cmdcycle_{k,i} = nocmds_{k,i}/nocycles_{k,i}$$

This metric can be meaningfully computed for a single search or averaged over a set of searches.

Similar measures will be found in Chapter 15, where we consider software metrics.

14.3.1.3 Measures Based on Records Retrieved

$setsize_{k,i,l}$ Set size; for set number l in search i, by searcher k.
$setsizefnl_{k,i}$ Final set size; size of the last set in search i, by user k. This may be a major factor in determining when to end a search or in characterizing how a given user performs.
$norecxm_{k,i,l}$ Number of records examined; or number browsed or read, from set l, in search i by user k.
$norecxmfnl_{k,i}$ Final number of records examined; or number browsed or read, of the final set created in search i by user k.

This is a major factor in Blair's *futility point* (Blair, 1980) and in Cooper's *expected search length* (Cooper, 1970).

14.3.2 Error Measures

In Chapter 12 we categorized error count as a process measure, but for users we feel errors should be in a class by themselves because they are so important in classifying or describing users. Most IRSYS command languages are so structured that a command statement begins with an imperative verb, optionally followed by an argument, the artificial equivalent of an adverb or object of the verb. In common usage, the word *command* can refer to either the verb or the entire statement, i.e., to FIND HYDROGEN or to FIND. In discussing errors, we shall use *command* to refer only to the verb and *statement* to refer to the entire command statement (which, like an English sentence, could consist only of the verb). We propose the following taxonomy of errors (Yuan, 1994), which can be extended in detail, given a specific language:

E1: *Invalid command.* This assumes the IRSYS was unable to recognize which command the user intended. Some systems assume a default, the basic search or set-creating command if none is given, in which case this type error cannot occur; e.g., PIRNT 5 would be treated as a search for records containing this phrase, not as a PRINT command. Since most systems that look for but cannot find a command do not check the argument, the error status of the argument is generally ignored under this category.

E2: *Valid command, invalid argument.* A valid command was detected or assumed, but its argument is invalid. It is tempting to further subdivide this class, but doing so probably creates as many ambiguities as it clears up. It is probably best left until a specific command language is selected for study. It is also tempting to try to distinguish between syntax errors and value errors, but these can easily be indistinguishable.

E3: *Valid command statement, invalid context.* The entire command statement is syntactically correct and its values appropriate, but it has no meaning in context, i.e., at the current point in a sequence of commands. For example, in DIALOG a PAGE command has no meaning unless the previous command has resulted in a multipage display.

E4: *Null set.* Technically, the generation of a null set is not an error. It simply means the IRSYS is reporting that no records meet the criteria stated in a set-forming command, and this may be valid, useful information. But, as a practicality, inexperienced searchers are more likely to create null sets than experienced ones, so their occurrence can serve as a measure of user skill. It might be worth distinguishing between null sets for a single word or phrase and for sets consisting of Boolean operations on other sets. The former is more likely to indicate poor choice of a term, or a misspelling; the latter simply means that a combination of otherwise valid terms is null.

E5: *Large set.* The mere creation of a very large set is even less an actual error than is a null set. But, again, on the assumption that experienced users will rarely generate sets so large as to be useless (say by creating a set for *education* in an educational bibliographic database), this error tends to indicate a lack of user skill. The threshold for error detection, the number of occurrences deemed to indicate an error, would depend on the magnitude of the database and is not a linear function of magnitude. If a single term occurs in as few as 5% of the records of a large (multimillion record) database, this could be overwhelming to a user. By contrast, 10% of records in a 50,000 record database could be a useful subset, even if still too many to read.

Measures of performance can be the frequency or relative frequency of occurrence of each error type. Once again, before using such data, it is important to establish statistical controls. A single user's performance, in terms of frequencies of errors, can be compared with others of like background, working under comparable circumstances. Two groups of users can be compared, if the circumstances of their work are similar. Two systems can be compared if the human subjects are comparable and the systems are alike enough to be meaningfully compared (it is not likely that errors made in the use of a statistical system could be readily compared with use of an information retrieval system).

14.3.3 Language Use Measures

The language used to express selection criteria in a query is usually artificial but may be natural. Artifical or not, it is a language and it can be subject to some linguistic or stylistic analysis as a means of differentiating among different types of users. Thus, quite apart from the actual logic expressed or the specific choice of words or attribute values, the manner in which a person uses a language is likely to reflect degree of knowledge of, and experience with, the language and perhaps with the subject domain.

Some of the measures to be introduced in the following are traditionally used in linguistics for analysis of natural language text. Others have been used only for artifical languages, but both have been used or tried as a means of differentiating between authors or language users, or groups of authors. None have been so successfully used to date, in information retrieval, that they can be said to be clearly reliable predictors of user behavior. Some have been able to be used to confirm differences in search behavior by users of backgrounds sufficiently different that behavioral differences of some kind were expected. In none of the cases do we have standards or enough experimental data that we can make a predictive statement of exactly how a given user will perform.

The measures are grouped as follows: traditional natural language linguistic measures, measures related to the selection of a command, measures related to command sequence, measures of terms used, and measures of the complexity of set-forming expressions.

14.3.3.1 Linguistic Measures

This group of measures represents an attempt to characterize the overall use of a language. Most of us recognize that we use a different style of language when in conversation with a child or close friend than when writing a document to be read by a critical, professional audience. Sentence structure in the latter type of communication will be tighter. We will use only full sentences, probably be terse, and will avoid excessive repetition of words. Oral conversation may well involve word sequences that are not proper sentences and a high degree of repetition of words. A sample of such measures was given in Chapter 8.

14.3.3.2 Command Selection Measures

The preceding measures characterize a person's use of language as a whole, particularly terseness and repetition. They were concerned with the overall pattern of term frequencies. Here, we deal with choice of specific commands to use. It is common, in any language, natural or artificial, that few users make use of all the known vocabulary elements. Which ones are chosen and with what relative frequency can be an important characterization of a language user. We can define:

$\{CMD_i\}$ Command vocabulary; the set of commands used in search i; or the set of command types occurring in the search.

This becomes a measure of what this user knows of the command language.

$fcmd_{j,i}$ Frequency of occurrence of command j in search i.
$pcmd_{j,i}$ Probability of command occurrence; or relative frequency of command j in search i.

$$pcmd_{j,i} = fcmd_{j,i} / ntkset_i$$

where $ntkset_i$ is the number of command tokens used in search i.
$rankcmd_{j,i}$ Rank of command j in search i. The command with highest frequency is assigned the rank of 1, the second highest rank 2, etc.

14.3.3.3 Measures Related to Command Sequence

Having looked at overall use of language and at the specific set of commands employed, let us now look to sequences of commands. Penniman (1975) was the first to use such a measure and he and subsequently others have shown that users of differing degrees of experience tend to string commands together differently. A sequence or chain of commands is a succession of commands issued as part of a search. Borrowing on usage of a closely related mathematical area of study, Markov chains or processes (Kemeny and Snell, 1963), the order of a sequence or chain is the number of elements between the first and the last. If a chain has three elements, it is of order one. A zero-order chain, with two elements, gives a state transition matrix; that is, it shows the probability of going from any one state to any other. A state, in this sense, is the state of having given or selected a particular command.

We are interested in the probability of moving from one state (having selected a given command) to another. We are also interested in the probability that, having selected commands c_1, c_2, c_3, the next command will be c_4, that is, the influence of all members of the chain on the selection of the next command.

A Markov process, strictly speaking, is one in which the value of a variable is determined by its value n steps previously, and n is then the order

14.3 User Performance Measures

of the chain. In database searching, and probably in the use of all computer command languages, we believe the choice of the next command is determined not by a single choice n steps back but by the entire sequence preceding the current one. Hence, our command sequences are not strictly Markov chains.

To use the method, Penniman compiles the frequency of occurrence of chains of commands, of all orders from zero up to a limit, L. For chains of orders above about 4, the probability tends to be so close to zero that it is hardly worth keeping the data. That is, everyone's frequency for virtually all chains above order 4 is so close to zero that they are all equal. Below this level, however, the distributions differ. A natural language analogy is that two writers on the same subject may use many words in common, and with about the same relative frequency, and may use a number of short phrases in common, but the likelihood of a complete sentence in one text matching a complete sentence in another is so low as to be not worth computing.

The measure, which is really a set of measures for any one text or set of commands from a search, is a frequency distribution for chains of order 0, 1, 2, 3, and possibly 4. The vocabulary used in chains is also of interest, i.e., the set of commands and their frequencies, irrespective of predecessors or successors.

$fchn_{o,i}$ *Frequency of occurrence of chain;* this is a chain of order o in search i.
$\{CMD_{i,m}\}$ *Chain vocabulary;* the set of command types comprising chain m in search i.

Greenberg and Witten (1988) report an interesting measure of command use, in this case with commands to the computer operating system UNIX. The measure is the probability of repetition of a command type as a function of distance from the repeated command. In the sequence of commands ABBAB, B occurs as the second command, then is repeated, with distance 1 from its predecessor; A is then repeated with distance 3; then B is again repeated, now with distance 2. Greenberg and Witten report a distribution showing some variation by experience characteristics of users, but a generally similar distribution for each user group. In each group the probability of repetition was strikingly higher for the distance 2 than for any other value. This gives rise to the possibility of using this type of measure as a means of discriminating among user groups. It has not been tested in the information retrieval context.

14.3.3.4 Measures of Term Usage

Term usage refers to search terms or attribute values used in set-defining commands. Since the syntax of these commands is normally quite simple, we focus interest only on the words or values used, not on sequences or chains. Hence:

$cmdf_{i,j,l}$ *Command term frequency;* the frequency of occurrence of term i in attribute j of command l. (See 8.2.3.1 for definition of frequency of occurrence of a term in a record.)

$\{TRM_{l,i}\}$ *Search vocabulary;* the set of term types used in command l of search i.

14.3.3.5 Measures of Expression Complexity

We have used a rather arbitrary measure of complexity, the number of punctuation marks or Boolean operators used in a search expression. First, count the number of terms used in a command argument. Then count the number of pairs of parentheses, Boolean operators or equivalent, and truncation or wild card symbols. A Boolean operator equivalent can be the comma or hyphen used between term values, as SMITH, SMYTH, SMYTHE to be taken as SMITH OR SMYTH OR SMYTHE, or SMI?–SMY? to indicate the selection of all terms from an alphabetical index that fall between the first term beginning with SMI and the last one beginning with SMY. The count can be used in an absolute form, or a relative form if the count is divided by the number of terms in the expression.

$|\ TRMtyp_{l,i}\ |$ *Number of term types in a set-forming command;* in command l of search i.

$|\ TRMtok_{l,i}\ |$ *Number of term tokens in a set-forming command;* in command l of search i. The difference between number of types and of tokens in a command is probably of no significance in a Boolean-type language, but may be highly significant if the query language permits natural language input.

$expcmpx_{l,i}$ *Expression complexity;* the count of punctuation or logic-indicating symbols in a command argument.

$relexpcmpx_{l,i}$ *Relative expression complexity;* the count of punctuation or logic-indicating symbols divided by the number of term tokens in the argument of command i.

$$relexpcmpx_{l,i} = expcmpx_{l,i} /\ |\ TRMtok_{l,i}\ |$$

Here, again, we will find in Chapter 15 that similar measures are used for software metrics.

14.4
Search Termination Measures

Cooper (1970) proposes a measure of *expected search length (esl)*, based on the number of irrelevant records a user must "search through" in order

14.5 Outcome Measures   **217**

to achieve the desired search result. Kraft and Lee (1979) propose a set of *stopping rules* for a search based, in one instance, on *saturation* (satisfaction of need) or *disgust* (giving up because of too many irrelevant records). Blair (1980) proposes a *futility point,* essentially the point at which the Kraft–Lee disgust stopping rule is triggered.

We believe the termination or stopping point cannot be predicted except by compiling behavioral data about individual users or users of similar characteristics. However, observation of the termination point and recording of the circumstances can be very valuable in understanding and categorizing user behavior. The circumstances should include those factors mentioned by the authors just cited: number of irrelevant records retrieved (which usually can only be estimated), number of irrelevant records read, number of relevant records retrieved or read, ratio of relevant to retrieved (*precision*). Also included may be elapsed time for the search ($timelaps_{k,i}$), funds expended or cost of a search (*costtot;*), number of search cycles ($nocycles_{k,i}$), and user's target in number of records. A measure of amount of relevance, after Tiamiyu and Ajiferuke (1988) (see Section 13.4.2), would also be useful.

Such statistics can characterize a single user or set of users (such as students in the first week of a searching course). To be predictive in an individual case, a great deal of information would be necessary about the user, the question, the database, and the time and funds available.

14.5
Outcome Measures

In Sections 14.2 and 14.3 we presented a set of measures descriptive of the user's actions. Now we can consider what the user *achieves.* Again, we must remind the reader of controversey surrounding all these measures.

14.5.1 Set Size

Bates (1984) described in a somewhat satirical way a mythical 30-item search that seems at times to be the goal of every searcher, at least of bibliographic files. In reality it is too simplistic to assume that any fixed number of records is always the goal. It depends on the end user, who rarely states an objective in terms of numbers of records. On the other hand, consistent failure to find anything satisfying a query, or consistently retrieving sets too large even to scan, may well indicate a lack of user skill. If a user can be induced to state a numeric goal, then final set size might be a useful measure of searcher skill, although the size of the database and its appropriateness to the search and resources available are also factors to consider.

Useful measures are: set size ($setsize_{k,i,l}$) and final set size ($setsizefnl_{k,i}$) as defined in Section 14.3.1.3. Regardless of the number of sets generated during a search, the last one is usually the one the user is either the most satisfied or discouraged with.

14.5.2 Precision and Recall

Precision and recall were defined in Section 13.2. They are popularly used system measures but are as applicable to the user. We do urge caution in their use. Professional searchers are likely to consider the retrieval of extraneous or nonrelevant material a mark of some lack of skill or of time and resources to do a proper search. That is, they will recognize that with persistence, a poor value of either P or R can be improved upon. They are also likely to use the topicality meaning of relevance when making judgments. We are inclined to believe (and we know of no convincing studies of this question) that end users are more interested in value for time, money, and effort invested. Again, we use as an example that an end user is likely to consider a search outcome that provides ten records, nine of which are of little use but one of which is of exceptional value, to be successful. The numeric value of P, here, would be close to 0.1, not traditionally seen as a commendable value.

On the other hand, end users have often been known to ask an intermediary for "everything" on a topic, an $R = 1.0$ search. The intermediary may know this to be practically impossible because it might involve thousands of items, but may not be able to convince the user until the large set is produced or its value displayed. These measures must be taken in context. Average values of relevance (average relevance value of items in a set) and P and R, as defined in Section 13.2, are useful when the context is fully known.

14.6
Summary

Measuring human performance is almost always difficult. Did a sprinter break a record for a particular distance in a race? It depends not just on what was recorded as this person's time but also on track and wind conditions and what the person may have infused before the race. The best approach is to try to control all relevant factors and allow only those under study to vary: use the same database and the same tasks for everyone involved in a retrieval study, assure that either all subjects have uniform backgrounds or that the differences are recognized as variables. Making sure that experimental subjects are equally motivated is most difficult because measurement of motivation is difficult.

Generally, experimenters or managers seeking measures of human performance in the use of information retrieval systems must accept a lesser degree of precision of measurement than may be customary in most other fields.

References

Bates, Marcia J. (1989). The design of berrypicking techniques for the online search interface. *Online Review*, 13(5), 407–424.

———. (1984). The fallacy of the perfect thirty-item search. *RQ*, 24(1), 43–50.

Bellardo, Trudi. (1985a) An investigation of online searcher traits and their relationship to search outcome. *Journal of the American Society for Information Science*, 36(4), 241–250.

———. (1985b) What do we really know about online searchers? *Online Review*, 9(3), 223–239.

Blair, David C. (1980). Searching biases in large interactive document retrieval systems. *Journal of the American Society for Information Science*, 31(4), 271–277.

Borgman, Christine L. (1983). Performance effects of a user's mental model of the information retrieval system. In Raymond F. Vondran, Anne Caputo, Carol Wasserman, Richard A. V. Diener, eds. *Productivity in the Information Age, Proceedings of the 46th ASIS Annual Meeting*. White Plains, NY: Knowledge Industry Publications, 121–124.

———. (1989). All users of information retrieval systems are not created equal: an exploration into individual differences. *Information Processing & Management*, 25(3), 237–251.

Burton, Richard R. and John Seeley Brown. (1978). Diagnostic models for procedural bugs in basic mathematical skills. *Cognitive Science*, 2, 155–192.

Carlisle, James H. (1974). *Man–Computer Problem Solving: Relationship Between User Characteristics and Interface Complexity*. Doctoral dissertation. New Haven: Yale University, School of Organization and Management.

Chignell, Mark H., Lee Jaffee, Philip J. Smith, Deborah Krawczak, and Stephen J. Shute. (1990). Knowledge-based search intermediaries for online information retrieval. In Rao Aluri and Donald E. Riggs, eds. *Expert Systems in Libraries*. Norwood, NJ: Ablex Publishing Corp., 170–191.

Cooper, W. S. (1970). On deriving design equations for information retrieval systems. *Journal of the American Society for Information Science*, 21(6), 385–395.

Fenichel, Carol H. (1981). Online searching: measures that discriminate among users with different types of experiences. *Journal of the American Society for Information Science*, 32(1), 22–32.

Fidel, Raya. (1987). *Database Design for Information Retrieval*. New York: John Wiley & Sons.

Gould, Stephen Jay. (1981). *The Mismeasure of Man*. New York: W.W. Norton & Co.

Greenberg, Saul and Ian H. Witten. (1988). How users repeat their actions on computers: principles for design of history mechanisms. *Proceedings of CHI, 1988 (Washington, May 15–19)*. New York: Association for Computing Machinery, 171–178.

Hockey, G. Robert. (1990). Styles, skills and strategies: cognitive variability and its implications for the role of mental models in HCI. In D. Ackermann and M. J. Tauber, eds. *Mental Models and Human–Computer Interaction 1*. Amsterdam: Elsevier Science Publishers, 113–129.

Huber, George P. (1983). Cognitive style as a basis for MIS and DSS designs: much ado about nothing. *Management Science*, 29(5), 567–579.
Kelly, George A. (1970). A brief introduction to personal construct theory. In D. Bannister, ed. *Perspectives in Personal Construct Theory*. New York: Academic Press, 1–29.
Kemeny, J. G. and J. L. Snell. (1963). *Finite Markov Chains*. Princeton, NJ: Van Nostrand.
Kraft, Donald H. and T. Lee. (1979). Stopping rules and their effect on expected search length. *Information Processing and Management*, 15(1), 47–58.
Latta, Gail and Keith Swigger. (1992). Validation of the repertory grid for use in modelling knowledge. *Journal of the American Society for Information Science*, 43(2), 115–129.
Meadow, Charles T., Joan M. Cherry, and Gary Marchionini. (1994). Speculations on the measurement and use of user characteristics in information retrieval experimentation. *Unpublished manuscript*.
Penniman, W. David. (1975). *Rhythms of Dialogue in Human-Computer Communication*. Ph.D. dissertation. Columbus: The Ohio State University.
Saracevic, Tefko, Paul Kantor, Alice Y. Chamis, and Donna Trivision. (1988). A study of information seeking and retrieving. I. Background and methodology. *Journal of the American Society for Information Science*, 39(3), 161–176.
Saracevic, Tefko and Paul Kantor. (1988). A study of information seeking and retrieving. II. Users, questions, and effectiveness. *Journal of the American Society for Information Science*, 39(3), 177–196.
Saracevic, Tefko and Paul Kantor. (1988). A study of information seeking and retrieving. III. Searchers, searches, and overlap. *Journal of the American Society for Information Science*, 39(3), 197–216.
Tiamiyu, Mutawakilu A. and Isola Y. Ajiferuke. (1988). A total relevance and document interaction effects model for the evaluation of information retrieval processes. *Information Processing and Management*, 24(4), 391–404.
Wolman, Benjamin B. (1985). *Handbook of Intelligence Theories, Measurements, and Applications*. New York: John Wiley & Sons.
Yuan, Weijing. (1994). Long-term monitoring of end-user searching behaviour in adapting to an information retrieval system. Manuscript.
Yule, G. Udny. (1944). *The Statistical Study of Literary Vocabulary*. Cambridge: Cambridge University Press, 47.

Five

Information Systems Measures

15

Software Metrics

15.1
Relation to Information Systems Measurement

Many modern information systems make use of computer systems to store and retrieve the records they contain and to dispense these to their users. Software that carries out these activities needs to be as efficient as possible so that costs can be held down and response times minimized. Software engineers are concerned with the application to software development of metrics, measurement, and models, and with metrics that will compare and predict software performance. These metrics are inherently valuable to the understanding of the performance of automated information systems and may have some more general application to the efficient construction of search strategies and file structures.

15.2
Software Physics and Measures

What are the measurable characteristics of software? In the days when we created programs in machine-readable form by punching holes into 80-column cards, it was clear that programs had size in physical dimensions. A count of the cards in the deck provided a unit of measure, their cardinality. The length of the deck in inches and even the weight of the deck in pounds were clear measures of size.

Ultimately, however, software has size in the number of characters or bits necessary for its representation. A program that will load into 10 kilobytes of random access memory is smaller than one that will require 100 kilobytes. In fact, it is one tenth as large, and we are dealing with a ratio scale. A more common metric is the number of lines of code in the program. The number of lines seems closer to a measure of programmer effort than the number of bits or bytes, since each line presumably has

223

some logical purpose not clearly related to the number of bits necessary to represent it.

Line count, however, is not such a clear measure either. Should comment lines be counted? Should blank lines be counted? If a line contains more than one statement should it be counted only once? Should the nonexecutable but descriptive statements in the environment division of a COBOL program be counted? The most common definition excludes blank lines and comments but includes all others (Conte et al., 1986, p. 35).

This solution means that some lines which "do more," which "are more difficult to code," are counted equally with all other lines. One way to overcome this problem is to look below the line level without going as far as the bit level. Halstead (1977) suggests token counts. The tokens are symbols or keywords, usually bounded by spaces or some other delimiter, and are classified as either operators or operands. A token that specifies an action is considered to be an operator, as are most punctuation marks. Other tokens are operands, which include variables, constants, and labels. We then count the number of operators and operands, as well as the number of unique operators and unique operands. In the language of Section 8.2.2, we call the counts of operator tokens N_1, operator types n_1, operand tokens N_2, and operand types n_2. Then:

pgmlen or N Program length; the number of commands in a program.

$$N = N_1 + N_2$$

pgmvoc or n Program vocabulary; the number of command types or different commands used.

$$n = n_1 + n_2$$

A measure of the bits necessary to encode a program with a vocabulary n and a length N is

pgmvol or V Program volume; the number of bits required to encode a program.

$$V = N \cdot \log_2 n$$

V is the number of tokens times the number of bits necessary to encode uniquely the number of types in the vocabulary of a program. N and V are little changed by varying definition rules and both appear to measure the same characteristic as an actual line count (Elshoff, 1978).

Since a great deal of programming involves the modification and utilization of old program statements, or *code,* it is often felt to be necessary to distinguish between old lines and new lines. Some would prefer to count *modules* or *functions* rather than lines or tokens. Modules are independently compilable sequences of lines of code, and functions are collections of execut-

15.2 Software Physics and Measures

able statements that perform a given task. Since both these terms are abstractions, with widely varying size characteristics, there is no easy means of measuring size. Programmers do tend to borrow modules and functions from other programs. Hence, it is useful to distinguish between the code of old and new modules or functions.

This leads to formulations which attempt to estimate a value that can be used to compare programming effort for tasks that involve differing amounts of preexisting code. Some adjustment factor must be used with the line counts of old code S_u so it can be meaningfully added to line counts of new code S_n. Thebaut (1983) suggests the measure

> S_e *Estimated effort;* a measure of the effort involved in revising an existing program.

$$S_e = S_n + S_u^k$$

where k is a positive constant no greater than 1 and, by regression analysis on existing data, approximately equal to 6/7.

Other formulas also exist, but agreement on their use does not.

Another way of viewing the complexity of software is by measuring the amount of data that must be entered into a program, the amount processed within the program, and the amount that is produced as output. A count of the amount of this sort of data associated with a particular piece of software is known as a *data structure metric*. For internal processing such metrics concentrate on counting variables and their occurrences. A variable, of course, is a character string in a program that is used to represent some value that changes during execution. Halstead's n_2 is the sum of the number of variables, unique constants, and labels used in a program. These make up the unique operands. N_2 is the sum of all occurrences of these operands. Thus n_2 and N_2 along with *vars* (a count of unique variable names) are data structure measures.

The complexity of a procedure may be measured by the number of items of which the programmer must be aware during the design of a procedure. Such a measure is

> $\overline{LV}$ Average number of *live variables;* where a variable's life is considered to begin with its first reference in a procedure and to end with its last.

$$\overline{LV} = \sum v_i / S$$

Simply by counting the number of variables in each executable statement v_i, and dividing their sum by the number of such statements S, we may compute the average. The number of statements between two symbol occurrences of the same variable is a measure of its importance in a program.

span$_{i,j}$ *Span;* the number of statements between successive occurrences of variable *j*, where *i* is the occurrence number.

There may be multiple spans for each variable; in fact, there will be one less span than there are statements that reference the variable in question.

Finally, the average of the spans for any variable may be more descriptive than any single case. Hence, we define

f$_j$ *Frequency of occurrence of variable j;* the number of times the variable is mentioned in a program.

and

avgspan$_j$ *Average span;* the average span for a given variable in a program.

$$avgspan_j = \sum span_{i,j}/f_j$$

This reflects how long a programmer must retain awareness of the value of each variable. An average of all *avgspan*$_j$ for a program would provide a rough measure of awareness of the programmer for the complete procedure.

15.3
Logical Complexity

Along with size and data structure we are also concerned with the complexity of the *logic structure* of a program. By this we mean the tests and branches in a program that cause different paths of processing to take place based upon available data. The most straightforward metric is:

decount *Decision count;* count of the conditional and loop controlling statements in a program.

However, even here we must be aware that compound conditionals exist, which lead to multiple decisions. If we say IF A AND B THEN C, two decisions (evaluating the truth of A and B) must be made before C can be executed. The simple decisions are called predicates and it is the predicates that must be counted to arrive at the decision count, *deccount.*

In order to visualize a computer program or algorithm, we can employ a *graph.* Mathematically, a graph consists of a set of *nodes* or *vertices,* V, and a relationship among some pairs of vertices, illustrated as a set of *edges,* E. Vertices are points on a graph; edges are lines connecting the points. For example, consider the vertices to represent people and the relationship represented by the edges to be parent-and-child. Thus, two vertices are related on the graph if the people they represent are a parent and that parent's child.

15.3 Logical Complexity

This relationship is not symmetric; if A is the parent of B then B cannot be the parent of A. Therefore, the edge must have a direction; it must go from the parent to the child. In such a case we have a *directed graph*. For purposes of visualization, vertices are often depicted as boxes in the shape of rectangles, diamonds, ovals, or circles. The edges are depicted as lines connecting the boxes. In a directed graph, the lines will have arrowheads indicating direction.

Here is an example of a computer program and its representation as a graph (flowchart). The following algorithm, written in generic programming language, is shown in graph form in Figure 15.1.

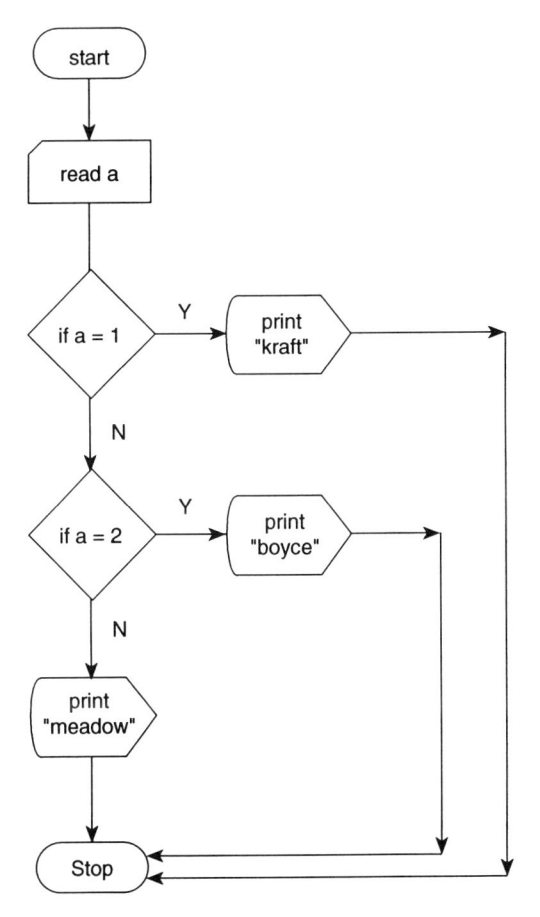

Figure 15.1
Flowchart of a computer program.

```
START
CLEAR SCREEN
READ A
IF A = 1 THEN PRINT "KRAFT"
    ELSE IF A = 2 THEN PRINT "BOYCE"
        ELSE PRINT "MEADOW"
        ENDIF
    ENDIF
STOP
```

If we consider the program's logic to be represented by a directed graph, G, then we may use standard software engineering notation to compute a *cyclomatic complexity number* (McCabe, 1976):

$v(G)$ *cyclomatic complexity number;* the number of connected components of a program.

$$v(G) = e - n + 2$$

where e is the number of edges, n the number of nodes, and 2 represents an assumed branch from the exit node to the entry node. Thus, $v(G)$ represents the number of connected components.

The phrase *cyclomatic number* is used because, from a graph theory perspective, it represents the number of edges that must be removed in order to reduce the graph to its "skeleton" which has no loops or cycles. Using the constant 2 in this definition also assures that a simple linear flowchart, where nodes will exceed edges by one, has a $v(G) = 1$. Since in this case $e = n - 1$, and any conditional has two edges going out, e will increase by 1 for each conditional. Thus

$$e = n - 1 + dec$$

or

$$e - n = dec - 1$$

so

$$v(G) = e - n + 2 = dec + 1$$

Thus we can use the easily computable *dec* to derive a number based on a complex graph analysis. It can also be shown that the cyclomatic complexity number for a program is the sum of the cyclomatic complexity numbers of its modules plus the number of modules (Conte et al., 1986, p. 70).

It is also possible to count the minimum number of paths, *NP*, from the first to the last node in a flowchart. Paths with backward loops that can be traversed more than once are not included in the computation since they could be infinitely large (Schneidewind and Hoffman, 1979). The same analysis yields:

R_i Reachability; a count of the number of paths for reaching any node.

An extension of this measure is

$\overline{R}$ Average reachability; the sum of the path counts divided by number of nodes.

$$\overline{R} = \sum R_i/n$$

The more deeply statements are nested in loops or conditional transfers controlled by other statements, the more complex and difficult to comprehend a program becomes. We may assign nesting levels to statements by assuming that those that sequentially follow the execution of a previous statement are on the same level as that statement, and those that are in the range of a loop controlled by the previous statement are at one level deeper. If we then add all the levels assigned to each statement and divide by the number of statements, we will have:

$\overline{NL}$ Average nesting level; the sum of all levels assigned to all statements divided by the number of statements.

Since the appearance of structured programming, a count of GOTO statements has been considered a measure of unnecessary complexity. If the GOTO is required for transfer in a language, then it is the uncontrolled use of the GOTO that should be counted. The metric for this is

knots Knots; the number of times that flow of control lines drawn in the margin of a program listing would cross. A high knot count demonstrates undue complexity.

The meaning of *knots* is illustrated in Figure 15.2, a slight variation of the program flowchart used earlier.

15.4
Algorithmic Complexity

When measuring the resources, e.g., time and memory or space, for executing a computer algorithm, several issues come to the front that are illustrative of the entire subject of measurement. For example, suppose we want to measure the resources required to accomplish a given task, e.g., sorting a file of m records. Moreover, suppose we want to select a reasonable

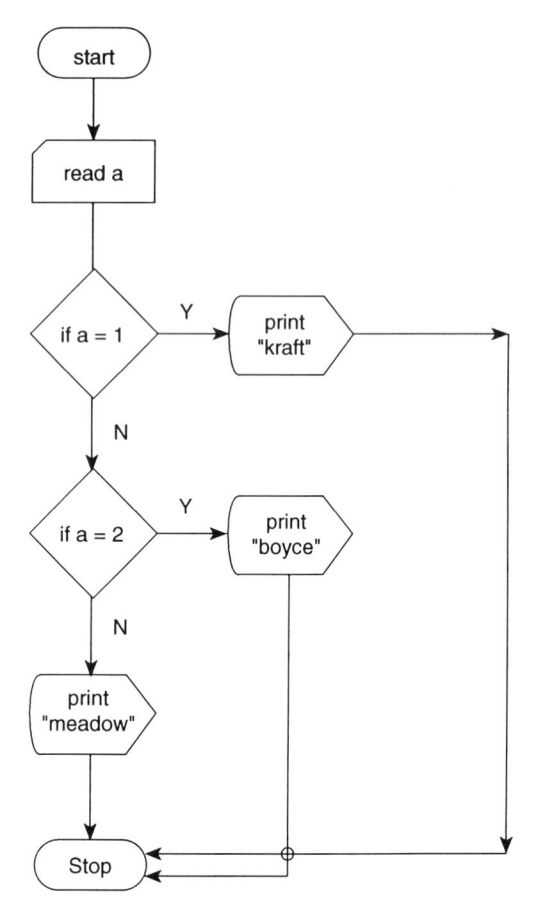

Figure 15.2
Knots in a flowchart.

sorting method that uses the minimum amount of resources and yet accomplishes this task.

We could develop several sorting algorithms, implement each in a program, compile each algorithm, and execute them on a convenient computer. We could measure the resources consumed by each algorithm and compare them, especially the time and space resources.

However, this is not very satisfactory. The problem is that it is rather difficult, if not impossible, to isolate and control all of the side effects of external factors. For example, the choice of computer could affect the time and storage of one sorting program versus another. The operating system used by the computer could come into play. If the operating system allows

15.4 Algorithmic Complexity

for multiple users, the total load on the computer at a given time can affect its efficiency as much as the individual sort program being tested. The choice of programming language can affect efficiency, too. Perhaps worst of all, the capabilities of the programmers who write the codes for the programs can influence efficiency. Yet, we are basically interested only in the efficiency of the various sorting algorithms rather than the influences of these other factors.

Thus, the notion of a formal, theoretical, analytic methodology, known as *algorithmic complexity*, came into being. This involves writing out a step-by-step description of the algorithm, using a programming language or *pseudo-code* (analogous to a programming language but without attention to syntactic details). Next, we count the number of steps, i.e., the number of statements to be executed if the algorithm is executed.

Complexity in an algorithm is generally viewed as the number of operations the procedure requires, given a certain number of inputs, m. Thus we might say that the complexity or efficiency of an algorithm is measured by a function:

$f(m)$ *Algorithmic complexity;* the maximum number of operations required when there are m input items to be processed by the procedure.

Then the count of elements of input becomes the unit of measure. If we have a simple serial comparison search, where we pass a file of m records against a search specification in order to find a match, the maximum number of operations (comparisons of the specification with each record) is m.

If we instead perform a search where there are two specifications, and each input element must be compared to both, the maximum number of operations is $2m$. In a binary search where we look in the middle of a sorted file, discard the half where the specification is not to be found, and iterate the procedure until we have a match, we find that the maximum operation count is $\log_2 m$. This sort of measure reflects efficiency without depending upon equipment, compilers, or operating systems which would affect actual run time tests.

Depending upon the algorithm of concern, we need to identify its key operation. The fact that our procedure may require a reformatting of the matched record, and its writing to another file, has no real effect in terms of operations based upon input items. If there are m input elements, ten operations to format the record and five to write it, then with a binary search we would have an $f(m) = \log_2 m + 15$ and with a serial search $f(m) = m + 15$. It is the operations that by their repetitive nature dominate the algorithm that are significant. If we must compare each input element with every other such element, before our formatting and writing operations we would generate m^2 comparisons and our function would be $f(m) = m^2 + 15$.

We have a sort of ordinal scale of efficiency or complexity of operation: $\log_2 m < m < 2m < m^2$. However, the difference between m and $2m$ is hardly comparable to that between m and $\log_2 m$, or between $\log_2 m$ and m^2. We can clarify the situation by using what is known as the *big O* notation. *Big O* is a form of function in which only the dominating term is identified and its constant multiples are eliminated along with the other terms. The *big O* is all that really matters when m is large. We would say $f(m)$ is of the order of $O(m)$ and in notation write, for example,

$$\text{if } f(m) = \log m \text{ then } f \text{ is } O(\log m).$$

The common *big O* sets of functions have names (Fenton, 1991, p. 211).

If a function f is:	then f has:
$O(1)$	*constant complexity*
$O(\log m)$	*logarithmic complexity*
$O(m)$	*linear complexity*
$O(m \log m)$	m *log* m *complexity*
$O(m^2)$	*quadratic complexity*
$O(m^p)$, (for $p > 0$)	*polynomial complexity*
$O(c^m)$, (for $c > 1$)	*exponential complexity*
$O(m!)$	*factorial complexity*

We can define the efficiency of an algorithm as $O(f(m))$ when it requires no more than $O(f(m))$ operations in the worst case.

15.4.1 Worst and Average Case Analysis

The *big O* is used to indicate the worst case complexity. Often an algorithm may meet its criterion for success prior to running its complete course. For instance, it is possible that in a binary search of an index, the initial probe to the middle of the file will locate the record. For this particular case $f(m) = 1$. Or, it is possible that the second cut of the file will locate the desired record. In this particular instance $f(m) = 2$. Clearly, on the basis of average operation, the worst case will not be the normal performance. With long operation the average search time will be less than $O(\log m)$. If we serially scan a random file of m records, attempting to match a single value, the average search time will be $m/2$, despite the fact that the search has linear complexity in the worst case where the desired record is the last examined.

As another example, consider the bubble sort algorithm seen in many freshman programming courses (Helman et al., 1991, pp. 307–309). It can be shown that in the best case, if the file of m records is already sorted, the algorithm will terminate in $O(m)$ steps. However, in the worst case, with the data sorted in reverse order, the algorithm requires $O(m^2)$ steps. The average case will be somewhere in between these extremes depending on the order of the data relative to the desired area. On the other hand, the quick sort algorithm is $O(m \log m)$ for the average case but $O(m^2)$ in the worst case (Naps and Pothering, 1992).

We might find in comparing algorithms that the worst case of one is far worse than that of a competing one, while the average case of the same algorithm is far better than that of the competition. This occurs when the worst case is exceedingly unlikely. Therefore, we may choose an algorithm whose worst case is very complex, if we believe that the worst case is quite unlikely to occur and that the average case is far less complex.

15.5
Applications

We will now look briefly at how these concepts can be applied to information retrieval problems. The reader will note that the some of the concepts discussed were used in a somewhat different form to address certain aspects of the measurement of users in Chapter 14.

15.5.1 Query Complexity

In their major study of information retrieval, Saracevic et al. (1988) made use of measures similar to software metrics in their study of search tactics and efficiency. These measures could be calculated from logs of search interactions. Since the system used in the study was command driven, that is, each user-initiated interaction with the system required a command with arguments, the *number* of *commands* was considered a measure of the complexity of the query interaction. This is essentially a statement count of user input to the system, and except in cases where particularly long sets of arguments are utilized is a line count of such input.

Since effective retrieval searching is normally an iterative process, the *number* of *cycles* was also considered as a complexity measure. A *cycle* was defined as a set of commands ending with a command that causes a display of results. Each display gives the user information on the current success of the strategy, assuming user evaluation of the materials displayed. The final display marks the completion of the search. Thus a count of commands generating displays of records is assumed to be a count of iterations, or reformulations with feedback, of the search.

A slightly different definition of *cycle* is offered by Penniman and Dominick (1980). They suggest that commands in a bibliographic search can be grouped by broad function and that they are usually entered in this sequence: database selection, term browsing and selection, set formation, and display or printing. A new cycle is deemed to start anytime a command is issued which is in a previous group to the previously entered command. As a practical matter, the main differences between this definition and that of Saravecic are that in the Penniman–Dominick definition, a new cycle starts if a user sees a set size displayed but does not look at any records before ending the cycle, and in the Saracevic definition, a new cycle does not start if, early in the search, a user backtracks.

The *number of search terms*, the *preparation time*, the *connect time*, and the *total time*, preparation plus connect, were also kept by the Saravecic team. Preparation time, of course, must be kept by separate record and is not available from a search interaction log.

We would presume that number of cycles would have some effect on search outcomes, since relevance feedback has been shown to be an effective retrieval technique. Indeed, Saracevic and Kantor (1988) found that a high number of cycles was associated with increased odds of relevance of retrieved items. High numbers of terms and long preparation time were correlated with *decreased* odds of relevance of retrieved items. None of these measures had any significant relationship with the traditional measures of precision and recall. These results call into question the meaningfulness of search tactics in improving retrieval results.

15.5.2 File Structures and Search Algorithms

The most direct application of software metrics to information retrieval systems concerns the efficiency of search algorithms and file structures. Characteristically, an automated information retrieval system will have a large and steadily growing file of documents. This means that there will be a regular need to update the file. There will also be a need to rapidly (usually interactively, without noticeable delay) identify small subsets of the file that match user specifications and display them. Whatever matching algorithm or logical storage structure is utilized, there are a limited number of physical file structures available. We will review these in the following sections in light of the retrieval environment.

When we search an index for a particular attribute, in order to determine which records are referenced by it, or when we search a file of document records to find a particular document by some unique identifier, we are carrying out the same algorithmic procedure. We know some definite characteristic of the record wanted, and we scanned the file of all records available for the purpose of identifying that record by matching its identifying characteristic with the search key.

15.5 Applications

If our file of n records is not ordered, or is ordered on some attribute other than the search key (the attribute we want to match), we shall have to search the whole file, examining all n records in turn in the worst case. If and only if there can be only one match, then we need only test an average of $n/2$ records. A file ordered on an attribute other than the search key will need to be considered randomly ordered for the desired attribute. If we are aware in advance of the attributes upon which we are likely to search, we will order the records in the file by these attributes and use the information inherent in that order to shorten the search process. Typically the attributes of interest are identified in advance, and their values are used as sort keys to organize the records.

An *index* is a file of the values of the searchable attributes sorted into a broadly accepted order like that of the Roman alphabet. Enumerated with each attribute value is a list of unique arbitrary identifiers for the records in question. These records are arranged by those unique identifiers in another file. An example is the alphabetical index at the rear of this book. The entries in this index represent words of interest on the pages of the book which make up the record file. The page numbers are listed with the entries if the page is appropriate. Instead of examining each page for references to the term *standard,* we need only find the term *standard* by examining the index and search only those pages of the text mentioned there. This is an *index–register* file structure, commonly used in information retrieval systems.

The index file, which is a serial file of records representing attributes, can be produced from a serial file of records representing the actual documents of interest. This is done by extracting each value of the desired attributes from the records in the original file, combining that value with a unique address for the record from which it was derived, and then combining these new records together if they have the same attribute value. The result is a record for each unique attribute value with a list of unique addresses for the original records appended. This process is sometimes called inversion and the result an *inverted file*. An example of this is the back-of-the-book index in this book. Words and phrases have been extracted from the pages on which they occurred, the page numbers appended, then the whole resequenced into word order.

It is also possible to cluster the documents in the file as described in Chapter 7. Each cluster will require some identifying value that can be matched to query specifications. The identifying value becomes an index entry for the file. The record identifiers in the cluster are all linked to the index entry for that cluster, and only these are examined in the initial search. Thus, we typically have two logical files: a relatively stable-sized index file and a growing, unbounded document file. It is possible that the document file will be only a surrogate file in which records merely represent documents, as in a library catalogue. In this case, we can anticipate that each actual record will indicate a location in a third file where the text of the documents may be found. How can these logical files be physically structured and searched?

If we do not wish to examine each document record or each index record in turn, we might use a unique attribute value to generate an actual, physical address in a file for the document records. Then, when searching for that attribute, we recompute the address and go directly to the indicated location. This means one accessible attribute value per record unless we store multiple duplicate records. This technique is quite useful when combined with an index, since each index record has only one attribute of interest, and the unique document addresses found in the index records could now be unique accession numbers from which physical addresses could be computed.

If the addresses in the index records are subject to frequent modification, with new document addresses being added to an entry point with no limit, such addresses could be stored in a *linked list*. This is a file structure in which each record has the address of the following record or an indication of the end of the list incorporated within it. Records can thus be stored wherever space is available, while logical order is maintained. One example of such a list is the set of murder mysteries written by the late Agatha Christie. Somone might recommend as a first book *Ten Little Indians*, which might have an advertisement on the back for *Murder on the Orient Express*, which has in turn an advertisement for *Death on the Nile*, and so on.

A special case of the list structure is the *balanced tree*. Each record has two or more pointers to other records. The initial record has a key in the middle of the sorted order of keys. Half the keys are greater than the initial record's key and are usually depicted down and to the right of the center. The other half are less and are shown down and to the left. This gives us a list structure that can sustain a binary search. A balanced tree using the first names of a series of colleagues to be arranged alphabetically is illustrated in Figure 15.3.

More detailed discussions of logical and physical data structures for retrieval are found in Meadow (1992), Miller (1987), and Korth and Silberschatz (1986).

15.5.3 Algorithm Comparisons

How should we measure and compare the utility of these structures for information retrieval applications? First we must determine the operational characteristics desired for our system. Next we must determine where the structures stand in relation to these characteristics. Information retrieval is likely to demand very high performance with large files at the time of search. Search and update operations are usually in conflict in that making

15.5 Applications

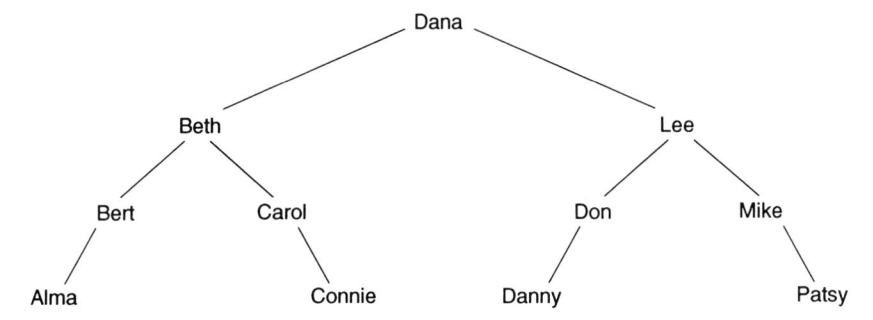

Figure 15.3
A balanced tree. The starting point is ideally the center or median value, i.e., one with half the others below it and half above. This tree is perfectly balanced. If a person named Leah were added, the right half would have more records than the left half and if this were to continue, it could begin to affect search time.

one faster is usually done at the cost of the other's slowing down. Hence, structures that are slow to update but quick to search are to be more valued. Naturally we would like to minimize both time and memory requirements. We would like to be able to match multiple attributes at time of search. Let us view the various search structures with these considerations in mind.

15.5.3.1 Linear Search

A linear search would normally be carried out if a file were randomly ordered in terms of the desired attribute, or search key. A linear search has linear complexity, $f = O(n)$. The average search time will be $n/2$ times individual record acquisition time. Since n is often larger than a million records, this can only be a very slow search process. If the file is unordered, then any new record can be added in any convenient location, appended to the end, say. Hence, update is independent of file size and quite rapid. This seems to be the direct opposite of our retrieval requirements. While search is slow, the memory required to store the file is minimal, just n times the average record size. There is no serious problem in matching multiple attributes in a single search. If there are x attribute values we wish to match, only a single examination of each record is required and $f = O(xn)$.

15.5.3.2 Binary Search

A binary search requires that the file be ordered on the attribute used as a search key. If an index file has been created, multiple attribute values may be combined in a single index file (by prefixing each value with the attribute name and a special symbol, e.g., "AU = ") or in separate files if desired, and multiple attribute value searches performed. Since the addition of new records will require the updating of the index file or files, which will need to be sorted and rewritten, update will be time-consuming. The binary search itself, however, has logarithmic complexity, $f = O(\log m)$, and is quite efficient. If there are x multiple attribute specifications in the search then $f = O(x \log m)$. This method will allow rapid search, multiple attribute value searches with limited deterioration of search efficiency, and will require a longer update time, say $f = O(m \log m)$, for a sort after new records are added. This seems to meet our requirements, but the overhead storage requirements will be large unless searches on the values of only a single attribute can be anticipated. If this is so, no index will be required and the file itself can be organized on the desired attribute value. We will still have the sort time penalty at update but no additional storage will be required. It is more likely that access by multiple attributes will be desirable and large index files will need to be stored.

15.5.3.3 Balanced Tree Search

The balanced tree search is rapid because it allows the same time reduction as the binary search, $f = O(\log m)$, while allowing records to be stored physically wherever necessary because of its list structure. Record size will grow because to each record there needs to be added at least two forward pointers and the attribute value which is to be matched. Since only one attribute can be used to order the records, the method is not useful for files where multiple attributes will need to be searched (unless, again, each attribute value is appended to a symbol for the attribute type or separate trees are maintained for each type). Each new record added to the file will require an $f = O(\log m)$ search to locate the proper logical position for insertion into the list. However, each record added will unbalance the tree slightly, and this can cumulate to degrade overall search performance significantly unless a balancing process regularly takes place. The cost of maintaining balance is not insignificant.

15.5.3.4 Indexed Sequential Search

In an indexed sequential file, the records are ordered in a sequence using the values of a chosen attribute. It employs the addressing mechanisms used in the formatting of disc drives. To locate a record or a position in which to place a record, we first look into an index record where an attribute value indicates which cylinder of the physical storage device holds those records that would sort before the search key. Thus this first level index must hold value and address records equal in number to the number of physical cylinders in use. Once the cylinder has been identified, the cylinder index is examined in the same way to find the proper track. Each track must be scanned sequentially to find the proper record. Gaps are normally left on the tracks so that new records can be added and overflow areas in each cylinder established so that new records can be added where no room exists on a track.

Given the attribute value, the proper cylinder can be located with a binary search of the index which will have a relatively small n, the proper track with a second such search, and the proper record by scanning the whole track, which the read head on the disc drive would need to do in any case. This is a rapid process well suited to the structure of disc storage devices. It uses little space. However, as new records are added and overflows of tracks occur, the physical order begins to diverge from the logical order. This will degrade performance and eventually the overflow areas will fill. Although updating is rapid, time-consuming reorderings will need to take place regularly.

An everyday example of an indexed sequential file is the telephone book, which is a file of peoples' names in alphabetical order, along with their addresses and telephone numbers. At the top of each page is the last name on that page. Thus, when looking for MEADOW, if the top name is KING we must look further in the file. However, if the top name were MELANCON and the top name on the previous page were LUNIN, we would know we had identified the correct page and now move into a linear search mode to find the desired name.

15.5.3.5 Direct Access Search

In direct access search the key attribute value is converted into a binary number and that number is then mapped into an address available on the storage devices in use. If there were as many external memory device addresses as there were attribute values, there could be a one-to-one mapping and each attribute value could be directly utilized. Since this is not normally the case, a process known as *hashing* maps attribute values into addresses. A common method is to divide the value by a prime number and use the remainder as an address. If two values map to the same address, a collision is said to have occurred, and a list will have to be created at that position using other available storage space. This means that collisions can now occur at addresses where records have been placed in the list structure (as a result of a previous collision) as well as in instances where the hashing algorithm produces a many-to-one mapping (Miller, 1987, pp. 205–260).

Thus we see that while direct search is very rapid, it does not collocate logically adjacent records either physically or logically, and it can lead to some real complexity in attempting to minimize collisions.

15.6
Summary

Software metrics provide us with means to measure the complexity of algorithms and implementations of those algorithms in computer programming languages. They can be used to estimate the time or cost to produce computer information systems.

In addition, there are a variety of file structures with which we can store information. The file size and structure can influence measures of effort required to create, add, delete, update, and search the file.

References

Conte, S. D., H. E. Dunsmore, and V. Y. Shen. (1986). *Software Engineering Metrics and Models*. Menlo Park, CA: The Benjamin/Cummings Publishing Company.

Elshoff, J. L. (1978). An investigation into the effect of the counting method used on software measurements. *ACM SIGPLAN Notices,* 13(2), 30–45.

Fenton, N. E. (1991). *Software Metrics: a Rigorous Approach*. London: Chapman & Hall,

Halstead, M. H. (1977). *Elements of Software Science*. New York: Elsevier.

Helman, P., R. Verhoff, and F. M. Carrano. (1991). *Intermediate Problem Solving and Data Structures: Walls and Mirrors,* 2nd ed. Redwood City, CA: Benjamin/Cummings.

Korth, H. F. and A Silberschatz. (1986). *Database System Concepts*. New York: McGraw-Hill Book Co.

McCabe, T. J. (1976). A complexity measure. *IEEE Transactions on Software Engineering,* SE-2(4), 308–320.

Meadow, C. T. (1992). *Text Information Retrieval Systems*. San Diego: Academic Press, 76–128.

Miller, N. E. (1987). *File Structure Using Pascal*. Menlo Park, CA: Benjamin/Cummings.

Naps, T. L. and G. J. Pothering. (1992). *Introduction to Data Structures and Algorithm Analysis with Pascal,* 2nd ed. St. Paul, MN: West Publishing.

Penniman, M. David and Wayne Dominick. (1980). Monitoring and evaluation of online information system usage. *Information Processing and Management,* 16(1), 17–35.

Saracevic, T, P. Kantor, A. Y. Chamis, and D. Trivison. (1988). A study of information seeking and retrieving. I. Background and methodology. *Journal of the American Society for Information Science,* 39(3), 161–178.

Saracevic T. and P. Kantor. (1988). A study of information seeking and retrieving. III. Searchers, searches, and overlap. *Journal of the American Society for Information Science,* 39(3), 197–216.

Schneidewind, N. F. and H. Hoffman. (1979). An experiment in software error data collection and analysis. *IEEE Transactions on Software Engineering SE-5,* (3), 276–286.

Thebaut, S. M. (1983). *The Saturation Effect in Large-Scale Software Development: Its Impact and Control*. Ph.D. thesis, Department of Computer Science, Purdue University, West Lafayette, IN.

16

Measures of Information Services

16.1
Output Services versus Inputs versus Intermediate Outputs

An information system exists to provide information services to more or less defined groups of people. One such group consists of the users of the system. A second consists of the managers and operators of the system, and a third are those who provide the money to operate the system, the funders. Users have information needs and want these satisfied for a reasonable expenditure of their time and effort. The manager–operator group determine whether or not the services provided are those desired, whether or not they are provided in a desirable and cost-effective manner, and whether they perceived by the users to meet their expectations. The funders are also concerned about cost-effectiveness, about providing required services, and about keeping costs within acceptable bounds. Each group has certain goals and outcomes in mind for the system. Each may define a concept such as "acceptable bounds" differently. Conceivably, any two groups, or even all three, may consist of the same individuals.

We would prefer, however, to have some ongoing measures of use, operation, and funding in order to keep track of performance in the short run. The presumption is that a decline in either can be stemmed by changes in system policy and performance if we become aware of the need for change at an early stage. Careful attention to income and to expenditures, particularly where income is linked directly to service provided, affords a real indication of service effectiveness. Ongoing measurement of service effectiveness and efficiency will make possible a regular improvement in service. The accumulated data will also allow a general evaluation of overall effectiveness.

Perhaps we should distinguish between effectiveness and efficiency at this point. An *effectiveness* measure is one which measures the ability of a system to achieve its goals. It is thus user oriented. An *efficiency* measure considers units of goods or services produced per unit of resources provided. The resource could be energy. The efficiency of a steam engine is measured by the ratio of mechanical energy output to heat energy input. Or, the resource could be people, leading for example to the measure *revenue per employee*. Or, it could be money, leading to a measure such as *output per dollar*, making the measure funder oriented. It should be noted that if goods and services production is not judged to be effective, efficiency has little meaning. The most extensive review of the information service measurement literature is to be found in Baker and Lancaster (1991). The general orientation of this work is toward library effectiveness, but most of the material is applicable to all information systems.

Outcomes are the results of a system's operations. Desirable outcomes are really the broad goals or objectives for which the information system was created. Examples might be to ensure that a legal staff has access to the most up-to-date case law, to save the time of our research staff and avoid duplication of effort, to support the curriculum of a school, or to provide the chief executive officer with real-time accounting data on demand. Undesirable outcomes are results that fail to meet these objectives. It would seem that user and funder satisfaction is the only real measure of such outcomes. Satisfaction can be studied and in some sense quantified through preference type surveys. Asking a user to rate a retrieved record for relevance is a form of preference survey. We have no way to make an objective, independent measure of how well a text meets a user's requirement. We can only ask the user. Outcomes are generally not tangible enough to be subject to other methods of measurement.

It is far easier to measure the inputs and outputs of the system. The staff size, the size of the collection of information sources, its cost, its growth rate, the number of questions received, the number of visitors who enter the facility all are input measures that indicate characteristics of the system which can be compared with other systems and thus provide some relative measure of its operation if not its performance. Typical output measures are the number of questions answered, the number of items circulated to users of the system, the number of in-house uses of materials, the number of known items not available when requested, and response times to meet various types of requests.

Intermediate outputs can also be utilized as measures. These are countable products of the system that are the result of its activities that prepare its staff, files, and procedures for the provision of information service. A library may count the number of books cataloged, or perhaps, to be more instructive, the number of books awaiting cataloging. A personnel system may count the number of training sessions held for its staff, or an accounting system record the number of transactions posted by a data entry operator in an eight-hour day. Such numbers indicate something about aspects of system performance but do not directly measure its ultimate value.

16.2
Values and Utilities

In Chapter 1 we discussed values and will briefly review our conclusions here. *Normative values* are standards against which goals are measured, but no clear scales are generally available for this purpose. Not only do we have difficulty finding normative value systems based upon anything but consensus, we find that economic values occur only in real situations where choices are apparent. The theory of economic value is based upon behavior; it does not provide guidelines for behavior. Normative value judgments are normally made by a reliance on a social consensus learned by the individual in his or her interaction with society, rather than by any calculus of underlying quantities. If we must make a general statement on the measurement of values, it is that it will be a matter of empirical choice where we consider the effects of the decision on ourselves and those around us.

As Orr (1973) points out, there is a difference between *quality* and *value* in information services. The highest-quality information system in the world on restaurants in Toronto has limited value if it is supported and can be accessed only in Baton Rouge. Value is associated with user and funder demand. Quality is based on ability to perform within the goals set for the system.

Thus, for the purposes of evaluation of information services we may assume that our values come to us from the users and funders of the system and are related to the outcomes they desire. A *utility* measure, on the other hand, is an attempt to quantify the benefit derived from a certain outcome. Classically, utility is the property of an object whereby it produces benefit or advantage. A positive value is assigned if the outcome leads toward the realization of the underlying goal. A negative value is assigned if it does not.

Utility, defined as market value, or what will be paid for a service, provides an excellent criterion for evaluation. It represents the service output quantitatively as a measure of how well it meets the desires of the users or funders. Unfortunately, at least from the point of view of evaluation, information services are often considered as public goods, or as part of the overhead of an operation, so that the price to users is not direct and apparent and does not affect the users' willingness to utilize the system. The price paid would not be just the fee charged by the service in any case. The user also invests time and effort in the process. Thus it becomes nearly impossible to determine what the user would really be willing to pay for a service not previously tested in the marketplace. On the largest scale we can presume that as long as the funders continue to support the cost of the system, they are willing to pay this price in order to receive the outcomes produced.

Nonetheless, both this gross value and net value, which is computed by subtracting the actual costs of the service, are often estimated to measure utility. In some cases the information service may be available from an external commercial enterprise. Should this be so, we can use the quoted price of the external service to measure the benefit derived from not having to use that service. This gross figure represents the market value of the service, and by subtracting the in-house cost we can derive a utility measure for the net benefit of maintaining the service. If the service would have to be carried out by the user personally, if not provided by the information system, then we might estimate the costs of the user's time as the gross value of the service and the net utility as this valuation less the cost to the system of the service. In the event that the information provided leads to the choice of a less costly alternative over a more costly alternative, then this differential benefit might also be used.

None of these methods is both general and totally objective. Along with these more or less standard methods of assigning utility measures, Lancaster (1988) suggests that savings through the avoidance of duplication and loss of productivity and income from the stimulation of invention are also possible measures. Although these are theoretically benefits of information services, it is not clear how these effects can be measured while controlling for other variables which could have great effect on their magnitude.

16.3
Costs

In the previous section we referred to costs as opposed to prices. The *price* of a service is what the user is willing to pay. *Costs* are the monies expended by the information system in order to provide its service. Such things as time, effort, and inconvenience to the system are included but these are reduced to money terms, if possible.

Although systems could be compared on the basis of single cost items, we normally compare them in terms of cost versus effectiveness or cost versus benefit. We may wish to weigh the total costs of an information system against its benefits, or to compare the costs of systems of varying utility or effectiveness. We presume that ineffective systems might cost less or more than effective systems but still not be preferable. For such purposes it is necessary to include all relevant costs as well as to judge effectiveness.

Effectiveness is normally the amount of some particular output or result over a unit of time. Assuming that all real costs of operating the

16.3 Costs

system have been identified, it is not difficult to produce a measure. Costs are tangible and quantitative for the most part. In theory we compound all costs for a time period, choose an output measure, and produce a coefficient which is average cost for a unit of output in that time period. The trick is identifying all relevant costs.

In understanding the determination of costs it is important to remember the principle of the free lunch. That is, zero cost, or any cost, is a point of view. All lunches and all activities have costs. The relevant question is who pays. If we wish to confirm a citation for this book, we can send a graduate assistant to the library to check the accuracy of our work, or we can go to the library ourselves and check, or we can access an online interactive retrieval system and locate the citation. Only the last alternative generates an actual money charge. Because our employer may pay this charge, however, we might consider this to be free from our point of view. Our own trip to the library clearly takes time away from the actual writing of the book, will annoy us, and could be costed at our hourly rate, either from our employer or from our projected income from the book. The two methods would result in strikingly different costs. Sending the graduate assistant will cause us the least inconvenience and will result in no personal cash outlay. It will, of course, result in a cost based on the graduate assistant's hourly rate, which is not free to our employer, but is a sunk cost which is paid whether or not the assistant performs the service.

This means that the use of cost comparisons for evaluation purposes in information services is extremely suspect unless all costs are recorded from the same point of view, with the same rules of inclusion. Except in controlled studies, and not always then, this is rarely the case. Once we have rules for cost inclusion, we can accumulate costs over a period of time, accumulate units of output over the same period, and produce an output per cost ratio which will serve as a measure of efficiency.

The distribution of costs in an organization providing multiple services is particularly difficult, or arbitrary, or easy to manipulate, depending on point of view. Suppose, for example, that an information service makes its service available free to certain schools in order to encourage sales in the distant future. To what is this cost allocated? To marketing? To charitable donations? Simply absorbed as a cost of production? These are all ethical choices. The issue is one of meaningful management accounting. Similarly, should all of a hospital's emergency room costs be attributed to the patients, or should some be assigned to the general tax rolls on the grounds that the existence of an emergency room is a benefit, even if unused, to all citizens of a community? It is perhaps interesting that fire departments tend take the latter approach; i.e., they are treated as community services and costed as such, not as services whose costs are borne only by those who suffered a fire.

16.4
Service Statistics

Service statistics normally reflect the quality or effectiveness of the system's performance, rather than its value to the users. The typical statistic that is used as a performance measure in an information system is a *fill rate* of some sort. A fill rate is a percentage of requests successfully met. In a library, a title or item fill rate refers to the percentage of known information-bearing items requested by name that are available at the time of the request. The question or reference fill rate is the percentage of questions received by the system that it is able to answer. A topic or subject fill rate is also sometimes used. In this case it is the percentage of topics upon which the system receives requests for which it can supply material. Similar measures exist for other types of institutions: number of court cases successfully disposed of by the prosecutor's office, number of houses sold by a real estate agency per client.

It is also possible to normalize by the potential user population rather than actual requests. Indeed, we might consider a question per capita rate, where the number of questions asked is treated as a percentage of the potential user population. The ratio of document holdings of an information system to its potential user population is another input measure of this nature, whereas the ratio of circulated materials in a time span to user population is an example of such an output measure. The use of the user population as a normalization factor makes such measures more reflective of value to users than of system performance.

Circulated materials might in addition be viewed as a ratio of items available for circulation. This is commonly known as a *collection turnover rate*. This measure also reflects utility more than quality operation. Holdings and collection size are other possible quantities that might be used to normalize questions asked or questions answered. Turnover rate also has meaning in retailing, as a measure of how well stock is moving off the shelves.

There are a great many such measures. Choices depend upon what areas of operation the information agency wishes to clarify and the points of view that are significant for its users and funders. Extensive lists of measures for libraries are given in two studies by Van House and others (1987, 1988). These may selectively and easily be adapted for the evaluation of other information systems.

16.5
Data Collection, Analysis, and Standards

From the previous discussion it seems clear what sort of data should be collected in order to measure information services provided. A *Management*

Information System (MIS) is the name given to the information system which is designed to capture and analyze such data. An MIS for an information system collects data on system costs, price fluctuations, collection size and growth, intermediate transaction times, size and characteristics of the population to be served, number and type of requests received, number and type of requests met successfully, counts of uses of materials, and time and personnel spent on defined tasks.

When systems are automated the possibility exists for capturing much of this data in real time and reflecting the complete population of transactions in the system. Even in manual systems a policy of manually recording transactions in order to provide management information is quite common. Some needed data, however, may not be easily captured from records of daily transactions. This is certainly true for information on potential system users, actual work practices, usage of materials outside the system that might influence acquisition decisions, and nearly any information on staff or patron attitudes and behaviors.

Such information is almost always gathered in ad hoc studies utilizing time- and space-limited samples. Indeed, much analysis of daily recorded management information is from samples rather than the complete data population. Hernon and McClure (1990) list a large number of collection techniques which are applicable to these studies. These include both expert and self-assessment, questionnaires, interviews, obtrusive and unobtrusive observation and testing, examination of logs, records, and recorded transactions, content analysis, and bibliometrics.

Once the desired measures have been identified, it is the MIS that collects the necessary data, calculates the measures, and makes them available to the management of the information system. It should be clear that an MIS is itself an information system that has wide applicability in the ongoing evaluation of any system of any sort. The successful MIS, like any information system, will be designed to provide for the information needs of its users and funders, collecting just the information that is appropriate and organizing it in a way which will produce necessary reports in a useful format.

The development of performance measures suggests a need for performance standards, just as the existence of standards implies the availability of measures. What does a particular fill rate mean? Is answering 10% of reference questions good service, or is 90% required? We know how large our collection of items is. How large should it be?

Although there are few standards for information systems in general, there certainly are standards for libraries. In fact, the areas and issues normally generalize to all information systems, if the particular standards, which often tend to great specificity, do not. Standards cover the physical proximity of service nodes to potential users, collection size, expenditures per user, public relations, staff training, working conditions, physical facilities, and nearly all of the measures referred to earlier in this section. Although national agencies often set prescriptive standards, the goals of the individual system should really be considered first. Then measures should be chosen that reflect those goals. Only at this point should we consider what the standard of performance relative to those measures might be.

The best standards are quantitative in nature, allowing some meaningful measurement to take place. Qualitative statements of standards are not uncommon but are really only expressions of the goals or desirable outcomes. A truly useful standard will be associated with a possible measurement of resources, activity, or output. In fact, it will be based upon an analysis of measurements of performance that reflect actual practice in similar systems.

This does not mean that standards should reflect the lowest common denominator of performance. A standard at least should reflect the minimal acceptable level of performance and, to be most effective, should indicate a level which, if not optimal, reflects a common reasonable level of performance. Thus, the most useful standards of performance are couched in terms of quantitative ranges from some minimal level to an optimal level. The limits of these ranges will reflect actual practice.

Standards for both input and output measures have real value. The most effective information system will meet optimal output standards, while staying as close as possible to the minimum input standards. It should be clear that effective performance can be categorized only by output measures, so output standards are clearly of greater importance in the evaluation of information services.

16.6
Decision Making

There is a systematic approach to decision making. In the first 10 steps of their 13-step description of the systems design process, Kraft and Boyce (1991) outline the process. They suggest that we begin with a four-step analysis phase. First, we produce a definition of the system and its boundaries, then a statement of the goals of the system, and the requirements for the achievement of these goals. Finally, we determine the current status of the system in terms of its fulfillment of the goals. At the completion of the analysis phase we should have an understanding of the problem and are ready to begin the design of possible solutions.

Quite often an information system manager has a firm understanding of the requirements and the current system's ability to meet them. It may well have been some failure in the current system that led to the decision problem in the first place. Nonetheless, a review of these first four steps cannot help but clarify the problem situation, in preparation for the design phase.

The first step of the design phase is the specification of alternatives. This is a listing of all possible alternatives to current procedures. The second step is a listing of constraints. Constraints are limiting factors that interfere with the attainment of objectives. Common constraints have to do with space, time, and money availability, but personal and political factors may also be important. In the final design step each alternative is tested against each constraint. If a constraint is violated the alternative under consideration is deemed unfeasible. Those alternatives remaining may then be considered feasible for evaluation.

The last three steps concern evaluation. In this phase, we must specify performance measures, use these measures to collect data on each of the feasible alternatives, and finally rank the alternatives with the choice going to the best performer.

> Strictly, one cannot determine optimal decisions . . . unless one knows what all these wants are, how effective (and how costly) alternative types of service arrangements are in each case, *and* what values should be assigned to generally rather intangible outcomes. It is likely that this will remain impossible to do in any strict manner. Yet, library administrators are continually making decisions based on assumptions, explicit or implicit, on precisely these matters. (Buckland, 1988, p. 204)

With these words Buckland summarizes his thoughts on the effect of measurement of information services on decision makers in information systems. More specifically, a page later, he continues, "The fundamental problem is that the sophistication of the manipulation of what is measured is in great contrast with—and, unfortunately, distracts attention from, the fundamental weakness of our understanding of what has been measured" (Buckland, 1988, p. 205). We do not seriously disagree with this assessment. The real meaning of citation counts, word counts, circulation counts, and more abstract measures like relevance and information is far from clear. Nonetheless, management decisions must be made and are being made on the basis of the information available. Alternatives cannot be evaluated, decisions cannot be made, on other than an arbitrary basis, without performance measures.

16.7
Conclusion

This work might well be dedicated to William Farish. In the last decade of the eighteenth century, Professor Farish, an engineer and Oxford tutor about whom very little else is known, first made the suggestion of assigning grades to student's papers (Hoskin, 1979). As Postman says of this suggestion, "his idea that a quantitative value should be assigned to human thought was a major step toward constructing a mathematical concept of reality. If a number can be given to the quality of a thought, then a number can be given to the qualities of mercy, love, hate, beauty, creativity, intelligence, even sanity itself" (Postman, 1992, p. 13).

When we speak of measurement of information, and of information systems, we owe a debt to Farish. There is very little in our world today that we do not attempt to measure. Once measurement moved beyond the realm of physical things, it was no longer restricted to the physical sciences, engineering, and technology. The possibilities of what might be measured now seem nearly boundless, and much of the work of social scientists and even humanists today deals with measurement.

There is a tendency in Western thought to equate learned activity with science and to bring to bear scientific methods wherever possible to further our understanding. The viewpoint can hardly be better expressed than by repeating our quotation, in Chapter 1, from Lord Kelvin, a contemporary of Farish.

> When you can measure what you are speaking about, and express it in numbers, you know something about it; but when you cannot measure it, when you cannot express it in numbers, your knowledge is of a meager and unsatisfactory kind: it may be the beginning of knowledge, but you have scarcely, in your thoughts, advanced to the stage of science, whatever the matter may be. Lord Kelvin (1889–1894)

We would not wish to indicate that the beauty of a sunset must be measured to be appreciated, but the particles in the air which produce the effect must be measured if we wish to truly understand the observed phenomena. There is a certain satisfaction, a certain beauty, in reaching such an understanding that does not diminish the direct aesthetic experience, but rather supplements and enhances it. We can say with Keats, who wrote only a generation after Kelvin and Farish:

> O Attic shape! Fair attitude!
> Thou, silent form, dost tease us out of thought
> As doth eternity: Cold Pastoral!
> 'Beauty is truth, truth beauty,—that is all
> Ye know on earth, and all ye need to know.'
> John Keats (1972, pp. 607–608)

References

Baker, S. L. and F. W. Lancaster. (1991). *The Measurement and Evaluation of Library Services*, 2nd edition. Arlington, VA: Information Resources Press.

References

Buckland, M. K. (1988). *Library Services in Theory and Context,* 2nd edition. Oxford: Pergamon Press.

Hernon, P. and C. R. McClure. (1990). *Evaluation and Library Decision Making.* Norwood, NJ: Ablex Publishing Corp., 88.

Hoskin, Keith. (1979). The examination, disciplinary power and rational schooling. *History of Education,* VIII(2), 135–146.

Keats, John. (1972). "Ode on a Grecian Urn." *The New Oxford Book of English Verse 1250–1950.* Oxford: Oxford University Press.

Kelvin, William Thomson. (1889–1894). *Popular Lectures and Addresses.* London: Macmillan, Vol. I, p. 73.

Kraft, D. H. and B. R. Boyce. (1991). *Operations Research for Libraries and Information Agencies: Techniques for the Evaluation of Management Decision Alternatives.* San Diego: Academic Press, 5–8.

Lancaster, F. W. (1988). *If You Want to Evaluate Your Library . . . .* Champaign, IL: University of Illinois, Graduate School of Library and Information Science, p. 56.

Orr, R. M. (1973). Measuring the goodness of library service: a general framework for considering quantitative measures. *Journal of Documentation,* 29(3), 315–332.

Postman, Neil. (1992). *Technology: The Surrender of Culture to Technology.* New York: Alfred A. Knopf.

Van House, N. A., B. Weil, and C. R. McClure. (1988). *Measuring Academic Library Performance: A Practical Approach.* Prepared for the Association of College and Research Libraries, Committee on Performance Measures, Ad Hoc. Chicago, IL: American Library Association.

Van House, N. A., M. J. Lynch, C. R. McClure, D. L. Zweizig, and E. J. Roger. (1987). *Output Measures for Public Libraries: A Manual of Standardized Proceedures.* Chicago, IL: American Library Association.

Appendix: Measurement Index[1]

$\bar{R}$	See *Average reachability*
$\bar{x}$	See *Mean*
$\bar{LV}$	See *Average number of live variables*
$\bar{NL}$	See *Average nesting level*
$\bar{f}$	See *Mean frequency*
$\bar{f}(t_{i,j})$	See *Mean frequency of type* $t_{i,j}$
Λ	See *Wilk's lambda*
μ	See *Mean*
ρ	See *Pearson's correlation coefficient*
σ	See *Standard deviation*
σ^2	See *Variance*
χ^2	See *Chi-square*
$asymovrlp_{1,2}$	See *Asymmetric overlap*
$attr$	See *Attributes*
$attr_d$	See *Number of attributes*
$attr_d$	See *Attributes contained*
$avgspan_j$	See *Average span*

Algorithmic complexity; the maximum number of operations required when there are m input items to be processed by the procedure. (15.4)

Asymmetric overlap; the ratio of the number of terms in common to two texts or sets to the number of terms in one of the texts.

$$asymovrlp_{1,2} = \frac{|S_1 \cap S_2|}{|S_1|} \qquad (13.5)$$

Attributes; the set of descriptors, fields, or data elements which describe an entity. (11.3)

---

[1] Entries are sequenced using the Word Perfect® 5.1 sort sequence.

Attributes contained; a nominal measure of the attributes of database d, really a listing of them. (11.5.9)

Average elapsed time for user k to perform a search.

$$\overline{timelaps}_k = \Sigma \; timelaps_{k,i}/n$$

where n is the number of searches by user k for which we have data. (14.3.1.1)

Average number of commands per cycle used by searcher k in search i.

$$cmdcycle_{k,i} = nocmds_{k,i}/nocycles_{k,i} \quad (14.3.1.2)$$

Average nesting level; the sum of all levels assigned to all statements divided by the number of statements. (15.3)

Average number of live variables; where a variable's life is considered to begin with its first reference in a procedure and to end with its last.

$$\overline{LV} = \Sigma \; v_i/S \quad (15.2)$$

Average reachability; the sum of the path counts divided by number of nodes.

$$\overline{R} = \Sigma \; R_i/n \quad (15.3)$$

Average span; the average span for a given variable in a program.

$$avgspan_j = \Sigma \; span_{i,j}/f_j \quad (15.2)$$

$bcof(t_{i,j}, t_{l,j}, k)$ See *Binary co-occurrence frequency*
$bf(k)_{i,j}$ See *Binary term frequency*

Binary co-occurrence frequency in record k; the frequency of co-occurrence of two terms, t_i and t_l, taking the value:
 1 if $t_{i,j,k}$ and $t_{l,j,k}$ both occur in record k,
 0 if $t_{i,j,k}$ and $t_{l,j,k}$ do *not* both occur in the record. (11.4.2)

Binary co-occurrence record frequency; the number of records in which $t_{i,j}$ and $t_{l,j}$ both occur. In information retrieval terms, it is *the size of a retrieval set* for the intersection of the sets containing $t_{i,j}$ and $t_{l,j}$.

$$rbcof(t_{i,j}, t_{l,j}) = \sum_{k=1}^{m} bcof(t_{i,j}, t_{l,j}) \quad (11.4.2)$$

Binary term frequency of term $t_{i,j}$ in record k; taking the value, for type i of attribute j of record k, of:
 1 if $t_{i,j}$ occurs in record k,
 0 if $t_{i,j}$ does *not* occur in record k. (11.4.1)

Binary record occurrence frequency; the number of records in the range $k = 1$ to m in which $t_{i,j}$ occurs. In information retrieval terms, this is the size of a retrieval set for the term $t_{i,j}$.

Appendix: Measurement Index 255

$$brf(t_{i,j}) = \sum_{k=1}^{m} bf(k)_{i,j} \qquad (11.4.1)$$

$brf(t_{i,j})$ See *Binary record occurrence frequency*

Chain vocabulary; the set of command types comprising chain m in search i.   (14.3.3.3)

Chi-square; the squared difference between the expected and observed number of occurrences in each cell in the table, divided by the expected number and summed over all cells.

$$\chi^2 = \Sigma_{i,j}(O_{ij} - E_{ij})^2 / E_{ij} \qquad (6.3.1.1)$$

$cmdcycle_{k,i}$ See *Average number of commands per cycle*
CMD_i See *Command vocabulary*
$CMD_{i,m}$ See *Chain vocabulary*
$cmdf_{i,j,l}$ See *Command term frequency*

Coefficient of kurtosis; the fourth moment which measures the pointedness of the peak of the probability distribution.

$$coekur = \Sigma(x_i - \mu)^4 / n \qquad (5.3.4)$$

Coefficient of skewness; calculated as the third moment. It measures the symmetry of the probability distribution.

$$coesk = \Sigma(x_i - \mu)^3 / n \qquad (5.3.4)$$

Coefficient of variation; the ratio of the standard deviation to the mean, used to measure the relative deviation.   (5.3.4)

$coekur$ See *Coefficient of kurtosis*
$coesk$ See *Coefficient of skewness*
$coevar$ See *Coefficient of variation*

Command term frequency; the frequency of occurrence of term i in attribute j of command l. (See 8.2.3.1 for definition of frequency of occurrence of a term in a record.)   (14.3.3.4)

Command time; the time required to select, enter, and execute command j of search i.   (12.3)

Command vocabulary; the set of commands used in search i; or the set of command types occurring in the search.   (14.3.3.2)

Confidence interval; the distance on either side of a sample mean in which the population mean is likely to fall, with probability equal to a set amount.

$$\begin{aligned} confint &= \bar{x} \pm 1.96 \cdot sem \\ &= \bar{x} \pm 1.96 \cdot \sigma / \sqrt{n} \end{aligned} \qquad (6.1)$$

confint   See *Confidence interval*

Connect time cost; a charge for a unit of time during which a user's computer is connected via telecommunications with that of an IRSVCE. (12.2)

Correlation coefficient   See *Pearson's correlation coefficient*

Cosine coefficient; measuring the angle between two vectors in the vector space model of a text. Its range is [0,1].

$$SIM3(T_1, T_2) = \frac{\Sigma(f_{i,k}) \bigcirc (f_{j,k})}{(\Sigma(f_{i,k})^2 + \Sigma(f_{j,k})^2)^{1/2}}$$

Summation, in all cases, is over the number of dimensions or possible terms, i.e., $k = 1$ to n. (7.2.3.2)

Cost; the price a user pays for a service. (11.3)

Cost of nonretrieval; the cost of not retrieving a record, whether or not it is relevant. (13.4.1)

Cost of retrieval; the cost of retrieving a record, whether or not relevant.

$$costret = P(\text{Rel} \mid a) \cdot C_{\text{Ret,Rel}} + P(\text{NonRel} \mid a) \cdot C_{\text{Ret,NonRel}} \quad (13.4.1)$$

costct$_d$	See *Connect time cost*
costdb$_d$	See *Database cost*
costfl$_d$	See *File size charge*
costnonret	See *Cost of nonretrieval*
costpr	See *Printing charge*
costrc$_d$	See *Record charge*
costret	See *Cost of retrieval*
costtc$_n$	See *Telecommunications cost*
costtot$_j$	*Total cost of search* j; the sum of all costs associated with a given search.
costtrm$_d$	See *Search term charge*

Cumulative probability of term type; or cumulative probability of occurrence of $t_{i,j,k}$ over the range of records, or the probability that the type occurs somewhere in the range.

$$pcum(t_{i,j}) = \sum_{k=1}^{s} p(t_{i,j,k}) = \sum_{k=1}^{s} f_{i,j,k} / ntyrec_{j,k} \quad (11.4.1)$$

Cyclomatic complexity number; the number of connected components of a program.

$$v(G) = e - n + 2$$

where e is the number of edges, n the number of nodes, and 2 represents an assumed branch from the exit node to the entry node. Thus, $v(G)$ represents the number of connected components. (15.3)

D	See *Discriminator function*
D_i	See *Discriminant coefficient*
$D(O_i, O_j)$	See *Object distance*

Database cost; the charge for a complete database, d, with few restrictions on use. (12.2)

| decount | See *Decision count* |

Decision count; count of the conditional and loop controlling statements in a program. (15.3)

Degrees of freedom.

$$df = (r - 1) \cdot (c - 1)$$

where r and c are the numbers of rows and columns, respectively. (6.3.1.1)

| df | See *Degrees of freedom* |

Dice's coefficient; twice the ratio of the number of co-occurrences to total number of occurrences of either value.

$$SIM1(T_1, T_2) = \frac{2[\Sigma(f_{i,k}) \bigcirc (f_{j,k})]}{\Sigma f_{i,k} + \Sigma f_{j,k}}$$

where T_1 and T_2 represent texts number 1 and 2; $f_{i,k}$ represents the frequency of occurrence of term (value) k in text i; $(f_{i,k}) \bigcirc (f_{j,k})$ is the number of co-occurrences of term k in text i and text j; and m is the magnitude of the database. (7.2.3.2)

Discriminant coefficient; a measure of the discriminating power of words and frequencies to separate document sets by subject classes.

$$D_i = \sum_{j=1}^{J} ((p_{i,j} - \bar{p}_i)^2 / \bar{p}_i)$$

D_i is the coefficient for word i, which appears in J groups, where j is the group number, $p_{i,j}$ is the probability of word i occurring in group j, and $\bar{p}_i$ is the mean probability of word i across all groups. (8.2.2)

| *Discriminating ability* | See *Selectivity* |

Discriminator function; used to separate entities according to values of a set of predictor variables.

$$D = w_1 x_1 + w_2 x_2 + \cdots + w_k x_k \qquad (7.2.1)$$

ec(a)   See *Expected cost of retrieval of a record*
effect1   See *Effectiveness* (Meadow)
effect2   See *Effectiveness* (Vickery)
effect3   See *Effectiveness* (Heine)
effect4   See *Effectiveness* (van Rijsbergen)
effect5   See *Effectiveness* (Shaw)
effect6   See *Effectiveness* (Goffman & Newill)
Effectiveness   (Goffman & Newill)

$$EGN = \frac{a}{a+c} + \frac{d}{b+d} - 1 \qquad (13.6.3)$$

Effectiveness   (Heine).

$$EH = 1 - \frac{1}{1/P_i + 1/R_i - 1}$$

where the subscript *i* indicates that the measure applies to an individual measure of *P* and *R*.   (13.6.3)

Effectiveness   (Meadow).

$$EM = 1 - \frac{\sqrt{(1-P)^2 + (1-R)^2}}{\sqrt{2}} \qquad (13.6.3)$$

Effectiveness   (Shaw).

$$ES = 1 - \frac{1}{1/2P + 1/2R} \qquad (13.6.3)$$

Effectiveness   (van Rijsbergen).

$$EVa = 1 - \frac{1}{\alpha(1/P) + (1-\alpha)\cdot(1/R)} \qquad (13.7)$$

where α is the relative importance or weight assigned by the user to *precision*, on a scale of [0,1]. Implicit is the assumption that the importance of *recall* is the complement $(1 - \alpha)$ of that of *precision*.

  (13.6.3)

Effectiveness   (Vickery).

$$EVi = 1 - \frac{1}{2/P + 2/R - 3} \qquad (13.6.3)$$

EGN   See *Effectiveness* (Goffman & Newill)
EH   See *Effectiveness* (Heine)

Elapsed search time; for search *i*. If only one search is being discussed, the subscript may be omitted.   (12.3)

Appendix: Measurement Index 259

Elapsed search time for user k to perform search i. (14.3.1.1)

EM   See *Effectiveness* (Meadow)
$errcnt_{i,j}$ See *Number of occurrences of an error message*
$errrate_{i,j}$ See *Rate of occurrence of an error message*
ES   See *Effectiveness* (Shaw)

Estimated effort; a measure of the effort involved in revising an existing program.

$$S_e = S_n + S_u^k$$

where k is a positive constant no greater than 1, and by regression analysis on existing data, approximately equal to 6/7. (15.2)

EVi   See *Effectiveness* (Vickery)
Expcost   See *Expected cost of retrieval of a record*

Expected cost of retrieval of a record.

$$ec(a) = \Sigma \ (f(r,a,h) \cdot costret(r(\qquad (13.4.1)$$

F   *Fallout;* the ratio of non-relevant records retrieved to total non-relevant records, or the proportion of the unwanted records that were nonetheless retrieved.

$$F = \frac{b}{b + d} \qquad (13.2)$$

$f(m)$ See *Algorithmic complexity*
$f(t_1 t_2)$ See *Frequency of co-occurrence*
$fchn_{o,i}$ See *Frequency of occurrence of chain*
$fcmd_{j,i}$ See *Frequency of occurrence of command*
$f_{i,j,k}$ See *Term frequency*
f_j See *Frequency of occurrence of variable j*

File size charge; a charge sometimes applied to a query, based on the number of records in the database being searched. (12.2)

Final number of records examined; or number browsed or read, of the final set created in search i by user k.. (14.3.1.3)

Final set size; size of the last set in search i, by user k. This may be a major factor in determining when to end a search or in characterizing how a given user performs. (14.3.1.3)

Frequency of co-occurrence; the number of records in which terms or values t_1 and t_2 both occur. (8.2.3.2)

Frequency of occurrence of chain; this is a chain of order o in search i. (14.3.3.3)

Frequency of occurrence of command j in search i; number of times command i occurs in the search. (14.3.3.2)

Frequency of occurrence of variable j; the number of times the variable is mentioned in a program. (15.2)

Geometric mean; the nth root of the product of n observed values. (5.3.3)

growth   See *Growth of a population*

Growth of a population; population size at a given time t, the product of the initial size times e (Euler's number, the number whose natural logarithm is 1) to the power of mt.

$$G(t) = G(t^0)e^{mt}$$

where t^0 indicates time zero and $G(t^0)$ the initial size of a population. (9.3)

H   See *Information*
halflife See *Half-life*

Half-life; the period of time in which half the total use for a set of items will have taken place. (9.4)

Harmonic mean; the number of observed values, n, divided by the sum of the reciprocals of all these values. (5.3.3)

Information; the number of bits of information in a system of n messages of probability p_i each.

$$H = - \sum_{1<=i<=n} p_i \log p_i \qquad (9.7)$$

Inverse document frequency weight; a weighting of word frequencies to reflect the difference between high rate of occurrence in all (most) documents and high in only a limited set of them.

$$W_{i,k} = F_{i,k}(\log_2(n) - \log_2 D_k + 1)$$

where F_{ik} is the frequency of occurrence of a type k in document i, D_k is the number of documents in the file in which type k occurs at least once, and n is the number of documents in the file. (8.2.2)

Jaccard's coefficient; reduces the denominator of SIM1 by the number of occurrences in common, hence it is a ratio of co-occurrences to non-co-occurrences, rather than to total occurrences.

$$SIM2(T_1, T_2) = \frac{\Sigma(f_{i,k}) \bigcirc (f_{j,k})}{\Sigma f_{i,k} + \Sigma f_{j,k} - \Sigma(f_{i,k}) \bigcirc (f_{j,k})} \qquad (7.2.3.2)$$

K   See *Yule's characteristic*
knots See *Knots*

Knots; the number of times that flow of control lines drawn in the

Appendix: Measurement Index   **261**

margin of a program listing would cross. A high knot count demonstrates undue complexity. (15.3)

List of the attributes represented in T. A set of attributes to be used to test a database. (11.5.6.1)

| $L_j(T)$ | See *Number of attributes in $L_j(T)$*
$L_j(T)$ See *List of the values of attribute $_j$ represented in T*
| $L_j(T·S)$ | See *Number of values of attribute $_j$ in common*
mad   See *Mean absolute deviation*

Mean absolute deviation or *MAD;* the mean of the absolute values of deviations of all observations from the mean. The use of absolute values limits the mathematical operations that may be used on the *mad*.
(5.3.4)

Mean or *average;* the sum of the values of a set of observations divided by the number of observations. The mean of a frequency distribution of the variable x is usually designated μ (Greek mu) if we are dealing with a complete population or $\bar{x}$ ("x bar") if this is a sample.
(5.3.3)

Mean frequency; the average frequency of occurrence of a word type in a text.

$$\bar{f} = 1/typetoken \qquad (8.2.4)$$

Mean frequency of type $t_{i,j}$; or average number of occurrences of the type $t_{i,j,k}$ over the full record range.

$$\bar{f}(t_{i,j}) = f_{i,j,k}/ntkset_j \qquad (11.4.1)$$

Median; the middle value of a distribution, the value where one half the observations precede and one half follow. (5.3.3)

Mode; the value of a distribution that occurs most frequently. (5.3.3)

n   See *Program vocabulary*
N   See *Program length*
N   See *Noise*
$nocmds_i$ See *Number of commands used in search*
$nocmds_{k,i}$ See *Number of commands used by searcher*
$nocycles_{k,i}$ See *Number of cycles*

Noise, fallout, or *false drop rate;* the ratio of nonrelevant records retrieved to total retrieved; the complement of precision $(1 - P)$. (13.2)

$norecxmfnl_{k,i}$ See *Final number of records examined*
$norecxm_{k,i,l}$ See *Number of records examined*
$ntkrec_{j,k}$ See *Number of term tokens in a record*
$ntkset_j$ See *Number of term tokens in a set*
$ntyrec_{j,k}$ See *Number of term types in a record*
$ntyset_j$ See *Number of term types in a set*

Number of attributes; the magnitude of the attribute list, or number of attributes of the database. (11.5.9)

Number of attributes in common to T and S. Count of attributes that occur in records of both databases. (11.5.6.1)

Number of attributes in $L_j(T)$; or the magnitude of $L_j(T)$. The number of attributes found in records of a database. (11.5.6.1)

Number of commands used by searcher k in search i. (14.3.1.2)

Number of commands used; in search i. (12.3)

Number of cycles used by searcher k in search i. (14.3.1.2)

Number of occurrences of an error message; for message type j in search i. (12.4)

Number of records examined; or number browsed or read, from set l, in search i by user k. (14.3.1.3)

Number of term tokens in a record; the number of tokens occurring in attribute j of record k. (Recurrences of the same type are counted each time.) (11.4.1)

Number of term tokens in a set; the number of tokens occurring in attribute j over the range of k.

$$ntkset_j = \sum_{k=1}^{s} ntk_{j,k}$$

where s is the magnitude of a subset of the database. If the set is the entire database, then $s = m$. (11.4.1)

Number of term types in a record; the total number of term types occurring in attribute j, in a single record k. (11.4.1)

Number of term types in a set or *vocabulary size* of attribute j; the total number of types in attribute j over a range of records.

$$ntyset_j = \sum_{k=1}^{m} ntyrec_{j,k}$$ (11.4.1)

O   See *Omission factor*

Object distance; the distance from one object to another measured in terms of values of various dimensions.

$$D(O_i, O_j) = [(x_j - x_i)^2 + (y_j - y_i)^2 + \cdots + (n_j - n_i)^2]^{1/2}$$

where i and j indicate the objects (documents, typically) whose distance is to be measured and $x, y, \ldots n$ are the dimensions in n-space. (7.2.3.1)

Omission factor; the portion of relevant *not* retrieved records; the complement of R. Like recall, O requires measurement of the number of relevant records not retrieved. (13.2)

Appendix: Measurement Index   **263**

overlap   See *Overlap*
*overlap*_j   See *Overlap*

Overlap; or comparability of one database or set with with another, measuring the extent to which two databases share entities in common.
(11.3)

Overlap; the number of records or entities in common divided by the average number of records in the two databases being compared.

$$overlap_j = \frac{2|A \cap B|}{|A| + |B|}$$ (11.5.9)

Overlap measure; the ratio of the number of terms in common to the number of terms in the text with the smaller number of terms.

$$SIM4(T_1, T_2) = \frac{\Sigma(f_{i,k}) \bigcirc (f_{j,k})}{MIN(\Sigma(f_{i,k}), \Sigma(f_{j,k}))}$$ (7.2.3.2)

P See *Precision*
$p(t_{i,j,k})$ See *Probability of occurrence of a type*
$pcmd_{j,i}$ See *Probability of command occurrence*
$pco(t_{i,j,k} \bigcirc t_{l,j,k})$ See *Probability of co-occurrence of two types*
$pcum(t_{i,j})$ See *Cumulative probability of term type*

Pearson's correlation coefficient; a measure of the mathematical similarity of two distributions.

$$r = \Sigma((x_i - \bar{x}) \cdot (y_i - \bar{y})/(n - 1)s_x s_y)$$

where x_i represents the *i*th x value and y_i represents the *i*th y value, $\bar{x}$ represents the sample mean of the x's and $\bar{y}$ represents the sample mean of the y's, s_x represents the sample standard deviation of the x's and s_y represents the sample standard deviation of the y's, and n is the number of sample pairs (x_i, y_i).
(6.3.1.2)

pgmlen   See *Program length*
pgmvoc   See *Program vocabulary*
pgmvol   See *Program volume*

Precision; the ratio of relevant records retrieved to the total number retrieved.
(13.2)

Printing charge; a composite measure used to help decide whether to ask for retrieved records to be transmitted online to the user or printed at the IRSVCE and mailed to the user.

$$costpr = (R/S) \cdot (costct_d + costtc_n)/3600 + onpr$$

where R is the length of a record, in bytes, S is the speed of communication in bytes per second, *costct* and *costtc* are charges per hour converted to per-second charges by the 3600 factor, and *onpr* is a one-time extra charge for offline printing that may be applied. (12.2)

Probability of command occurrence; or relative frequency, of command *j* in search *i*.

$$pcmd_{j,i} = fcmd_{j,i}/ntkset_i$$

where *ntkset_i* is the number of command tokens used in search *i*.
(14.3.3.2)

Probability of occurrence of a type; relative frequency of type *i* in attribute *j*, in record *k*.

$$p(t_{i,j,k}) = f_{i,j,k}/ntyrec_{j,k} \qquad (11.4.1)$$

Probability of co-occurrence of two types; $t_{i,j,k}$ and $t_{l,j,k}$.

$$pco(t_{i,j,k}Ot_{l,j,k}) = rcof(t_{i,j}Ot_{l,j})/m \qquad (11.4.2)$$

Program length; the number of commands in a program.

$$N = N_1 + N_2 \qquad (15.2)$$

Program vocabulary; the number of command types or different commands used.

$$n = n_1 + n_2 \qquad (15.2)$$

Program volume; the number of bits required to encode a program.

$$V = N \cdot \log_2 n \qquad (15.2)$$

|R| *Quantity or amount of relevance;* to provide an indication of how much relevant material has been retrieved.

$$|R| = \sum_{k=1}^{a} r_k$$

r   See *Pearson's correlation coefficient*
R   See *Recall*
R_i See *Reachability*
range   See *Range*

Range; the difference between the value of the highest and lowest observations in a distribution.

$$range = x_{max} - x_{min} \qquad (5.3.4)$$

$rankcmd_{j,i}$ See *Rank of command*

Rank of command; j in search *i*. The command with highest frequency is assigned the rank of 1, the second highest rank 2, etc. (14.3.3.2)

$ratecmds_i$ See *Rate of command entry*
$ratecmds_{k,i}$ See *Rate of entry of commands*

Appendix: Measurement Index   **265**

Rate of command entry; in search i.
$$ratecmds_i = nocmds_i / timelaps_i \qquad (12.3)$$

Rate of entry of commands by searcher k in search i.
$$ratecmds_{k,i} = 1/\overline{timelaps}_k \qquad (14.3.1.1)$$

Rate of occurrence of an error message; for message type j in search i.
$$errrate_{i,j} = errcnt_{i,j}/nocmds_i \qquad (12.4)$$

rbcof($t_{i,j} \mathrm{O} t_{l,j}$)   See *Binary co-occurrence record frequency*

Reachability; a count of the number of paths for reaching any node. (15.3)

Recall; the ratio of the number of relevant records retrieved to the number of relevant records existing in the database. (13.2)

Record charge; charge for viewing or retrieving a record of database d, or a portion thereof. This may be a variable depending on the format, or portion of the record viewed or downloaded. (12.2)

Relative specificity; the number of attributes in common divided by the mean number of attributes in the two databases.

$$relspec_j(T,S) = \frac{2 \cdot | L_j(T \cdot S) |}{| L_j(T) | + | L_j(S) |} \qquad (11.5.6.1)$$

reliab   See *Reliability*

Reliability; a term without a precise definition in terms of database content. (11.3)

relspec(T,S)   See *Relative specificity*
s See *Standard deviation*
S See *Specificity*
s^2 See *Variance*

Scope; the intended population of entities about which records are acquired or maintained. (11.3)

S_e See *Estimated effort*

Search term charge; a charge sometimes applied on each term used in a query. (12.2)

Search vocabulary; the set of term types used in command l of search i. (14.3.3.4)

selectent   See *Selection of entities*

Selection of entities; the measure of the reality of the selection process compared with the intent. (11.3)

Selectivity; or *discriminating ability*, is the ability of an information system to make distinctions between records or entities. (11.3)

selectvy	See *Selectivity*
setdist	See *Set distance*
setsizefnl$_{k,i}$	See *Final set size*
setsize$_{k,i,l}$	See *Set size*

Set distance; the complement of *overlap* expresses how different two sets are, in terms of the entities included.

$$setdist = 1 - overlap = 1 - \frac{2\,|A \cap B|}{|A| + |B|} \quad (11.5.9)$$

Set size; for set number *l* in search *i*, by searcher *k*. (14.3.1.3)

$SIM1(T_1, T_2)$	See *Dice's coefficient*
$SIM2(T_1, T_2)$	See *Jaccard's coefficient*
$SIM3(T_1, T_2)$	See *Cosine coefficient*
$SIM4(T_1, T_2)$	See *Overlap measure*

Span; the number of statements between successive occurrences of variable *j*, where *i* is the occurrence number. (15.2)

Specificity; the proportion of nonrelevant records not retrieved, or rejected. This measures the ability of a system to reject what we want to reject. (13.2)

Standard deviation; represented by the letter σ or *s*, or sometimes as the *root mean square* or *RMS*. Clearly, the higher the standard deviation the more the observations vary about the mean. (5.3.4)

stress	See *Stress*

Stress; loss of accuracy in multidimensional scaling.

$$stress = [\Sigma\,|d_{i,j} - d'_{i,j}|^2 / \Sigma\,|d_{i,j} - \bar{d}|]^{1/2}$$

where $d_{i,j}$ = the configuration distance between objects *i* and *j*, possibly the taxi-cab distance, but possibly another like measure;
$d'_{i,j}$ = the target distance (observed distance in *n*-space) based on the data; and
$\bar{d}$ = the mean of the configuration distances. (7.3)

Taxi-cab distance; the distance is the sum of the various distances *p* over the number of segments required.

$$td_{i,j} = \Sigma\,|x_{ip} - x_{jp}| \quad (7.3)$$

$td_{i,j}$	See *Taxi-cab distance*

Telecommunications cost; charge for long-distance telecommunications,

Appendix: Measurement Index

using network service n, from user's location to the IRSVCE's computer; typically a fixed rate within a country, independent of actual distance. (12.2)

Term co-occurrence1; the frequency of co-occurrence of the terms, divided by m, the number of records in the database (its *magnitude*).

$$termco_1(t_1,t_2) = f(t_1 \bigcirc t_2)/m \qquad (8.2.3.2)$$

Term co-occurrence2; this form takes into account the relative frequencies of occurrence of the t's within a single record. More weight is given to a pair of terms that occur frequently together, multiple times in each of n records, than occur once only in each of the n records.

$$termco2(t_1,t_2) = \frac{\Sigma f(t1,i \oplus t_{2,i})}{\Sigma f(t_{1,i} \cdot t_{2,i})}$$

where $\oplus$ is the operation of counting the total frequency of occurrence of t_1 and t_2 in record i, the denominator is the total number of occurrence of the terms, and summation is over all records. (8.2.3.2)

Term frequency; the frequency of occurrence of term type i of attribute j in record k. Whereas an attribute such as *publication date* will only occur once in a record, an attribute such as *named person* may occur many times in the text of a news article. (8.2.3.1)

$termco1(t_1,t_2)$ See *Term co-occurrence1*
$termco2(t_1,t_2)$ See *Term co-occurrence2*

Time for the system to process command j of search i for user k.
(14.3.1.1)
Time for user k to enter text of command j of search i. (14.3.1.1)
Time for user k to plan command j of search i. (14.3.1.1)
Time for user k to select, enter, and execute command j of search i.

$$timeexe_{k,i,j} = timeplan_{k,i,j} + timeent_{k,i,j} + timeproc_{k,i,j} \quad (14.3.1.1)$$

Time to enter the command; or to enter the selection or message for step j of search i. (12.3)

Time to plan; to consider or think about the action to be taken as step, or command, j of search i. (12.3)

Time to process; the time for the IRSYS to process the command or message entered at step j of search i. (12.3)

$timecmd_{i,j}$ See *Command time*
$timeent_{i,j}$ See *Time to enter the command*
$timeent_{k,i,j}$ See *Time for user k to enter text of command*
$timeexe_{k,i,j}$ See *Time for user to select, enter, and execute command*

$timelaps_i$	See *Elapsed search time*
$timelaps_k$	See *Average elapsed time*
$timelaps_{k,i}$	See *Elapsed search time*, user k

Timeliness; the elapsed time between the occurrence of an event and its recording in a database. (11.3)

$timels$	See *Timeliness*
$timeplan_{i,j}$	See *Time to plan*
$timeplan_{k,i,j}$	See *Time for user k to plan*
$timeproc_{i,j}$	See *Time to process*
$timeproc_{k,i,j}$	See *Time for the system to process command*

Total number of errors; the combined number of occurrences of all error types in search i.

$$totalerr_i = \sum_{j=1}^{J} errcnt_{i,j}$$

where J is the number of possible error types for the IRSYS under study. (12.4)

$totalerr_i$	See *Total number of errors*
$TRM_{1,i}$	See *Search vocabulary*

Type-token ratio; the ratio of the number of word types appearing in a text (the number of different words used) to the number of tokens, the number of word occurrences, including repetitions. (8.2.4)

$typetoken$	See *Type-token ratio*
V	See *Program volume*
$v(G)$	See *Cyclomatic complexity number*

Variance; usually represented by the use of the lowercase Greek letter σ^2 (sigma squared) for the population or s^2 for the sample variance.

$$\sigma^2 = \sum \frac{(x_i - \mu)^2}{n} \qquad s^2 = \sum \frac{(x_i - \bar{x})^2}{n - 1} \qquad (5.3.4)$$

$W_{i,k}$	See *Inverse document frequency weight*

Wilk's lambda; an inverse measure of the discrimination power in the variables not yet removed.

$$\Lambda = t^2_{11} \cdot t^2_{22} \cdots t^2_{pp}$$

where the t_{ii} are diagonal elements of the quantitative variables matrix. (7.2.1)

Word frequency ratio; the ratio of the number of occurrences of any word to the number occurring once.

Appendix: Measurement Index

$$I_n/I_1 = 2/n(n+1)$$

where I_n indicates the number of words occurring n times. (8.2.4)

wordfreq   See *Word frequency ratio*
$\bar{x}_g$ See *Geometric mean*
$\bar{x}_h$ See *Harmonic mean*

Yule's characteristic; a measure devised by Yule (1943, p. 47), somewhat similar to $\bar{f}$ but bringing the dispersion of word frequencies more into play.

$$K = 10,000 \frac{\sigma^2 - \bar{f}}{\bar{f}}$$

where σ^2 is the standard deviation of the frequency distribution and the constant 10,000 is used to avoid small numbers. (8.2.4)

Z score; the deviation of an observation from the mean divided by the standard deviation, expressed in number of standard deviations by which the observation differs from the mean. (5.3.8)

$zd_{i,j}$ See *Zero metric*

Zero metric; a simplification of the taxi-cab distance.

$$zd_{i,j} = \Sigma \, | \, x_{ip} - x_{jp} \, |^{\,0}$$

where

$$| \, x_{ip} - x_{jp} \, |^{\,0} = 0 \text{ if } | \, x_{ip} - x_{jp} \, | = 0$$
$$= 1 \text{ if } | \, x_{ip} - x_{jp} \, | > 0 \qquad (7.3)$$

Recommended Reading

Baker, Sharon L. and F. Wilfrid Lancaster. (1991). *The Measurement and Evaluation of Library Services*. Arlington, VA: Information Resources Press.
Bragg, Gordon M. (1974). *Principles of Experimentation and Measurement*. Englewood Cliffs, NJ: Prentice-Hall, Inc.
Brillouin, L. (1956). *Science and Information Theory*. New York: Academic Press.
Conte, S. D., H. E. Dunsmore, and V. Y. Shen. (1986). *Software Engineering Metrics and Models*. Menlo Park, CA: The Benjamin/Cummings Publishing Company.
Crosby, Philip B. (1979). *Quality Is Free: the Art of Making Quality Certain*. New York: McGraw-Hill.
Egghe, L. and R. Rousseau. (1990). *Introduction to Informetrics: Quantitative Methods in Library, Documentation and Information Science*. Amsterdam: Elsevier.
Fenton, N. E. (1991). *Software Metrics: A Rigorous Approach*. London: Chapman & Hall.
Fidel, Raya. (1987). *Database Design for Information Retrieval*. New York: John Wiley & Sons.
Frakes, William B. and Ricardo Baeza-Yates, eds. (1992). *Information Retrieval: Data Structures & Algorithms*. Englewood Cliffs, NJ: Prentice Hall.
Gould, Stephen Jay. (1981). *The Mismeasure of Man*. New York: W. W. Norton & Company.
Harman, H. H. (1967). *Modern Factor Analysis*. Chicago: The University of Chicago Press.
Hernon, P. and C. R. McClure. (1990). *Evaluation and Library Decision Making*. Norwood, NJ: Ablex Publishing Corp., 88.
Holsti, Ole R. (1969). *Content Analysis for the Social Sciences and Humanities*. Reading, MA: Addison-Wesley.
Korth, Henry F. and Abraham Silberschatz. (1986). *Database System Concepts*. New York: McGraw-Hill, 21–44.
Kraft, Donald H. and Bert R. Boyce. (1991). *Operations Research for Libraries and Information Agencies*. San Diego: Academic Press.
Losee, Robert M., Jr. (1990). *The Science of Information, Measurement and Applications*. San Diego: Academic Press.
Martin, Paul and Patrick Bateson. (1993). *Measuring Behavior, an Introductory Guide*, 2nd edition. Cambridge: Cambridge University Press.
Meadow, Charles T. (1992). *Text Information Retreieval Systems*. San Diego: Academic Press.
Morris, C. W. (1946). *Signs, Language, and Behavior*. New York: Prentice Hall.
Morrison, D. G. (1974). Discriminant analysis. In R. Ferber, ed. *Handbook of Marketing Research*. New York: McGraw-Hill.
Osgood, C. E., G. J. Suci, and P. H. Tannebaum. (1957). *The Measurement of Meaning*. Urbana, IL: The University of Illinois Press.
Salton, Gerard. (1989). *Automatic Text Processing*. Reading, MA: Addison-Wesley.
Salton, Gerard and Michael J. McGill. (1983). *Introduction to Modern Information Retrieval*. New York: McGraw-Hill.

Schiffman, Susan, M. L. Reynolds, and F. W. Young. (1981). *Introduction to Multidimensional Scaling*. New York: Academic Press.

Shannon, Claude E. and Warren Weaver. (1949). *The Mathematical Theory of Communication*. Urbana: The University of Illinois Press.

Sirohi, R. S. and Rada Krishna, H.C. (1983). *Mechanical Measurement*. New York: John Wiley & Sons.

Soergel, Dagobert. (1985). *Organizing Information: Principles of Data Base and Retrieval Systems*. Orlando: Academic Press.

Sparck Jones, K., ed. (1981). *Information Retrieval Experiment*. London: Butterworths.

Spark Jones, K. and M. Kay. (1973). *Linguistics and Information Science*. New York: Academic Press.

Sydenham, P. H. (1979). *Measuring Instruments: Tools of Knowledge and Control*. Stevenage, U.K.: Peter Peregrinus Ltd.

Tenopir, Carol and Jung Soon Ro. (1990). *Full Text Databases*. New York: Greenwood Press.

van Rijsbergen, C. J. (1979). *Information Retrieval*, 2nd edition. London: Butterworth & Co.

Vickery, B. C. (1961). *On Retrieval System Theory*. London: Butterworths.

Vickery, Alina and Brian C. Vickery. (1987). *Information Science in Theory and Practice*. London: Butterworths.

Williams, Martha E., ed. *Annual Review of Information Science and Technology*. Published annually. New York: Knowledge Industry Publications.

Yule, G. Udny. (1944). *The Statistical Study of Literary Vocabulary*. Cambridge: Cambridge University Press.

Zipf, George Kingsley. (1949). *Human Behavior and the Principle of Least Effort*. Cambridge: Addison-Wesley Press.

Index

A

80/20 rule, 118
Aboutness, 177
Absolute scale, 44
Accuracy, 31
 of measures, 29–34
Adler, Irving, 44, 96
Aggregation of data, 81
Ajiferuke, Isola Y., 183, 187, 189, 201, 217, 220
Algorithmic complexity, 229, 231
Algorithms, comparisons of, 236–238
 search, 234–236
 single-link, 89
 single-pass, 90
Allen, Thomas J., 158, 167
Allophones, 100
Analysis of variance, 77
Anomalous state of knowledge (ASK), 178, 187
Antisymmetric relationship, 39, 40
Aptitude, 204
Archimedes, 23
Aristotelian class, 80
Arithmetic mean, 59
Ascher, Marcia, 146, 167
Ascher, Robert, 146, 167
ASK, see Anomalous state of knowledge
Association, measures of, 72–78
Associativity, 36–37
Asymmetric overlap, 191
Attribute representation languages, 133
 values, 36, 106–107, 151, 160–161
Attributes, contained in a database, 165
 of an entity, 36, 132, 149
 representation in a database, 155–156, 159
Auster, Ethel, 134, 144
Authority list, 133

Availability elsewhere of a journal, 124
Average case analysis, 232–233

B

Baker, Sharon L., 182, 200, 242, 250
Balanced tree, 236
 search, 238
Bar-Hillel, Y., 123, 127
Barraclough, Elizabeth D., 169, 174
Barry, Carol L., 187, 200
Bates, Marcia J., 177, 200, 207, 217, 219
Bayes' theorem, 136
Beghtol, Clare, 178, 200
Belkin, N. J., 178, 200
Bellardo, Trudi, 203, 206, 219
Benefits, 139, 169
Bentham, Jeremy, 19, 20
Berkeley, George, 21
Berry, M. M., 200
Bibliographic phenomena, measures of, 112–128
Bibliometrics, 99, 112
Big O notation, 232
Bimodal distribution, 58
Binary search, 237–238
Binet IQ test, 15
Biological measures, 203–204
Blair, David C., 182, 200, 211, 217
Bolinger, Dwight, 100–101, 110
Boltzman, 122
Bookstein, Abraham, 99, 110, 136, 137, 144, 177, 189, 200
Boolean algebraic statements, 136
 model of information retrieval, 135, 137
 operators, 216
 query, 136
Booth, Andrew D., 109, 110, 118, 127
Borgman, Christine L., 203, 206, 208, 219

273

Boyce, Bert R., 14, 20, 57, 66, 77, 79, 119, 124, 127, 143, 144, 171, 174, 186, 200, 248, 251
Bradford bibliograph, 120
Bradford, S. C., 112, 119, 126, 127
Bradford's Law, 119–120
Bragg, Gordon M., 29, 30, 33
Brillouin, L., 123, 127
Broadus, R. N., 112, 127
Brookes, B. C., 99, 110, 119, 120, 127, 157
Brooks, H. M., 134, 145
Brown, John Seeley, 208, 219
Brown, Rowland C. W., 12, 20
Buckland, M. K, 249, 251
Buckley, Chris, 190, 201
Budd, J. M., 112, 114, 127
Buell, D. A., 137, 144
Bureau International de l'Heure, 4
Burton, Richard R., 208, 219

C

Calibration, 31
Cardinal scale, 42
Carlisle, James H., 207, 219
Carnap, R., 123, 127
Carrano, F. M., 240
Carroll, John M., 143, 144
Central limit theorem, 68
  tendency, measures of, 58–60
Chain vocabulary, 215
Chains, frequency of, 215
Chamis, Alice Y., 145, 167, 201, 220, 240
Chebyshev's inequality, 64
Cherry, Joan, 145, 220
Chi-square statistic, 73–75, 82
Chignell, Mark, 140, 144, 205, 219
Christensen, Howard B., 47, 66
Citation indexing, 114
Citations, 112–114
Clarity, 147
  of a question, 148, 191
Class interval, 53
Classification, 7, 80–81, 133
Cleverdon, Cyril, 139, 169, 176, 196, 200
Cliques, 89
Cluster analysis, 84, 104
Clustering, 85–90
Co-occurrence, frequency, 107
  of values, 107

Coefficient, cosine, 87
  Dice's, 86–87, 164
  Jacquard's, 87
  of correlation, 75–76
  of kurtosis, 63
  of skewness, 62–63
  of variation, 62
Cole, F. J., 112, 127
Collection maintenance, 125
  turnover rate, 246
Command frequency, 214
  sequence, measures of, 214–215
  vocabulary, 214
Commands
  number of, 169, 173, 211, 214, 233
  rate of, 172, 173, 210
  selection of, 214
Commutativity, 36–37
Comparability of databases, 164–166
Complement of a set, 36–37
Complementarity, 187
Complete ordering, 40
Completeness, 148
Complexity, algorithmic, 229–233
  logical, 226
  of a procedure, 225
  of a query, 233–234
  of a question, 148, 191
  of a search, 237, 238
  of a search expression, 216
Composite measures *see* Measures, composite
Computational linguistics, 100
Conditional probability, 49
  statements, 135
Condon, E. U., 108, 110
Confidence interval, 68–69
Connect time, 234
  cost, 170
Consistency, 147
Conte, S. D., 224, 228, 240
Contingency table, 73, 180
Continuance, 147
Continuous variables, 53
Controlled vocabulary, 105, 133
Cooper, W. S., 23, 28, 139, 144, 177, 182, 196, 200, 211, 216, 219
Coordinated Universal Time (UTC), 4
Correlation coefficient, 75–76
  measures of, 73–76
Cosine coefficient, 87

Index

Cost, 139–140, 150, 163, 170–171
   expected, 189
   monetary, 169
   of a search total, 171, 217
   of nonretrieval, 189
   of retrieval, 188–189
   of service, 244
   of use of a system, 141
   telecommunications, 170
Cost-benefit, 139
Cost-effectiveness, 139, 241
Cost-performance-benefit, 139
Covariation, 73
Coverage, 139–140
Croft, W. B., 134, 145
Crosby, Philip B., 12, 20
Cumulative advantage distribution, 115
   frequency, 54
Cycles, 210
   number of, 233
   number used in a search, 211, 217
Cyclomatic complexity number, 228
   number, 228

D

Data aggregation, 81
   analysis, 246–248
   collection, 125–126, 246–248
   declaration languages, 155
   standards, 246–248
   structure metric, 225
Database, 5, 132–133, 146
   characteristics, 147–148,
   cost, 170
   measures, 139–140, 149–151, 154–166
De Santo, Carmine, 47, 66
Decision count, 226
   making, 248–249
Degrees of freedom, 74
DeMorgan, A., 37, 44
DeMorgan's laws, 37
Dervin, B., 178, 200
Descriptive statistics, 47
Deviation from the mean, 61–63
Dewey Decimal Classification, 133
Dice's coefficient, 86–87, 164, 191
Difference of sets, 36–37
   scale, 44
Dillman, Don A., 25, 28
Dillon, Martin, 110

Direct access search, 239
Discrete variables, 53
Discriminant analysis, 81–83
   coefficient, 104
Discriminating ability of a database, 150
Discriminator function, 82
Disgust with search results, 217
Disjoint sets, 37
Dispersion measures, 61–63
Dissimilarity measures, 85
Distance between sets, 88
Distance, measures of, 85–86
   object, 86
   target, 92
   taxi-cab, 91
Domain expressiveness, 148, 191
   of a subject, 148
   specificity, 148
Dominick, Wayne, 233–234, 240
Dunsmore, H. E., 240

E

Earles, W. B., 112, 127
Ease of learning, 141
Economic value, 16, 18–19
Education, 204
Effectiveness, 139, 169, 241
   measures of, 196–198
Efficiency, 147, 241
Effort, estimated, to revise a program, 225
Egghe, L., 77, 79, 121, 127
Eigenvalue, 84
Eisenberg, M. B., 143, 145, 184, 186, 200
Elshoff, J. L., 224, 240
End user, 206
Entities, 35–36, 131–132, 151
Entity-relation maps, 155–156
Entropy, 122
Entry points 7–8
Equivalence class, 40
   relations, 40
   statements, 135
Errors, 67–69, 162, 173–174
   measurement of, 163, 173, 211–213
   messages, rate of occurrence of, 174
esl, see Expected search length
Estoup, J. B., 108, 110
Evans, G. Edward., 24, 28
Exclusive union of sets, 36
Expected cost, 189

Index

Expected search length (*esl*), 211, 216
Experience, 140, 204–207
Experimental procedures, 143
Expression complexity, 216
Extensive measurement, 44
Extrinsic quality, 14

F

Factor analysis, 83–84
  loadings, 83–84
  rotation, 84
  score, 84
Fallout, 181
False drop rate, 181
Farish, William, 249–250
Feedback, 187–190
  relevance, 190
Fenichel, Carol H., 207, 219
Fenton, N. E., 240
Fidel, Raya, 147, 167, 206, 219
Fields of a record, 36
File, definiton of, 36, 151
  size charge, 170
  structures, 234–236
Fill rate, 246
Flexibility, 147
Foskett, A. C. 41, 44
Free text, 105
  indexing, 106
Frequency, cumulative, 54
  distributions, 53–54
  function, 53
  measures, 52–53
  polygons, 55
  relative, 54
  table, 53
Functions of a program, 224
Funk, Mark, 124, 127
Futility point, 182, 211, 217
Fuzzy sets, 93–95, 132
  model of information retrieval, 135, 137
  theory of, 93–95

G

Gap, in knowledge, 178
Garfield, Eugene, 113, 127
Gatekeeper, 156
Geometric mean, 59–60

Gillen, Edward J., 171, 174
Goals of a search, 183–184, 206
Goffman, W., 115, 117–118, 127, 198, 200
Gordon, Michael, 194, 200
Gould, Stephen Jay, 15, 20, 204, 219
Grammars, 101
Graph, 226
  theoretic measures, 89
Graphical portrayal of statistics, 55–58
  user interface, 135
Greenberg, Saul, 215, 219
Gribbin, John, 30, 33
Griffith, B. C., 92, 96, 113, 127
Groos, O.V., 120, 127
Groos' droop, 120
Gross, E. M., 112, 127
Gross, P. L. K., 112, 127
Growth, 114–116
Growth of a population, 114
Growth of the scientific literature, 115
GUI, *see* Graphical user interface

H

Hadley, G., 84, 96
Half-life, 116
Hall, Arthur D., 19, 20
Halstead, M. H., 224, 225, 240
Hancock-Beaulieu, M. N., 196, 201
Harman, H. H., 83, 96
Harmonic mean, 60
Harter, Stephen P., 186, 194, 200
Hawthorne effect, 23–24
Heath, T. L., 22, 28
Heine, M. H., 197, 200
Heisenberg, Werner, 29
Helman, P., 232, 240
Hernon, P., 247, 251
Hickey, Thomas B., 166, 167
Hiero's crown, 22
Histograms, 55
Hockey, G. Robert, 203, 219
Hoffman, H., 229, 240
Hollander, Myles, 76, 77, 79
Holsti, Harold, 166, 167
Hoskin, Keith, 250, 251
Hu, X., 184, 186, 200
Huber, George P., 203, 219
Hulme, E. W., 112, 127
Hypothesis testing, 69–71

Index

I

Impact factor, 113
Imputed value, *see* Economic value
Index, of a file, 235
  terms, 105
Indexed sequential search, 238–239
Indexing, 102–105, 133
Inferential statistics, 47, 52
Information, content of a message, 122
  measure of, 123
  need statement (INS), 178, 187
  retrieval, management, issues in, 142–143
    measurement in, 131–145
    models, 131–138
    service, (IRSVCE), 7, 132
    service, operation of, 141–142
    system (IRSYS), 7, 131–138
  services, inputs to, 241–242
    intermediate outputs of, 241–242
    measures of, 241–251
  systems, 5–8, 123–124
    measures of, 223–251
  theory, 100, 121
Informetrics, 99–100
Innis, Harold, 146, 167
Inputs to information services, 241–242
INS, *see* Information need statement
Intermediaries, 134
Intermediary, 7, 206
Intermediate outputs of information services, 241–242
International System of Units, 4
Intersection of sets, 36–37
Intersubject agreement, 9
Interval scales, 42
Intrinsic quality, 13
Intrinsicality, 147
Inverse document frequency weight, 103, 187
Inverted file, 235
IRSVCE, *see* Information retrieval service
IRSYS, *see* Information retrieval systems

J

Jacquard's coefficient, 87
Jaffee, Lee, 144, 219
Janes, Joseph W., 140, 145
Johnson, Norman L., 82, 96
Joint probability, 49
Joos, M., 102, 110
Journal selection, 124
Joyce, James, 108

K

Kachigan, S. K., 51, 66, 75, 79
Kantor, Paul, 145, 167, 201, 220, 234, 240
Kaplan, Abraham, 4, 9, 20
Kay, M., 106, 110
Keats, John, 250–251
Keen, M., 200
Keillor, Garrison, 185, 200
Kelly, George A., 209, 220
Kelvin, William Thomson, 8–9, 20, 250, 251
Kemeny, J. G., 214, 220
Kendall rank correlation, 77
Kent, Allen, 180, 200
Kessler, M. M., 113, 127
Klett, C., 76, 79
Klotz, Samuel, 82, 96
Knots, 229
Knowledge, as user characteristic, 204–207
  information seeking, 205
  of system, 205
Knuth, D. E., 118, 127
Kochen, Manfred, 194, 200
Kolmogorov-Smirnoff test, 77
Korth, Henry F., 155, 167, 236, 240
Kraft, Donald H., 7, 20, 57, 66, 119, 124, 127, 137, 144, 182, 220, 217, 248, 251
Krawczak, Deborah, 144, 219
Kuhns, J., 136, 145
Kurtosis, coefficient of, 63

L

Lancaster, F. W., 139, 145, 169, 174, 182, 200, 242, 244, 250, 251
Language, logical power of, 141
  measures of, 99–111
  use of, 213–216
Large numbers, law of, 63–64
Large sets, 211
Larson, Ray R., 78, 79
Latta, Gail, 209, 220
Law of large numbers, 63–64
Law of source yield, 118–119
Learning, ease of, 141

Least squares method, 76
Lee, T., 182, 217, 220
Leimkuhler, F. F., 119, 127
Length of program, 224
Leuhrs, F. U., 200
Lexemes, 101
Line, M. B., 116, 117, 128
Linear regression, 76
    search, 237
Linguistic measures, 213
Linked list, 236
Live variables, 225
Logic of an information system, 132–135
Logical complexity, 226
    power of language, 141
Logistic curve, 115
Losee, R. M., 123, 127, 187, 201
Lotka, 112, 121, 126
Lotka's law, 120–121, 125
Lovins, J. B., 104, 110
Lynch, M. J., 251

M

MAD *see* Mean absolute deviation
Magnitude of a database, 149, 151, 158
    of a measure, 4
    of a set, 36–37
Malthusian parameters, 115
Management information system, 246–247
    of information retrieval, issues in, 142–143
Mandelbrot, Benoit, 108, 110
Mann-Whitney test, 77
Marchionini, Gary, 145, 220
Marcus, Richard S., 134, 145
Marczewski, E., 164, 167, 197, 201
Market value *see* Economic value
Markov chains, 214–215
Maron, M. E., 136, 145
Marsh, Catherine, 25, 26, 28
Matching functions, 92–93, 136
Matthew effect, 115
McCabe, T. J., 228, 240
McClure, C. R., 247, 251
McGill, Michael J., 7, 20, 96, 103, 105, 110, 186, 190, 194, 201
McKillip, Jack, 26, 28
Meadow, Charles T., 109, 110, 134, 140, 145, 173, 175, 196, 201, 207, 220, 236, 240

Mean, 59
    absolute deviation (MAD), 61
Meaning, measurement of, 101–102
Measure of overlap, 87–88, 140, 150, 164
    of set size, 211, 218
Measurement, absolute, 3
    and human behavior, 10–11
    destructive, 23
    devices, 29–31
    in information retrieval, 131–145
    methods of, 21–28
    nature of, 3–5
    of relevance, 183–184
    of databases, 146–167
    of error, 163
    of human behavior and skills, 15–16
    of meaning, 101–102
    of opinion, 23–28
    of quality, 12–14
    of questions, 191–192
    of retrieval outcome, 176–201, 217–218
    of users, 202–220
    of values, 16–19
    quantitative and qualitative aspects of, 3–20
    reasons for, 8–9
    relative, 3, 11
    scale for relevance, 184–185
Measures, accuracy and reliability of, 29–34
    biological, 203–204
    composite, 9–10, 23
    goals of, 138–142
    linguistic, 213
    of association, 72–78
    of bibliographic phenomena, 112–128
    of central tendency, 58–60
    of correlation, 73–76
    of databases, 139–140, 149–151
    of dispersion, 61–63
    of dissimilarity, 85
    of distance and similarity, 85–86
    of information services, 241–251
    of information systems, 223–251
    of language, 99–111
    of occurrence of values, 152–153
    of query language, 141
    of record or text similarity, 86–88
    of retrieval outcome, overall, 196–198
    of search termination, 216–217
    of set membership, 80–96
    of term usage, 215–216
    of text, 99–111

of the retrieval process, 168–175
of time, 210
of user process, 209–211
psychological, 203–204
types of, 138–142
Median, 59
Mediation process, 102
Membership function, 132
Mendel, Gregor, 13
Mental models, 142–143, 208–209
Mill, John Stuart, 19
Miller, N. E., 236, 238, 240
Mode, 58
Models in information retrieval, 131–138
Modules of a program, 224
Molyneux, Robert E., 114, 128
Monothetic sets, 80
Morphemes, 100
Morris, C. W., 101, 110
Morrison, D. G., 82, 96
Multidimensional scaling, 90–92
Multiple regression, 77
Multivalued relevance scales, 182–183

N

n-tile, 61
Naps, T. L., 233, 240
Negation of a set, 36–37
Nesting level, 229
Newill, A., 198, 200
Nickens, John M., 26, 28
Nodes of a graph, 226
Noise, 181
Nonmonetary resources, 141
Nonparametric statistics, 77
Nonprocedural language, 135
Nonsymmetric relationship, 39
Noriega, P. P., 28
Normal distribution, 57
Normative value, 16–18
Null sets, 212

O

O notation, big, 232
O'Neil, Edward, 110, 120, 128
Object distance, 86
Objectives of a search, 183–184
Observation, direct, 21–22
Observation, indirect, 22–23
Obsolescence, 116–117

Olson, J. R., 143, 144
Omission factor, 181
One-tailed test, 70
Operation of an IRSVCE, 141–142
Opinion, measurement of, 23–28
Ordering, basis of, 41–42
  strong, 40
  weak, 40
Organizational factors in user behavior, 207
Orr, R. M., 13, 14, 20, 243, 251
Osgood, C. E., 102, 110
Outcome, general measures of, 192–199
  measurement of, 176–201, 217–218
Output services, 241–242
Overall, J. E., 76, 79
Overall measures of retrieval outcome, 196–198
Overlap, 87–88, 140, 150, 164
  asymmetric, 191

P

Paice, C. D., 104, 110
Pao, M. L., 113, 121, 128
Partial ordering, 40
Patterns of command use, 169
Pearson's correlation coefficient, 75–76
Penniman, W. David, 209, 214–215, 220, 233–234, 240
Percentile, 61
Perceptual map, 92
Perry, J. W., 200
Personnel evaluation, 125
Phoenemes, 100
Poisson distribution, 64–65
Pollens, J. S., 124, 127
Polls, 25
Polythetic sets, 80
Population, 51–52
Porter, M. F., 104, 110
Postman, Neil, 250, 251
Pothering, G. J., 233, 240
Pragmatic meaning, 101
Precision, 31, 180–181, 217, 218
  relationship to recall, 193–196
Preparation time, 234
Presupposition in a question, 148, 191
Price, D. J. de Solla, 115, 128
Price of use, 170, 244
Principal components analysis, 84
Printing charge, 171
Pritchard, A., 99, 110

Probabilistic model of information retrieval, 135–137
Probabilities of events, 49–51
Probability of occurrence of a type, 153–154
Process measures, user, 209–211
Program, length of, 224
  vocabulary, 224
  volume, 224
Pseudo-code, 231
Psychological measures, 203–204
  relevance, 186
Punctuation marks, 216
Purga, A. J., 28

Q

Quality, and value, 243
  measurement of, 12–14
Quartile, 61
Queries, 132, 135, 178, 187, 197
  complexity of, 233–234
  interpretation of, 141, 148
  language measures for, 141
  relationship to record, 143
Question, in information retrieval, 135
  measurement of, 191–192
Questionnaires, 24–27
Quine, Willard V. O., 37, 44

R

Rada Krishna, H. C., 31, 34
Random samples, 52
Range, 53, 61
Rank correlation, 77
Ranking, 187–190
Rao, I. K. R., 60, 66, 74, 77, 79
Ratio scale, 42–44
Reachability, 229
Recall, 181, 198, 218
  relationship to precision, 193–196
Records, 151
  charge for, 170
  similarity measures of, 86–88
  structure of, 151
  examined, 211
  retrieved, 211
Regression, 76–77
Reintjes, J. F., 134, 145
Relatedness, 177
Relationships, 140

Relative frequency, 54
  specificity, 159
Relevance, 177–179
  as a relative and variable measure, 186–187
  feedback, 190
  function, 189
  meaning of, 185–186
  measurement of, 183–184
    scale for, 184–185,
    uncertainties in, 179–180
  measures derived from, 180–183
  none retrieved, 198–199
  of a journal, 124
  psychological, 186
  quantity of, 183, 189–190
  scales, multivalued, 182–183
  system computed, 187–190
Reliability, 140, 147, 150, 161–162
  of measures, 29–34
Repertory grid technique, 208–209
Representability, 147
Representation of atributes, 133
Reproducibility, 31
Resolution, 30, 147
Resources, nonmonetary, 141
  used, 170–171
Retrieval outcome, overall measures of, 196–198
  process, measures of, 168–175
  status value (rsv), 132, 136, 180, 189
Reynolds, M. L., 96
Robertson, S. E., 196, 201
Root of a word, 104
Rousseau, R., 77, 79, 121, 127
Royse, David, 25, 28
rsv, see Retrieval status value
Russell, Bertrand, 21, 27–28, 33, 34
Rypka, David J., 166, 167

S

Salton, Gerard, 7, 20, 86, 96, 103, 105, 110, 186, 190, 194, 201
Salvia, Anthony A., 47, 66
Sample spaces, 48–52
Samples, random, 52
  statistical, 51–52
Sandison, A., 116, 117, 128
Saracevic, Tefko, 135, 145, 148, 167, 177, 185, 191, 201, 220, 234, 240
Saturation of need, 217

Scales, 35-44
  absolute, 44
  cardinal, 42
  concept of, 37-38
  difference, 44
  interval, 42
  nominal, 38-39
  ordinal, 39-42
  ratio, 42-44
Scaling, multidimensional, 90-92
Scatter diagram, 75
Scattering, 117
Schiffman, Susan, 90, 96
Schneidewind, N. F., 229, 240
Scientometrics, 99
Scope of a database, 149, 154
Search, algorithms for, 234-236
  goals, objectives, standards of, 183-184
  length, expected, 211, 216
  linear, 237
  term charge, 170
  termination measures, 216-217
  terms, number of, 234
  vocabulary, 216
Searcher, *see also* User
  end user, 206
  individual characteristics, 206
  role in information retrieval, 206
Seglen, Per, 114, 128
Selection of entities of a database, 149, 156-157
Selectivity of a database, 150, 159-161
Semantic differential, 102
  integrity, 147
  meaning, 102
Sensitivity, 198
Service statistics, 246
Sets, 35-44
  definitions of, 35-36
  distance of, 164
  fuzzy, 93-95, 132
  large, 211
  membership in, 93
  membership measures of, 80-96
  null, 211
  operations on, 36
  size of, as a measure, 211, 217-218
  universal, 35
Shannon, Claude E., 100, 110, 121-123, 128
Shaw, W. M., Jr., 164, 167, 197, 198, 201
Shen, V. Y., 240

Shi, Xirong, 174, 175
Shute, Stephen J., 144, 219
Significance level, 70
Silberschatz, Abraham, 155, 167, 236, 240
Similarity measures, 85-86
Simon, H. A., 115, 128
Single-link algorithms, 89
Single-pass algorithms, 90
Sirohi, R. S., 31, 34
Skewness, coefficient of, 62-63
Skill, 140, 205
Small, H. G., 113, 128
Smith, Philip J., 144, 219
Smith, Richard Austin, 147, 167
Smith, Robert P., 162
Smithson, Michael, 93, 96
Snell, J. L., 214, 220
Soergel, Dagobert, 134, 145
Software, IRSYS, 141
  metrics, 223-240
  physics, 223-226
Source yield, law of, 118-119
Span, 226-227
Sparck Jones, K., 106, 110, 186, 201
Spearman rank correlation, 77
Specificity, 148, 182, 191, 198
  of a question, 148
  relative, 159
Stamboulie, M., 110
Standard deviation as a measure, 63
  defined, 62
Standard error of the mean, 68
Standards, 27-28
  data, 246-248
  of a search, 183-184
Statistical measures, 47-66
  tests, 67-79
Steinhaus, H., 164, 167, 198, 201
Stemming, 104
Stephens, David, 110
Stop list, 104
Stopping rules for a search, 217
Stress, measure of, 92
Strong ordering, 40
Structure of a record, 151
  of an information system, 132-135
Struminger, Leny, 146, 167
Subject domain knowledge, 140-141, 205-206
  of a question, 148
  relatedness, 187, 188
Subjective judgements, 148

Substitutability, 187
Suci, G. J., 110
Surrogate records, 178
Surveys, 24–27
 descriptive, 25
 exploratory, 25
Swets, J.A., 201
Swigger, Keith, 209, 220
Sydenham, P.H., 31, 34
Syllables, 100
Symmetric relationship, 39
Syntactic meaning, 101
Syntax, 101
System design process, 248–249
System to be measured, 192–193
Système Internationale (SI), 4

T

Tannebaum, P. H., 110
Target distance, 92
Taxi-cab distance, 91
Telecommunications cost, 170
Tenopir, Carol, 146, 164, 167
Term co-occurrence, 107, 153–154
Term, frequency of, 106, 152, 216
 tokens, number of, 152–153, 216
 types, number of, 152, 216
 usage, measures of, 215–216
 value, 106, 151
Text, characteristics of, 108–109
 measures of, 99–111
 similarity measures, 86–88
Thebaut, S. M., 225, 240
Thesauri, 8
Thompson, R. H., 134, 145
Tiamiyu, M. A., 183, 187, 189, 201, 217, 220
Time, 141, 169, 172, 210
 of a search, elapsed, 210
 to enter a command, 172, 210
 to execute a command, 210
 to plan, 172, 210
 to process a command, 172
 to select a command, 210
Timeliness, 140
 of a database, 149, 150, 158–159
Token of a word or symbol, 103, 106, 152
Tolerances, 31–33
Topicality, 187

Total probability, law of, 50
 relevance function, 189
 time for a search, 234
Totoro, Michael, 47, 66
Transitivity, 39
Trivision, Donna, 145, 167, 201, 220, 240
Trueswell, R. W., 118, 128
Turnover rate of a collection, 246
Two-tailed test, 70
Type, frequency of, 153
 of a word or symbol, 103, 106, 152
Type-token ratio, 109

U

Ulysses, 108
Union of sets, 36
Universal set, 35
Universe of discourse, 35
Usage of a journal, 124
Use of resources, 169
Users, characteristics of, 202–209
 language of, 134–135
 measurement of, 202–220
 performance measures of, 209–216
 process measures of, 209–211
Utility, 177–179, 187, 243–244

V

Value, economic *see* Economic value
 measures of occurrence of, 152–153
 normative *see* normative value
 of attributes, 36, 151
 of an information system, 243–244
 of retrieved records, 177, 185, 187
Value-in-use, *see* Economic value
Van House, N. A., 246, 251
van Rijsbergen, C. J., 80, 86, 96, 138–139, 145, 176, 196, 197, 198, 201
Variables, frequency of occurrence of, 226
 live, 225
Variance, 62
 analysis of, 77
Vector space model, 87, 137–138
Ven, A. H. G. S. van der, 92, 96
Verhoff, R., 240
Vertices of a graph, 226
Vickery, B. C., 134, 139, 145, 169, 175, 180, 196, 198, 201

Index

Virgo, J. A., 114, 128
Vocabulary, control of, 105–106
　controlled, 133
　of a program, 224
　of a search, 216
Volume of a program, 224

W

Wallace, Danny P., 77, 79
Wang, J., 110
Warren, K. S., 115, 117–118, 127
Waters, Samuel T., 134, 145
Weak ordering, 40
Weaver, Warren, 100, 110, 121–122, 128
Weil, B., 251
Western Electric Co., 24
Weyer, Stephen, 134, 145
Wheelwright, Philip, 18, 20
Whitehorn, J. C., 108, 111
Whorf, Benjamin, 135, 145
Whorf hypothesis, 135
Wilk's lambda, 82
Wilkinson, E. A., 119, 128
Williams, J. H., 104, 111

Williams, Philip W., 134, 145
Wilson, Patrick, 177, 201
Witten, Ian H., 215, 219
Wolfe, Douglas A., 76, 77, 79
Wolman, Benjamin B., 203, 220
Word association, 105–106
　frequency ratio, 109
Worst case analysis, 232–233

Y

Young, F. W., 96
Yuan, Weijing, 211, 220
Yule, G. U., 109, 111
Yules' characteristic, 109

Z

z score, 65
Zero metric, 91
Zipf distribution, 118
Zipf, G. K., 108, 111, 112
Zipf's law, 108, 119
Zukav, Gary, 29, 34

Library and Information Science

(Continued from page ii)

Nancy Jones Pruett
Scientific and Technical Libraries: Functions and Management
Volume 1 and Volume 2

Peter Judge and Brenda Gerrie
Small Bibliographic Databases

Dorothy B. Lilley and Ronald W. Trice
A History of Information Sciences 1945–1985

Elaine Svenonius
The Conceptual Foundations of Descriptive Cataloging

Robert M. Losee, Jr.
The Science of Information: Measurement and Applications

Irene P. Godden
Library Technical Services: Operations and Management, Second Edition

Donald H. Kraft and Bert R. Boyce
Operations Research for Libraries and Information Agencies: Techniques for the Evaluation of Management Decision Alternatives

James Cabeceiras
The Multimedia Library: Materials Selection and Use, Second Edition

Charles T. Meadow
Text Information Retrieval Systems

Robert M. Losee, Jr. and Karen A. Worley
Research and Evaluation for Information Professionals

Carmel Maguire, Edward J. Kazlauskas, and Anthony D. Weir
Information Services for Innovative Organizations

Karen Markey Drabenstott and Diane Vizine-Goetz
Using Subject Headings for Online Retrieval

Bert R. Boyce, Charles T. Meadow, and Donald H. Kraft
Measurement in Information Science

John V. Richardson
Knowledge-Based Systems in General Reference Work